Social Security's Looming Surpluses

Social Security's Looming Surpluses

Prospects and Implications

Edited by Carolyn L. Weaver

The AEI Press

Publisher for the American Enterprise Institute
WASHINGTON, D.C.

1990

Distributed by arrangement with

University Press of America, Inc.
4720 Boston Way
Lanham, Md. 20706

3 Henrietta Street
London WC2E 8LU England

Library of Congress Cataloging-in-Publication Data

Social security's looming surpluses/[edited by] Carolyn L. Weaver.
    p. cm. — (AEI studies ; 511)
  Includes bibliographical references and index.
  ISBN 0-8447-3729-1 (c). — ISBN 0-8447-3730-5 (p)
  1. Social security—United States—Finance. 2. Budget deficits—
United States. I. Weaver, Carolyn L. II. Series.
HD7125.S5998   1990
368.4'301'0973—dc20

90-43709
CIP

1 3 5 7 9 10 8 6 4 2

AEI Studies 511

The AEI Press
Publisher for the American Enterprise Institute
1150 Seventeenth Street, N.W., Washington, D.C. 20036

Printed in the United States of America

Contents

LIST OF FIGURES

Contributors

CAROLYN L. WEAVER is a resident scholar at the American Enterprise Institute and director of AEI's Social Security and Pension Project. She has been a senior research fellow at the Hoover Institution and a member of the Economics Department and research associate of the Center for Study of Public Choice at Virginia Polytechnic Institute. From 1981 to 1984, she served as chief professional staff member on social security for the U.S. Senate Finance Committee. She also served as a senior adviser to the 1983 National Commission on Social Security Reform and as a member of the 1987–1988 Disability Advisory Council, the 1989 Disability Advisory Committee, and the 1989 Public Trustees' Working Group on the Measurement of Trust Fund Solvency. She is the author of *Crisis in Social Security: Economic and Political Origins*, as well as many articles on social security and political economy. Ms. Weaver received her Ph.D. in economics from Virginia Polytechnic Institute.

ALAN S. BLINDER is the Gordon S. Rentschler Memorial Professor of Economics and chairman of the Department of Economics at Princeton University. He is also the vice president of the American Economic Association. Mr. Blinder has written extensively on macroeconomics, stabilization policy, and income distribution and is the author of nine books, including, most recently, *Hard Heads, Soft Hearts: Tough-Minded Economics for a Just Society*. He is a columnist for *Business Week* and the *Boston Globe* and testifies frequently on matters of economic policy before various committees of Congress. In 1975, Mr. Blinder was deputy assistant director, Fiscal Analysis Division, Congressional Budget Office. He received his Ph.D. in economics from the Massachusetts Institute of Technology.

BARRY P. BOSWORTH is a senior fellow at the Brookings Institution. Before joining Brookings in 1979, he was the director of the Council on Wage and Price Stability. He is the author of numerous books and articles on economic policy, his most recent being *Can America Afford to*

Grow Old? (co-written with Henry Aaron and Gary Burtless). Mr. Bosworth holds a B.A. and a Ph.D. from the University of Michigan.

JAMES M. BUCHANAN, recipient of the 1986 Nobel Prize in economic science, is Harris University Professor and advisory general director of the Center for Study of Public Choice at George Mason University. Mr. Buchanan has written or co-written hundreds of articles in professional journals and more than a dozen books, including *Democracy in Deficit: The Political Legacy of Lord Keynes* (with Richard E. Wagner), *The Power to Tax: Analytical Foundations of a Fiscal Constitution* (with Geoffrey Brennan), and his seminal work with Gordon Tullock, *The Calculus of Consent: Logical Foundations of Constitutional Democracy*. He received his Ph.D. in economics from the University of Chicago.

W. MARK CRAIN is professor of economics and research associate, Center for Study of Public Choice, at George Mason University. Since completing his Ph.D. at Texas A&M University, he has published many articles and books in economics and politics. He is the creator of Billcast, an electronic government information database that projects the chances of passage for bills in the U.S. Congress. In 1987–1988, Mr. Crain served as special assistant to the director at the U.S. Office of Management and Budget. He received his Ph.D. in economics from Texas A&M University.

ARTHUR T. DENZAU is a professor in the department of economics, research associate in the Center for the Study of American Business, and fellow in the Center for Political Economy at Washington University at St. Louis. Mr. Denzau has published widely in public economics and public finance, with a concentration on resource allocation in representative democracies. He also works and teaches in the fields of econometrics, urban economics, and the economics of education and finance. Mr. Denzau has taught at Virginia Polytechnic Institute and the University of Arizona. He received his Ph.D. from Washington University.

STEPHEN J. ENTIN is a resident scholar at the Institute for Research on the Economics of Taxation. From 1981 to 1988, he served as deputy assistant secretary for economic policy at the Treasury Department. In this capacity, he participated in the preparation of economic forecasts for the president's budgets and in the development of the 1981 tax cuts, including the tax indexing provision. He also represented the Treasury Department in the preparation of the Annual Reports of the Social Security Board of Trustees and conducted research into the long-run outlook for social security. Before joining the Treasury Department, Mr. Entin was staff economist with the Joint Economic Committee of the Congress. Mr. Entin is a graduate of Dartmouth College and received his graduate training in economics at the University of Chicago.

C. NICOLE ERNSBERGER is a student at Stanford Law School. Previously she was a senior research assistant at the Federal Reserve Bank of Boston, where she conducted research and contributed to two articles (by Alicia Munnell) in the area of public finance. She received her undergraduate degree in economics from Mount Holyoke College.

LAURENCE J. KOTLIKOFF is chairman of the Department of Economics at Boston University and a research associate of the National Bureau of Economic Research. He received his Ph.D. in economics from Harvard University and subsequently taught at the University of California, Los Angeles, and at Yale University. In 1981–1982, he served as a senior economist with the President's Council of Economic Advisers. Mr. Kotlikoff has published extensively on issues relating to the deficit, the tax structure, social security, pensions, saving, and insurance. His books include *What Determines Savings?*, *Dynamic Fiscal Policy* (with Alan Auerbach), and *The Wage Carrot and Pension Stick* (with David Wise).

HERMAN B. LEONARD is the Baker Professor of Public Sector Financial Management at Harvard University's Kennedy School of Government. He conducts research and teaches courses on corporate finance, finance theory, financial markets, financial management, and state and local fiscal issues. He has served on many government advisory committees, including the Governor's Council on Economic Policy for the State of Alaska, the Governor's Advisory Council on Infrastructure in Massachusetts, and the U.S. Senate Budget Committee's Private Sector Advisory Committee on Infrastructure. He has also been chief financial officer and chief executive officer of a human services agency and a director of several firms. He is a member of the board of the Massachusetts Health and Educational Facilities Authority. Mr. Leonard is the author of *Checks Unbalanced: The Quiet Side of Public Spending*. He received his Ph.D. in economics from Harvard University.

LAWRENCE B. LINDSEY is special assistant to the president for policy development. From 1984 through January 1989, he was on the faculty of the Department of Economics at Harvard University and was a faculty research fellow at the National Bureau of Economic Research. He is the author of a number of articles in books, journals, and newspapers on public finance and tax policy. From 1981 to 1984, Mr. Lindsey served as an economist with the President's Council of Economic Advisers. He received his Ph.D. in economics from Harvard.

JOHN H. MAKIN is director of Fiscal Policy Studies at the American Enterprise Institute and former professor of economics and director of the Institute of Economic Research at the University of Washington at Seattle. He has served as a consultant to the U.S. Treasury, the Federal Reserve Board, the International Monetary Fund, the Congressional Budget Office, and the Bank of Japan. He writes for major newspapers and is an associate editor of the *Review of Economics and Statistics*. He received his Ph.D. in economics from the University of Chicago.

MICHAEL L. MARLOW is associate professor of economics at California Polytechnic State University in San Luis Obispo, California. From 1983 to 1988, he was senior financial economist at the U.S. Treasury Department, where he conducted research on monetary policy and the economics of budget deficits in the offices of the under secretary for monetary affairs and the assistant secretary for economic policy. From 1979 to 1983, he was an associate professor of economics at George Washington University. Mr. Marlow has published widely on the causal relation between government spending and taxation and on the economics of government growth. He received his Ph.D. in economics from Virginia Polytechnic Institute.

DAVID G. MATHIASEN is special assistant to the assistant comptroller general of the General Accounting Office. Previously, he held various staff and executive positions in the Office of Management and Budget and its predecessor, the Bureau of the Budget, the most recent of which was assistant director for budget review. He was on leave from March 1988 to March 1989 to serve as executive director of the National Economic Commission. Between career assignments in public finance, Mr. Mathiasen worked for the Agency for International Development on economic issues of third world countries. He served overseas from 1965 to 1972 in Turkey, India, and Pakistan. Mr. Mathiasen holds an M.A. from the Woodrow Wilson School of Public and International Affairs at Princeton University. He has published and lectured on budget matters.

ALICIA H. MUNNELL is senior vice president and director of research for the Federal Reserve Bank of Boston. She has published extensively on tax policy, social security, and pensions. Her books include *The Economics of Private Pensions* and *The Future of Social Security*. She is cofounder and former president of the National Academy of Social Insurance and a member of the Institute of Medicine, the National Academy of Public Administration, and the Pension Research Council of the Wharton School of Finance and Commerce. She has also served as staff director for the National Planning Association's Joint Committee on Public Pensions and as a member of the Carnegie Corporation's Commission on College Retirement. Ms. Munnell received her Ph.D. in economics from Harvard University.

WILLIAM D. NORDHAUS is the John Musser Professor of Economics at Yale University and on the staff of the Cowles Foundation for Research in Economics. From 1986 to 1988, he served as the provost of Yale University. Mr. Nordhaus has engaged in economic research on a wide range of problems, including productivity, inflation, and economic growth and, more recently, energy and natural resources. He is the author of numerous books and articles. In 1985, he joined Paul Samuelson as co-author of *Economics*, the classic introductory textbook on economic theory and policy. He is a member of the Brookings Panel on Economic Activity and a research associate of the National Bureau of Economic Research. From 1977 to 1979, Mr. Nordhaus was a member of President Carter's Council of Economic Advisers. He received his Ph.D. in economics from the Massachusetts Institute of Technology.

JAMES M. POTERBA is professor of economics at the Massachusetts Institute of Technology, where he has been on the faculty since 1983. He has published widely on public finance and corporate finance. Mr. Poterba is the co-editor of the *Rand Journal* and associate editor of four journals, including the *Journal of Finance* and the *Journal of Public Economics*. In 1988, he was a visiting professor in the Graduate School of Business at the University of Chicago. Mr. Poterba received his D.Phil. in economics from Oxford University.

JOHN B. SHOVEN is professor of economics at Stanford University, where he has been a member of the economics faculty since 1973. He is director of the Center for Economic Policy Research and a codirector of the National Bureau of Economic Research. Mr. Shoven's research interests include public and private pensions, corporate finance, international cost-of-capital comparisons, federal personal and corporate income taxation, and applied general equilibrium analysis. In addition to teaching at Stanford, he has held posts at Yale, Harvard, and Kyoto universities. He is a frequent adviser to government agencies. Mr. Shoven received his Ph.D. in economics from Yale University.

1

Introduction

Carolyn L. Weaver

The financial condition of the social security system (Old-Age and Survivors Insurance, Disability Insurance, and Hospital Insurance) is a source of concern to some and confusion to many. On the one hand, the system is sitting atop a reserve fund in 1990 of $280 billion, twice its size in 1988 and four times its size in 1985.[1] Growing at a rate of $1.6 billion weekly in 1990 (and more thereafter), reserves are projected to reach a half-trillion dollars in 1992 and $1 trillion in 1996.[2] Some have been led to wonder whether social security will amass such a large reserve of U.S. government bonds that it will hold the entire national debt. If the size of the social security reserves can be taken as a measure of financial well-being, social security is in better shape than it has been in the past twenty years.

On the other hand, the social security system poses an enormous long-range liability, on the order of $25 trillion in present value terms ($15 trillion excluding hospital insurance).[3] According to the social security board of trustees, this liability cannot be met with the current structure of taxes and benefits. Interest earnings on trust fund reserves, together with all future tax revenues, will not be sufficient to cover future benefits. With the reserves invested entirely in government bonds and the federal government operating in the red, moreover, it is not immediately obvious whether the social security surpluses are being saved and invested for future years or spent on current consumption.

For the first time in many years, serious questions are being raised about the way the social security system is financed and its assets are invested. Are the reserve funds being productively saved and invested for future years? Are the excess taxes now being collected enhancing benefit security for baby-boom retirees? Will advance funding increase real incomes and lighten the burden of future benefits? If the answer to these questions is no, what policies can be put in place to promote these goals? This book addresses each of these questions head-on.

1

To put some of the issues addressed in this book into perspective, a brief review of the present and projected financial condition of the social security trust funds follows.

The Financial Outlook

Tables 1–1 and 1–2 summarize the social security surpluses (or deficits) and the accumulated reserves of the Old-Age, Survivors, and Disability Insurance (OASDI) and Old-Age, Survivors, Disability, and Hospital Insurance (OASDHI) trust funds.[4] The data are displayed in nominal and in real 1989 dollars, as well as in relation to program size and gross national product. Future projections are based on the social security board of trustees' intermediate economic and demographic assumptions, which are the ones traditionally used by policy makers.[5]

As the tables reveal, social security is projected to run very large surpluses, measured in nominal dollars, over the course of the next thirty years. In OASDI, the surplus in 1990 is $69 billion, projected to rise to $203 billion in 2000 and to peak at nearly $500 billion in 2015. Trust fund reserves, which reflect the accumulated balances over time, are thus projected to grow continuously over the next four decades, reaching approximately $12 trillion in 2030.

When the figures are adjusted for inflation, the same patterns are observed, although the dimensions of the looming surpluses are less impressive (or forbidding, depending on perspective). In real 1989 dollars, the annual surplus in OASDI peaks at $187 billion in 2010, and the reserve fund peaks at $2.8 trillion in 2020.

These trends in OASDI financing generally extend to the system as a whole, including hospital insurance, except that the combined surpluses are projected to be somewhat larger through the mid-1990s and smaller thereafter, with the total reserve funds peaking about a decade earlier. The generally more adverse long-range financial picture of HI takes its toll by reducing projected trust fund accumulations from a peak of $12 trillion to a peak of just $5.8 trillion. In real 1989 dollars, the annual surplus peaks at $126 billion in 2005, with total reserves peaking at $1.9 trillion in 2015.

If the reserves are evaluated relative to the size of the programs, it can be seen that the reserves of the OASDI trust funds, estimated at the start of 1990 to be 77 percent of annual outlays, are the equivalent of about nine months' worth of benefits. Reserves are projected to rise to about five years' worth of benefits, or 546 percent of outlays, in 2015. Reserves last amounted to five or more times outgo in the early 1950s and have been less than 100 percent of outgo since the early 1970s. The reserves of the OASDHI trust funds, estimated to be 87 percent of

TABLE 1–1

ANNUAL SOCIAL SECURITY SURPLUSES AND DEFICITS, 1960–2060

| | Annual Surplus or Deficit | | | | |
Year	Current dollars (billions)	Real (1989) dollars (billions)	As % of GNP	Interest as % of income	Net balance as % of GNP
		OASDI			
1960	1	3	.13	5	.02
1970	4	12	.38	5	.21
1980	−4	−6	−.14	2	−.23
1990	69	66	1.25	6	.91
1995	125	97	1.64	12	.93
2000	203	130	1.97	15	1.01
2005	308	162	2.21	17	1.06
2010	431	187	2.31	21	.86
2015	494	176	2.02	23	.35
2020	448	131	1.40	24	−.32
2025	278	68	.67	23	−.92
2030	−4	−1	−.01	19	−1.30
2035	−372	−60	−.52	14	−1.43
2040	−836	−112	−.90	9	−1.40
2045	−1,558	−171	−1.28	2	−1.38
2050	−2,780	−250	−1.75	a	−1.43
2055	−4,745	−351	−2.29		−1.51
2060	−7,673	−467	−2.83		−1.57
		OASDHI			
1960	1	3	.13	5	.02
1970	5	14	.45	5	.26
1980	−3	−5	−0.12	2	−.25
1990	82	79	1.49	7	.99
1995	127	99	1.67	11	.83
2000	179	115	1.74	13	.73
2005	240	126	1.72	14	.62
2010	278	120	1.49	16	.25
2015	197	70	.81	16	−.44
2020	−109	−32	−.34	13	−1.35
2025	−719	−173	−1.73	7	−2.23
2030	−1,684	−332	−3.10	a	−2.84
2035	−3,048	−495	−4.28		−3.12
2040	−4,931	−658	−5.29		−3.15
2045	−7,669	−841	−6.29		−3.15
2050	−11,776	−1,061	−7.41		−3.22
2055	−17,871	−1,324	−8.61		−3.32
2060	−26,702	−1,625	−9.83		−3.39

NOTE: The annual surplus (or deficit) is total income minus total outgo. The net balance excludes interest income. Projections, beginning in 1990, are based on the Trustees' intermediate II-B assumptions.

a. Reserves are exhausted and there is no interest income.

SOURCE: For OASDI, see *1989 Annual Report of the Board of Trustees of the Federal Old-Age and Survivors Insurance and Federal Disability Insurance Trust Funds.* Author's computations for OASDI are based on data contained in *1989 OASDI Trustees' Report* and underlying interest rate and CPI assumptions.

TABLE 1–2

SOCIAL SECURITY RESERVES, 1950–2060

(billions of dollars)

	Current Dollars		Real (1989) Dollars		As a % of Outlay	
Year	OASDI	OASDHI	OASDI	OASDHI	OASDI	OASDHI
1950	12	12	60	60	1,156	1,156
1955	21	21	93	93	405	405
1960	22	22	92	92	186	186
1965	21	21	83	82	110	110
1970	34	37	114	122	103	96
1975	46	55	113	136	66	68
1980	30	44	51	73	25	29
1985	46	62	55	74	24	26
1990	195	280	195	280	77	87
1995	646	786	523	636	188	174
2000	1,428	1,535	952	1,022	312	247
2005	2,651	2,580	1,451	1,412	431	301
2010	4,473	3,923	2,012	1,765	522	324
2015	6,817	5,260	2,521	1,945	546	299
2020	9,276	5,768	2,819	1,753	505	224
2025	11,269	4,161	2,815	1,039	428	112
2030	12,182	−1,201[a]	2,501	−247[a]	336	−23
2035	11,526	−12,139	1,945	−2,049	239	−176
2040	8,894	−30,852	1,234	−4,279	143	−342
2045	3,543	−60,505	404	−6,898	44	−517
2050	−6,275[b]	−105,610	−588[a]	−9,896	−60	−691
2055	−23,562	−175,542	−1,815	−13,520	−170	−875
2060	−52,437	−281,022	−3,319	−17,790	−289	−1,069

NOTE: Reserves are the accumulated assets at start of year. Projections, beginning in 1990, are based on the Trustees' intermediate II-B assumptions.

a. Reserves are exhausted. Negative figures show the cumulative amount of money that would need to be borrowed to pay benefits. (The trust funds do not have the authority to borrow from one another or from the general fund of the Treasury.)

SOURCE: For historical data, see *Social Security Bulletin: Annual Statistical Supplement*, 1988, tables 4.A3 and 7.A1. OASDI projections are based on data contained in *1989 Annual Report of the Board of Trustees* of the *Federal Old-Age and Survivors Insurance and Federal Disability Insurance Trust Funds*, and data supplied by the Office of the Actuary, Social Security Administration. HI projections are author's computations based on income and outgo data contained in the *1989 OASDI Trustees' Report*, and the underlying interest rate and CPI assumptions.

annual outlays at the start of 1990, are projected to peak at 324 percent in 2010.[6]

A clearer picture of the size of the surpluses can be gained by evaluating the annual balances in relation to gross national product (see table 1–1). Two figures are shown for both the OASDI and OASDHI trust funds, one that is evaluated using total income and one that excludes interest income. Including interest income, the OASDI surplus is projected to average 1.96 percent of GNP over the next twenty-five years, peaking at 2.31 percent in 2010. These figures are substantially larger than in the past; between 1960 and 1985, the average annual balance was less than 0.1 percent of GNP. If the OASDHI trust funds are combined, the annual surplus peaks at 1.74 percent of GNP in 2000. Excluding interest income, the average annual OASDI surplus (referred to as the net balance in table 1–1) over the next twenty-five years is cut by over half, from 1.96 percent to 0.90 percent of GNP. This figure compares with a net balance in the period 1960–1985 of less than 0.1 percent. The net OASDHI surplus is projected to average 0.5 percent of GNP over the next twenty-five years as compared with 0.01 percent in the period 1960–1985.

For purposes of comparison, the federal budget deficit averaged 2.3 percent of GNP in the period 1960–1990; over the same period, the deficit excluding social security averaged 2.45 percent of GNP.[7]

While the social security surpluses may not be as large as popularly believed—and may not last as long as policy makers would hope—they nevertheless are with us and already are of a size unprecedented in the history of the program. The chapters in this book assess the likely effects of these surpluses on the economy, on federal tax and budget policy, on the security of future benefits, and, ultimately, on the well-being of present and future workers and retirees.

Looming Deficits

Important to understanding the financial condition of social security is the fact that the surpluses the system now enjoys are not expected to last indefinitely. Even if we ignore the possibility that the actuaries' projections prove too optimistic or that Congress enacts benefit increases or tax cuts down the road that undermine financing, long-range demographic trends are such that deficits are very likely to emerge before today's younger workers have retired. Indeed, the social security financing picture is expected to change quite dramatically when the baby-boom generation moves into retirement. After about 2020 or 2030, the social security board of trustees projects a string of deficits growing in magnitude over time. Selling off the bonds held by the trust funds will be the way benefits are met, but this can work only so long. Under the trustees' intermediate assumptions, the combined OASDHI trust funds will be insolvent in 2030; the OASDI trust funds will be insolvent in 2046.

TABLE 1–3

THE CHANGING DEMOGRAPHICS OF U.S. WORKERS, 1960–2060

Year	Number of Workers (thousands)	Number of Beneficiaries (thousands)	Workers per Beneficiary	Percentage 65 and Older
1960	72,530	14,262	5.1	9.1
1970	93,090	25,186	3.7	9.7
1980	112,212	35,119	3.2	11.1
1990	130,708	39,618	3.3	12.4
2000	142,124	44,212	3.2	12.7
2010	150,989	50,566	3.0	13.5
2020	151,591	64,129	2.4	17.1
2030	150,613	76,151	2.0	20.9
2040	151,192	79,381	1.9	21.6
2050	150,776	80,780	1.9	21.7
2060	150,606	82,920	1.8	22.5

NOTE: Projections, beginning in 1990, are based on the trustees' intermediate II-B assumptions.
SOURCE: The *1989 OASDI Trustees' Report*, tables 30 and A1.

The pattern of large annual surpluses followed by growing annual deficits is a natural byproduct of long-term demographic trends coupled with the way social security is financed. As revealed in table 1–3, in the span of just two decades, 2010 to 2030, the number of people on the benefit rolls is expected to grow by 26 million, or roughly half, while the number of workers is expected to remain virtually constant. The ratio of workers to beneficiaries is thus projected to fall from 3:1 to 2:1. This will put real pressure on the cost of benefits in the next century. In addition, social security benefits are computed in a way that causes their real dollar value to rise over time.[8]

Figures 1–1 and 1–2 illustrate the cost of OASDI and OASDHI as projected by the social security board of trustees under three sets of assumptions: alternative I, alternative II-B, and alternative III, referred to as optimistic, intermediate, and pessimistic.[9] Cost is expressed as a percentage of taxable payroll in the economy since this provides a convenient measure of the payroll tax (employee and employer rate combined) that would need to be levied to meet benefit costs on a pay-as-you-go basis. After a brief period in the 1990s in which the relative cost of benefits declines (as a result of the low birth rates in the 1930s), costs rise quite rapidly under each of the three projections. Under the intermediate assumptions, the cost of OASDI jumps by roughly one-half, from 10.25 percent to 15.23 percent of taxable payroll,

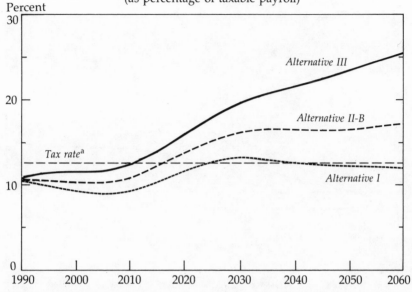

FIGURE 1–1

OASDI COST RATE AND TAX RATE, 1990–2060
(as percentage of taxable payroll)

a. Employee and employer rate combined.
SOURCE: 1989 Trustees' Reports.

in the period 2005–2025. The average cost of social security, including HI, reaches 21 percent of taxable payroll in 2025 and rises to 23–24 percent after about 2030. Under pessimistic assumptions, the long-range cost of OASDHI mounts even more rapidly and ultimately reaches a very high level—just over 30 percent of taxable payroll in 2030 and 40 percent of taxable payroll in 2060. As figures 1–1 and 1–2 make clear, costs remain high after the retirement of the baby-boom rather than returning to their prebulge level.

Given this pattern of costs, the flat payroll tax now in the law virtually guarantees that today's surpluses and reserve accumulation will give way to deficits and reserve depletion in the future. Under the 1983 Social Security Amendments, the payroll tax rate in 1990 and thereafter is 12.4 percent (15.3 percent including HI, employee and employer rate combined). This is projected, using the trustees' intermediate assumptions, to generate more revenues than needed to meet OASDI benefits for the next two to three decades but substantially less than needed to meet benefits thereafter. Interest earnings on the bonds purchased during the surplus years are expected to supplement future

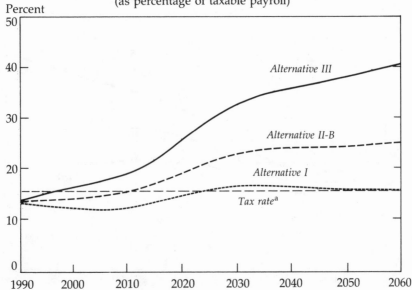

FIGURE 1–2

OASDHI COST RATE AND TAX RATE, 1990–2060

(as percentage of taxable payroll)

a. Employee and employer rate combined.
SOURCE: 1989 Trustees' Reports.

tax revenues and allow benefits to be met for a decade beyond the
point at which taxes alone would be sufficient. When benefits can no
longer be met with the available tax and interest income, projected by
the trustees to occur around 2030, the Treasury would be called on to
redeem the bonds held by the trust funds—and to continue to do so
until the trust funds are exhausted. The pattern of surpluses and
reserve accumulation followed by deficits and reserve depletion is
observed under each set of assumptions used by the trustees. The
trust funds become insolvent before the end of the long-range measuring period (2065) under the intermediate and pessimistic cost assumptions.

These projections suggest two questions addressed throughout
this book. First, does the current structure of benefits present a realistic
cost burden in the next century? Second, can future costs be met without increasing national saving (for example, through meaningful advance funding of social security) or in other ways increasing the
productive capacity of the United States in the next century?

8

The Growing Role of Interest

One consequence of the (partial) advance funding of social security is that interest earnings—as distinct from payroll tax revenues—play a growing role in the long-range solvency of social security. As illustrated in table 1–1, interest earnings are projected to account for 15 percent of income to the OASDI trust funds in 2000, or nearly half the surplus in that year, rising to 24 percent of income in 2020, which is more than the surplus in that year. Interest will account for just 6 percent of income to OASDI in 1990, and this will be a thirty-year high.

Since interest is an obligation of the general fund of the Treasury—and thus must be financed either by cuts in federal spending, increases in income or other federal taxes, or by new federal borrowing—questions have been raised about whether advance funding reduces the burden of social security or simply redistributes it among taxpayers.[10] Questions have also been raised about how to measure the impact of social security on the federal budget and ultimately on the economy since social security can, and periodically does, run surpluses due entirely to interest and other intragovernmental transfers. In these situations—trust fund surpluses notwithstanding—tax income is insufficient to cover benefit costs, and the government must borrow to meet the balance of benefits.

Some economists argue that the proper measure of the impact of social security on the budget is shown by excluding interest payments. This is the view presented, for example, in the 1989 *Economic Report of the President*.[11] Alicia Munnell takes the other position, arguing that interest payments (and intragovernmental transfers generally) should be included.[12] In her view, these payments amount to outlays the government otherwise would have made to the public. Because of the trust fund surpluses, and the ability of the government to borrow from the trust funds rather than from private individuals, total federal spending in future years is lower than it otherwise would be.

Which assessment is correct—and, indeed, whether advance funding reduces the burden of social security—turns on whether decisions regarding social security and the rest of the federal budget are largely independent. If fiscal decisions are independent—and the social security surpluses have no effect on the level of income taxes or spending on other federal programs—then the surpluses reduce the amount of outstanding debt held by the public (and increase government saving) dollar for dollar. Fiscal decisions are dependent if, by contrast, the surpluses relax fiscal restraint in the rest of the budget, causing income taxes to be lower than they otherwise would be or spending on

TABLE 1–4
SOCIAL SECURITY AND THE FEDERAL BUDGET, FISCAL YEARS 1990–1995
(billions of dollars)

	1990	1991	1992	1993	1994	1995
OASDI surplus	66	74	85	98	112	128
On-budget deficit[a]	204	212	221	239	242	246
Total budget deficit	138	138	135	141	130	118
Deficit targets	100	64	28	0	b	b

a. Excludes social security (OASDI) and Postal Service.
b. Gramm-Rudman targets effective fiscal years 1988–1993.
SOURCE: U.S. Congressional Budget Office, *The Economic and Budget Outlook: Fiscal Years 1991–1995* (January 1990).

other programs to be higher; in the extreme, the surpluses could be fully spent on deficit increases in the rest of the budget.

Social Security and the Budget

Under present law, the OASDI trust funds are technically "off budget," in the sense that data on trust fund income, outgo, and balances are reported separately from data on the rest of the federal budget in the president's annual budget. They are, however, included in federal budget computations for purposes of the Gramm-Rudman-Hollings legislation, which requires balance in the overall federal budget by fiscal year 1993. The HI trust fund is on budget for both purposes.[13] A one-dollar increase in the social security surpluses thus reduces by one dollar the amount of savings (or new revenues) the government must achieve in the rest of the budget to meet the deficit reduction targets in Gramm-Rudman.

Table 1–4 shows the federal deficit including and excluding OASDI, based on projections by the Congressional Budget Office, in relation to the Gramm-Rudman deficit reduction targets now in the law. As illustrated, the social security surpluses are expected to play a significant role in keeping the total budget deficit in check in the next few years. In fact, according to these CBO projections, were it not for the social security surpluses, the federal deficit would rise in each of the next five years rather than move toward balance as required by the law. Projected increases in the deficit in the rest of the budget are more than offset by the growing surpluses in the social security trust funds. These trends have raised concerns that the surpluses are relaxing fiscal restraint in the rest of the budget and, as a result, are being spent on current consumption rather than being saved.

While views differ on how to interpret these trends, the chapters in this book clearly suggest that a proper understanding warrants more than a casual look at a set of budget numbers. Issues that must be considered are the construction of the Gramm-Rudman targets (were they, for example, influenced by the size of the projected trust fund surpluses?), the nature of the interest payments, the relationship between tax and spending decisions in the various components of the budget, and, generally, the path of surpluses and deficits relative to the size of the economy. The current and proper relationship between social security, the federal budget, and Gramm-Rudman is an important theme throughout this book.

A Word about the Moynihan Proposal

Sen. Daniel P. Moynihan, who participated as a member and helped develop the recommendations of the 1983 National Commission on Social Security Reform, recently proposed cutting the social security payroll tax and returning the system to a pay-as-you-go basis. Under his proposal, the payroll tax would be rolled back from 15.3 percent (employee and employer combined) to 15.02 percent in 1990 and to 13.1 percent in 1991, remaining at that level until 2012. The tax would then be increased in stages to 19.1 percent in 2045. This schedule of taxes is projected, using the trustees' intermediate economic and demographic assumptions, to allow OASDI benefits to be paid while maintaining a reserve of approximately 100 percent of annual outgo for the next seventy-five years.[14] Senator Moynihan argues for this change on the grounds that the conduct of federal budget policy is effectively undermining any real saving of the social security surpluses. Without saving, the excess payroll taxes needed to sustain advance funding are, in his view, undermining the progressivity of the federal tax system and placing an undue burden on middle- and low-income workers.

The interest in—if not support for—the Moynihan proposal is a measure of the salience of the social security financing issue to American workers and retirees. For many of the over 130 million workers who pay social security taxes, these taxes are higher than federal income taxes.[15] Some 39 million people, or about one in seven Americans, receive a check each month from the Social Security Administration. The solvency of the system and the investment of and rate of return on taxes are of direct concern to millions of Americans.

The chapters in this book, while written before Senator Moynihan introduced his proposal, fully anticipated the possibility of this type of proposal. The book provides a careful evaluation of the problems and prospects of advance funding relative to pay-as-you-go financing and raises serious questions about the political sustainability of the social security surpluses.[16]

And a Word about HI

The chapters in this book generally focus on the OASDI portion of social security, excluding HI. In part this is because the 1983 amendments, which helped bring about the reserve accumulation now being observed, were addressed to OASDI. While the legislation included some significant changes that affected HI, its purpose was to shore up the short- and long-range financing of the OASDI trust funds. In addition, there are important differences in the key factors affecting the long-range cost of OASDI and HI. Different kinds of reforms therefore may be appropriate for the two portions of the system. With that said, however, the economic arguments for and against advance funding— or the likely economic, fiscal, and political effects of advance funding— are largely the same for OASDI and HI. A realistic assessment of the cost of social security or of the intergenerational wealth transfers implied by the system necessitate an examination of the OASI, DI, and HI programs combined, which pose a substantially larger long-range liability than OASI and DI alone.

The Plan of the Book

The four parts of this book deal with the following aspects of the economic, budgetary, and political consequences of the social security surpluses. Part one examines the desirability of increasing national saving through the social security trust funds and the problems of assessing the stance of fiscal policy with the official measures of deficits and debt now in use. Part two looks at the budgetary politics of the social security surpluses. How are the surpluses likely to affect congressional decisions on taxes and spending, and could these effects undermine the purposes and objectives of advance funding? Part three presents empirical evidence on the effect of social security on government budgets and national saving in the United States and abroad. (A few countries have attempted, with more or less success, to advance fund their social security systems.) Finally, part four explores future directions for policy and policy making.

While the opinions and research presented in this book represent a broad spectrum of views, common themes emerge. First, advance funding—properly structured—offers the potential for increasing national saving in anticipation of the retirement of the baby-boom and the strains that that will inevitably place on the federal budget and the economy at that time. Second, advance funding does not necessarily or automatically increase national saving or in other ways lighten the burden of future benefits. To the contrary, it poses risks to today's workers and future taxpayers as well as to long-term economic performance. Third, without changes in the way social security's assets are invested or more basic changes in the way the system operates, the success or failure of advance funding will be determined by fiscal policy actions outside the social security system, not just by actions involving social security.

The chapters in this book represent the culmination of a two-year research project sponsored by the Pew Charitable Trusts. This project brought together a group of distinguished scholars from around the country to conduct research and to participate in a major public policy conference on various aspects of the social security trust fund accumulation. The conference was held at the American Enterprise Institute in March 1989.

PART ONE
Promoting National Saving through the Social Security Trust Funds

2

The Social Security "Surpluses"—New Clothes for the Emperor?

Laurence J. Kotlikoff

The current debate over how to interpret the impending social security "surpluses" is symptomatic of a widespread fallacy, namely that the government "deficit" is a well-defined and useful measure of fiscal policy. Since the projected social security "surpluses," like the unified budget "deficit," have no real economic import, it would be unproductive to take these numbers seriously. Instead, I take as my first task to set forth a conceptual framework for judging the stance of fiscal policy and social security's role in fiscal policy and as my second task to explain why the so-called social security surpluses in particular and fiscal deficits in general do not necessarily reveal anything useful about the stance of fiscal policy. This approach will permit a meaningful discussion of current and possible future social security policy as a component of U.S. fiscal policy.

In a consideration of future policy, the social security surpluses are important not because they tell us anything we want to know but because so many people are paying attention to them. These meaningless auguries lead people to believe that we will have tight fiscal policy in the 1990s. As a result, there is a clear danger that fiscal policy will be greatly loosened in the 1990s at a time when fiscal policy would not be particularly tight anyway. Such a decision could further reduce U.S. saving.

The belief that the deficit tells us something meaningful about the stance of fiscal policy is, unfortunately, thoroughly ingrained in the public's perception as well as in the perceptions of most economists. Our fixation with the deficit is the result of a half-century's infatuation

I am grateful to Jane Gravelle for helpful comments.

with the Keynesian model in which the deficit plays such a key role. While the Keynesian model is easy to use, it has no precise grounding in microeconomics; as a consequence, it is fraught with fiscal illusion.[1]

When the public is systematically fooled by fiscal labels and misreads fiscal policy, it is deceived by a fiscal illusion. For example, suppose the federal government decided to label as "taxes" all the money it says it is "borrowing" this year and to label as "transfer payments" what was previously described as the repayment of "principal plus interest" on this "borrowing." While the words the government used to describe its receipts and payments would differ, the real policy would be unaffected. Those previously "lending" money to the government would find themselves "taxed," and by the same amount, and rather than receiving in the future the "return of principal plus interest" on these "loans," they would receive equivalent "transfer payments." If the individuals making these payments today and receiving these payments in the future are rational, their behavior will not be affected by this change in labels. According to the Keynesian model, however, this change in labels would result in a reported federal government deficit for this year of zero and a whopping change in economic behavior.

The notion that the Keynesian model embeds fiscal illusion and that there is a deep problem in using the deficit to measure fiscal policy is hardly new. It has been lurking in fiscal policy discussions since the mid-1970s, when Martin Feldstein pointed out that the government had accumulated vast unfunded social security liabilities without ever showing them on the books.[2] Others were quick to point to civil service and military pensions whose unfunded liabilities were also left out of the official national debt. Still others cited an array of government obligations, some legal and some simply economic (such as the clear commitment to maintain the National Park System), that might well be added to official debt. The question of where to draw the line in making such corrections has left many people with the uneasy feeling that the entire enterprise of defining government debt is simply arbitrary. It is.

Fortunately, this unease has been very greatly heightened by the projections of social security–induced budget surpluses. The questions typically raised are these: Do the huge impending surpluses mean we will be running tight fiscal policy starting in the 1990s? If so, what has changed or will change to transform the very loose current fiscal policy into a tight fiscal policy? How can we safeguard the trust funds and the welfare of baby-boom retirees?

The answers to these questions are straightforward, even if unpopular with those who fashioned the 1983 reforms. First, the impending social security surpluses tell us nothing about the stance of fiscal policy in the 1990s, just as the current budget deficits tell us nothing about the current stance of fiscal policy. Second, determining the stance of fiscal policy requires understanding how different generations are being treated and will be treated by the government. Tightening fiscal policy, for example, means making earlier (older) generations pay for a larger fraction of the government's current and projected consumption. Since the basic treatment of different generations is not projected to change in the next decade, at least under current law, we have no reason to project a tightening of fiscal policy in the 1990s. Third, the only way to safeguard the welfare of the baby-boom generation is to understand comprehensively their treatment by the government and to require that that treatment not worsen.

Fiscal Policy and Generational Accounts

One of the important lessons of Hans Christian Andersen's *The Emperor's New Clothes* is that mistaken beliefs, if repeated often and loud enough, can become accepted truth.[3] Another is that mistaken beliefs attract their own constituencies (the emperor's tailors). A third is that sometimes the less one knows about an issue, the better (it takes a child to see clearly). A fourth, and perhaps the most important, is that asking fundamental questions is important.

The fundamental question about "deficits" and "surpluses" is, Who will pay for the government's current and future consumption—present or future generations? The answer to this question is of particular importance for national saving. A decision to make future generations pick up more of the tab—to run loose fiscal policy—means that current generations can afford to consume more. If current generations do consume more, the nation will save less. If, as appears to be the case in the United States, the nation's investment depends on its saving, passing the bill to the next generation also means less current investment.

Over time, the "crowding out" of saving and investment through redistribution to earlier generations will raise real interest rates and depress real wages. This change in interest rates and wages constitutes a second round redistribution that also runs from later to earlier generations. In their old age earlier generations benefit from the higher real interest rates but do not suffer from the depressed real wages experienced by younger people.[4]

Notwithstanding its popular use, the official government deficit tells us nothing about the share of the government's consumption paid for by different generations. Hence, it tells us nothing that we need to know to determine if policy is tight or loose or if policy will "crowd in" or "crowd out" national saving.

What is needed is a method of accounting that reveals how different generations are being treated and are expected to be treated by the government. Such accounts would reflect the basic intertemporal budget constraint of the economy, namely that the economy's resources (the sum of its human and nonhuman wealth) equal the sum of the present value of private consumption plus government consumption.[5] The present value of private consumption, in turn, equals the sum of each generation's present value of consumption. I refer to each generation's present value of consumption as its "generational account."

In graphic terms, the economy's budget constraint says that there is a pie (the present value of the economy's resources) to be consumed by the government (both current and future governments) and the private sector (current and future generations). Since the size of the pie is fixed, the government's decision to consume a bigger slice of the pie leaves less pie to be divided among current and future generations. The government determines both the amount of pie consumed by the private sector and, given that decision, the size of the slices consumed by each generation. A decision to give earlier generations larger slices and later generations smaller slices corresponds to loosening fiscal policy. A side effect of running loose policy is that if crowding out occurs, earlier generations will also get to consume more because interest rates and wages will change in a way that will give them indirectly more pie at the expense of later generations.

Generational accounts would state, quite simply, the amount of pie available for each generation to consume. In convenient double-entry bookkeeping fashion, these accounts would add up to the total pie less the government's slice. Given an existing set of such accounts, the generational implications of any change in fiscal policy would be easy to observe by looking at changes in the accounts. Consider, for example, a decision by the government to consume more in present value. By looking at the changes in the accounts of different generations, one could immediately determine which generations were slated to pay the bill for the government's increased consumption. Alternatively, consider a policy in which the government does not alter its consumption but enacts legislation favorable to earlier generations and unfavorable to later generations. These changes would appear in the generational accounts as positive changes (larger slices of pie) for some generations and negative changes (smaller slices of pie) for others.

Generational accounts would be constructed by adding together, for each generation, three components: (1) its nonhuman wealth; (2) the present expected value, through the maximum age of death, of its human wealth; and (3) the present expected value, through the maximum age of death, of the (possibly negative) net payments the generation expects to receive from the government. The present expected value of each generation's lifetime resources is the present expected value of what each generation can afford to consume over its lifetime.

The major advantage of generational accounts is that, unlike the official deficit, they do not vary with the government's choice of fiscal labels. For example, a decision to label social security contributions as taxes, rather than loans from the private sector, and social security benefits as transfers, rather than repayment of principal plus interest on social security loans, would have no impact on generational accounts. A second advantage of generational accounts is that they would tell us not only about current policy but also about projected future policy. In other words, they would describe, in present value terms, the government's intended time path of policy. In contrast, official deficits describe, in a completely arbitrary manner, only the government's cash flow at a particular time and reveal nothing about the projected time path of policy. A third advantage of generational accounts is that they correspond to the lifetime budget constraints of generations in the life cycle model.[6] As such, the life cycle model allows the economic implications of policy-induced changes in the generational accounts to be readily evaluated.

While such generational accounts remain to be constructed, the concept of generational accounts is, by itself, extremely useful. It provides a framework for understanding fiscal policy and for judging the problems in using official deficits.

The Social Security "Surpluses" as Indicators of Fiscal Policy

There are many ways to see that the social security surpluses do not reveal anything useful about the true stance of fiscal policy. To begin, suppose that the 1983 Social Security Amendments had mandated no change in social security payroll taxes, including the earnings ceiling, until the year 2000 but that it had mandated larger increases in payroll taxes after the year 2000 that would have left the 1983 generational accounts roughly unchanged. This alternative timing of social security cash flows, while leaving basically unchanged the generational accounts and therefore the stance of fiscal policy, would indicate much smaller official surpluses and indeed possible deficits in the 1990s. Hence, social security deficits in the 1990s could be associated with the same real fiscal policy as social security surpluses.

As a second example, suppose that the government chooses, starting this year, to label the lifetime social security contributions of all new young workers as government borrowing, giving these workers social security bonds in exchange for their contributions. Suppose also that the government labels the future social security benefit payments to these individuals as repayment of principal plus interest plus a tax that corresponds to the difference between actual benefits and principal plus interest on contributions.

To see what is involved here, consider a worker who contributes $50,000 to social security during his working years and receives $60,000 in benefits during retirement. Suppose that principle plus interest on the $50,000 contribution corresponds to $70,000 in benefits. Then the government could label the $50,000 contribution as borrowing from the worker, and it could label the $60,000 benefit payment as a $70,000 repayment of principal plus interest on the $50,000 previously borrowed plus a tax of $10,000. The careful reader might object to this nomenclature because possible changes in law make the return on social security contributions uncertain. To accommodate this possibility and to make the $50,000 borrowing identical to other government borrowing in the risk properties of its payoff, the government simply guarantees the repayment of principal plus interest on the social security bonds while adapting to any future change in policy by adjusting the social security tax. In terms of the example, if benefit payments ultimately total only $50,000, the government labels the benefit payment as a $70,000 repayment of principal plus interest and a $20,000 social security tax. If benefit payments ultimately total, say, $80,000, the government labels this payment as a $70,000 repayment of principal plus interest plus a social security transfer payment (a negative tax) of $10,000.

Note that this change in labeling will have no economic implications if workers and other participants in the economy are rational. Workers contribute the same amount they would otherwise contribute and receive the same payments they would otherwise receive. The only difference is the labels. This relabeling would, however, greatly reduce the time path of reported social security surpluses and lead to much larger official deficits in the 1990s and the early part of the next century than are currently projected. Those who fear that the social security surpluses will lead to a misguided loosening of fiscal policy over the next few decades may view this relabeling scheme as a clever way to show more debt on the books.

Any economist who thinks the "deficit" tells him or her anything useful about fiscal policy should be greatly troubled by this illustration of alternative fiscal labeling. The fact that the government has chosen one set of labels and is not likely to adopt the alternative labeling scheme does not preclude economists from considering this equally valid alternative time series on deficits in thinking about the stance of fiscal policy. Indeed, by changing the labeling of receipts and payments, economists can contemplate a virtually infinite array of alternative time series on deficits, each of which corresponds to the same underlying real fiscal policy. These alternative time series on the deficit would be dramatically different from one another; furthermore, their changes from one year to the next would, in many cases, be opposite in sign. How then does an economist use them to judge the stance of fiscal policy? Stated differently, how do we know the United States has not been running enormous surpluses in the 1980s? The answer is we do not. The official U.S. deficit is only one of a myriad of equally useless time series.

Generational Accounts, the 1983 Social Security Amendments, and Fiscal Policy in the 1980s

Although complete generational accounts are not yet available, we can think through how the 1983 Social Security Amendments, taken alone, would have changed the accounts for now living generations. Recall that the 1983 amendments did not greatly alter the treatment of current elderly recipients. While it did include a provision to tax under the income tax the social security benefits of upper-income elderly, this change did not and will not affect the great majority of people who are already elderly.

The real import of the 1983 amendments lies in their treatment of the baby boom and future generations. The 1983 amendments significantly reduced the generational accounts of the baby-boom by: (1) advancing the normal social security retirement age from sixty-five to sixty-seven; (2) raising payroll taxes; and (3) subjecting a growing fraction of future social security benefits to income taxation. This third provision works through "bracket creep," since the level of income beyond which social security benefits are taxed is not indexed.

In reducing the generational accounts of members of the baby-boom generation, the 1983 amendments implicitly increased the generational accounts of the children of the baby-boom and subsequent generations. It did this by reducing the amount they will have to pay over their lifetimes to finance baby-boom retirees.

From a generational accounts perspective, the 1983 amendments were fiscally very conservative. According to the estimates of the Social Security Administration's Office of the Actuary, the 1983 amendments reduced the generational accounts of adults over age eighteen by roughly $1 trillion.[7] Since the present expected value of government consumption was not altered by the 1983 amendments, this represents a $1 trillion present value gain to future generations.

To gain some perspective on this fiscally conservative policy, let us compare the magnitude of its generational accounts with the budget deficits incurred during the Reagan administration. The buildup of official debt during the Reagan years was roughly $1 trillion. Assuming, for the sake of argument, that none of the burden of paying off this liability falls on current generations, the Reagan deficits represent an increase in the generational accounts of current generations of roughly $1 trillion at the expense of a decline in the generational accounts of future generations of the same amount. Hence, roughly speaking, the social security amendments and the Reagan "deficits" cancel in terms of their combined impact on generational accounts, suggesting no loosening (and perhaps some tightening if current generations pay off some of the new official debt) of fiscal policy during the 1980s.

Evidently, a generational accounts approach provides a very different perspective on the stance of fiscal policy during the 1980s[8] since generational accounts capture all policies that redistribute across generations, including policies that do not alter the official deficit.

Tight Fiscal Policy Now or in the 1990s?

As noted, the 1983 Social Security Amendments reduced the generational accounts of the baby boom to the benefit of their children. An important question to ask is whether this fiscally conservative legislation has already tightened fiscal policy and, if not, when it will. The answer, according to the life cycle model, is that the legislation tightened policy as of 1983. In the life cycle model, households make current consumption decisions based on the present value of expected lifetime resources. When the 1983 amendments were signed, the present expected value of resources of the baby-boom generation was reduced despite the fact that many of the provisions will not take effect until the future. Thus the change in fiscal policy occurred in 1983, and its impact is predicted, by the life cycle model, to have begun affecting consumption choices starting in that year. The fact that large social security surpluses will begin to accumulate in the 1990s does not have any bearing on when the legislation tightened fiscal policy.

Given that the tightening of fiscal policy occurred in 1983, do the larger surpluses in the 1990s mean that fiscal policy in the 1990s will be tighter than in the 1980s? Assuming no major changes in the generational stance of fiscal policy, changes in the generational accounts between now and the 1990s will reflect only changes in endogenous variables, such as the human wealth of different generations, not changes in fiscal policy per se. Since at the moment nothing indicates a major change in the stance of fiscal policy in the next decade, generational accounts in the 1990s will probably not reflect any fiscal policy other than the currently projected time path of policy. Hence, the projected surpluses in the 1990s will not signal any change in the stance of fiscal policy compared with fiscal policy in the 1980s.

The Risks of Misreading Fiscal Policy in the 1990s

As an economist reasoning from well-defined economic models, I do not know nor do I care whether we will be running "surpluses" or "deficits" in the 1990s; judging from the wholly arbitrary data the government now compiles, one can choose his labels and take his pick. The problem, however, is that everyone is focusing on one deficit series—namely, the official deficit—out of the infinite number of possible "deficit" series. While it is as meaningless and misleading as any unofficial series, the mistaken belief that the stance of fiscal policy is measured by the official series could well lead to a loosening of fiscal policy in the next decade. The loosening of policy can take many forms.

• First, the government may spend the trust fund surpluses by raising social security benefits for retirees. This would alter generational accounts, increasing the accounts of the current elderly and reducing the accounts of the current young and middle-aged as well as those of future generations.
• Second, the government may respond to the surpluses by reducing income taxes or by simply not increasing them as much as would otherwise be the case. This would raise the accounts of current generations and lower the accounts of future generations.
• Third, the government might cut payroll taxes and delay raising them until the baby-boom retires. This would raise the accounts of the baby-boom at the cost of lowering the accounts of the children, grandchildren, and subsequent descendants of the baby-boom.

Regardless of the form the loosening of policy takes, it is likely to spell a decline in U.S. saving and investment from what would otherwise be the case. By expanding the accounts of current generations at the expense of future generations, a looser policy will induce more current aggregate consumption and, therefore, less national saving. This is a perilous prospect for a country whose national saving rate is already among the lowest of the industrialized countries.

One response to this concern is that if we just remove social security from the Gramm-Rudman-Hollings targets in the 1990s and make sure the deficit in the rest of the budget is small, we will somehow be safeguarded against a loosening of fiscal policy. The problem is that just as we have not understood the generational account implications of trying to balance the budget including social security, we do not understand the generational account implications of balancing the budget with social security off the books.

What we do know is that meeting the Gramm-Rudman-Hollings targets with social security excluded would require very large spending cuts—on the order of 100 percent of nondefense, non-social-security, and noninterest spending.

The dilemma is that leaving social security in Gramm-Rudman-Hollings, while it lets people think about the size of the official deficit (as silly as that may be) in a way that they are accustomed, invites a loosening of fiscal policy along the lines of the second method described above. The alternative—taking social security out—leaves the budgeters adrift with no anchor; since budget balance is unthinkable, there will be no clear benchmark (as silly as it may be) against which to figure the appropriate size of the non-social-security deficit (as silly as it may be). Stated differently, with social security out of budgetary thinking, deficits on the order of 6 to 10 percent of GNP may come to be viewed as reasonable.

My guess is that once the objective of a balanced budget and the notion of a natural zero deficit are discarded and people get accustomed to the idea of running quite large deficits relative to GNP, any fiscal restraint currently in play will go by the wayside. Without a meaningful index of fiscal policy, namely generational accounts, we face the possibility of unrivaled fiscal irresponsibility in the next few years.

Summary and Conclusion

Perhaps for the first time in its fiscal history the United States is engaged in some long-term present value planning. The decision to accumulate a social security trust fund to pay for the retirement of the baby-boom seems like sound generational policy. Unfortunately, it is being implemented without any measure of the rest of generational policy and, therefore, without any guarantee that other government policies will not offset the social security policy. The 1983 Social Security Amendments, which were a major piece of fiscal policy based on present value, not cash flow, objectives, have thrown a huge wrench into the works. It is slowly becoming clear that one cannot sensibly mix present value thinking with cash flow accounting. It is also becoming clear that there is something uncomfortably arbitrary about the deficit:

unless we devise a conceptual framework for really understanding fiscal policy, we can easily break loose from the moorings.

Many would argue that we have already broken loose from the moorings. Dwight Eisenhower, John Kennedy, and Lyndon Johnson would all be thunderstruck to think of the United States running peace-time deficits as large as those in the 1980s. Yet we have run such deficits, and the public is now getting used to them. We face the clear and proximate danger that policy will be greatly loosened in the 1990s largely because people simply do not know how tight policy needs to be to keep the ship moored to the dock. The answer, unfortunately, cannot be found by looking at official deficits, whether they include or exclude social security. The answer lies in radically revised fiscal accounts—ones that embody economically meaningful present value generational accounts rather than economically arbitrary cash flows.

Generational accounts can provide the strong anchor needed by the system. By construction, generational accounts show which generations gain and which generations lose by any change in fiscal policy. In loosening or tightening fiscal policy, the government would be forced to declare publicly, through its official generational accounts, how it plans to hurt some generations to help others. It would also be forced to show precisely which generations would be tagged to pay the bill for any increase in government consumption.

While I am optimistic that official generational accounts will ultimately replace the official deficit as the standard measure of fiscal policy, the process will take time. Old notions make comfortable bed-fellows, and many people have already declared the beauty of this particular set of clothes for the emperor. In this vein it is sobering to close with the last paragraph of *The Emperor's New Clothes*:

> "Why, he hasn't got anything on!" the whole crowd was shouting at last; and the Emperor's flesh crept, for it seemed to him they were right. "But all the same," he thought to himself, "I must go through with the procession." So he held himself more proudly than before, and the lords in waiting walked on bearing the train—the train that wasn't there at all.[9]

Social Security, Budget Deficits, and National Saving

A Commentary by Barry P. Bosworth

Laurence Kotlikoff's chapter highlights many ambiguities of the federal budget and questions the economic meaning of current measures of the budget deficit. He is correct in arguing that examining the implications of government taxation and expenditures in terms of their impact on generational cohorts is informative. That does not mean, however, that we should replace the current budget with a set of intergenerational accounts, as he argues. I believe that he may overstate the magnitude of the problem. The issue does not have much quantitative significance beyond the treatment of retirement accounts where the government does face substantial future liabilities that are not recognized in the current budget.

In a discussion of social security, we should not focus on the distribution of the economic pie to the extent that we ignore the importance of expanding the pie. Clearly, by just taking the federal budget, dividing it into generational accounts, and balancing the burden across generations, the government will not have made the greatest contribution it can to maintaining economic growth and expansion.

In my view, we care about the budget deficit over an extended time primarily because of its implications for national saving. If we adopt the view of Robert Barro that private individuals adjust their saving to take full account of the actions of government, perhaps we care only about relative tax burdens on different age cohorts. But if we do not adopt that view, we must be concerned from a public policy perspective about the adequacy of the current rate of national saving and the role of the government budget in affecting that saving rate.

Nothing that Kotlikoff mentions affects the measurement of the national saving rate. Instead, the issues he raises affect the partitioning of that saving between government and the private sector. It is possible that by misstating the amount of government saving, principally by ignoring the accumulation of future liabilities, we may mislead the private sector into making the wrong saving decisions today. The usefulness of intergenerational accounts depends critically on the assumption that every American is a neoclassical individual who acts with full understanding of the future implications of his and others' actions. By simply presenting Americans with such information, they will optimize their own lifetime saving plans. Many of us, however, act in a very myopic fashion and have difficulty discerning the future.

The basic issue that this conference examines is the implications of the coming buildup of a substantial reserve in the social security system resulting from a significant shift in the demographic structure of the population. Because of a large baby-boom generation of workers, the inflow of revenues to the system, at current tax rates, will exceed expenditures on retirees for several decades; but after about 2020 or 2030 the situation will turn around, and the surplus will be dissipated by increased expenditures. Although I agree that the projections are highly uncertain, the basic pattern of a large buildup of a reserve followed by a rapid decline is not. While we might argue that the projections of real income growth are too optimistic, the assumption on the other side of a 2 percent real rate of interest is equally pessimistic. The projections are, on balance, more conservative than those of private pension plans.

Social security is basically a mature retirement system in which current tax rates are roughly at the level required to finance the benefits promised to current workers. Those benefits are specified at a level, approximately the poverty-income cutoff, at which there is little general public pressure to increase or reduce them. Essentially, current workers are required to pay for a pension sufficient to keep themselves out of severe poverty when they retire. If they want to do better than that, they are expected to make their own private provision. Perhaps it was a mistake to allow a generation of workers to receive greater benefits under a pay-as-you-go system than those they would have received under a fully funded system; but, since that generation is dying off, the issue is moot today.

Thus, I believe that the standards for managing the financing of the system are very much the same as those for a private retirement plan. Current taxes or current promises of future benefits should be adjusted as required to maintain the system in close actuarial balance on a present value basis. I would hope that we would not play the type of games suggested by Kotlikoff's accounting that would allow the fund to be restored to balance (in the event of an imbalance) by promising to raise taxes twenty years in the future. While, in general, legislated future tax and benefit changes should be recognized in our fiscal accounts, recognizing tax changes scheduled to take effect in the far future creates special problems. Those changes lack credibility and fall on the wrong generation of workers relative to benefits received.

Social security is in basically sound condition, with current taxes on workers being close to the level required to finance their future benefits. Administrators of the system need not worry about what is done with the proceeds of the bonds that they purchase for the reserve. They simply want to ensure that they can get their money back when they need it to pay future benefits.

There is a problem for the rest of government, however. Can we simply borrow the surplus of the social security system to pay for today's consumption, the operating fund deficit? Or should we set aside the social security surplus and allow it to add to national saving and wealth in recognition of the future liabilities it must finance? That is, in evaluating the long-run goals of fiscal policy, should we focus on the budget deficit inclusive of social security, assuming that any surplus in that account can be borrowed to finance spending in others? Or should we emphasize a measure of the budget deficit that excludes social security? If social security were in the private sector, this issue would not arise. I have not heard anyone suggest that larger budget deficits are acceptable because private pension funds are currently accumulating reserves. In fact, we would expect the nation's saving rate to rise in anticipation of the aging of the population.

We should worry about the decline in national saving from the rate we seemed to agree was already less than optimal. I do not understand the basis for believing that the decline is the outcome of rational private decisions. Rates of return on capital do not appear to have been declining in the 1980s, and the demographic trends have been in the opposite direction. In addition, much of the decline in saving is concentrated in the public sector where the notion of rational calculations of trade-offs between current and future consumption seem particularly suspect. In the 1980s the United States has saved an average 3 percent of income compared with about 6 percent in prior decades. The domestic investment rate has averaged 6 percent, also below the historical average, but by a smaller amount. A nation that invests 6 percent of its income and saves only 3 percent must borrow overseas, hence the current account deficit with other nations. Does it not seem reasonable to suggest that the world's richest nation ought to be able to finance its own capital formation, particularly when it is a paltry 6 percent of income?

The current debate over the social security surplus can be reduced to three options: we can spend it, we can save it, or we can eliminate it.

Clearly the current pattern is to spend it. The Gramm-Rudman-Hollings targets are stated in terms of a budget that includes social security. Inclusive of social security, we claim that the budget deficit has declined and will gradually fade away. The social security surplus already exceeds $50 billion, however, and it will grow to $100 billion annually in the mid-1990s. Excluding social security, the projected budget deficit actually increases. If we compiled a federal budget on the same basis as state and local governments and private institutions, excluding all the retirement accounts, the federal deficit would top $300 billion by the mid-1990s.

We cannot change this picture by restating the budget to take account of the effects of inflation on debt repayments because inflation has actually declined in the 1980s, compared with the 1970s. Nor can it be altered by developing a public capital budget: investment-type outlays have born the brunt of the cuts in public expenditures in the 1980s. We are simply using a regressive tax that falls heavily on low-wage workers to finance regular government programs, such as national defense, that benefit the rest of us. And we camouflage this dramatic shift in relative tax burdens through the gimmick of a financial transfer between social security and operating funds.

The second option of setting aside the surplus to add to national saving has enormous appeal from an economic point of view. It provides a means of responding to the inadequate national saving and to the excessive trade deficit. Adding the surplus to national saving would recognize the increased saving required for an aging future population. Anyone examining the studies of the rates of return on physical capital, research and development, and education is impressed by the large future benefits that could be achieved from an increase in the national saving rate.

We can take some time debating this second option because it is not a realistic option in the next several years. We already have a long way to go to meet the Gramm-Rudman deficit targets. No one is suggesting that the goal of saving the social security surplus should imply a faster rate of reduction in the budget deficit over the next few years than called for in Gramm-Rudman. A reduction of $30–50 billion annually was judged to be a rate that could be absorbed without precipitating a recession. The issue is something that would extend the targets after the mid-1990s to move toward balance in the operating budget, rather than balance in a budget including the social security surplus. Or, alternatively, some might wish to restate the targets to move toward a surplus of 1–2 percent of national income in a budget that includes social security. The question of whether social security is on or off-budget is not fundamental to this debate. It is simply a device for explaining the targets for public saving, and implicitly national saving, in public discussions.

In view of the political difficulties of dealing with the budget financing issue within the context of the current ideological battle over taxes and expenditures, we may have to consider seriously the third option: having built up a reserve against future liquidity crises, move back toward a pay-as-you-go system by cutting the payroll tax now and raising it in future decades to keep income in line with outgo. While I much prefer the second option of saving the surplus, I strongly agree that this third option is better than the current decision to use the social security reserve to finance other government consumption programs. What possible sense can it make to have low-income workers pay a disproportionate share of the cost of national defense and other government programs?

Boosting National Saving through U.S. Fiscal Policy

A Commentary by James M. Poterba

Laurence Kotlikoff argues for a radical change in the measurement of U.S. fiscal policy. He suggests that traditional measures of the federal deficit based on the difference between cash inflows and outflows should be replaced with a system of generational accounts designed to reflect the net effect of tax and spending policy on the lifetime budget constraint of individuals in different age groups. Who can doubt that these accounts would provide new insight on the nature of fiscal policy, since they would synthesize information on taxes and spending across generations? This does not, however, imply that traditional measures of fiscal deficits should be abandoned. For a number of reasons that are not well captured by the neoclassical paradigm, the differential between current government outlays and current receipts provides an important indicator of the government's fiscal stance. Large deficits are likely to have expansionary macroeconomic effects, while small deficits or surpluses are relatively contractionary.

This more traditional view of public finance implies that accumulation of social security trust fund surpluses in the 1990s *is* a contractionary fiscal policy. The reduction in disposable income for individuals employed at that time will, holding constant the level of social security and other government outlays, reduce the level of economic stimulus emanating from government activity.

I will examine the potential limitations of the generational accounts approach to measuring fiscal policy. I will then briefly discuss the role of impending surpluses in raising national saving and elaborate my views on the appropriate benchmark for fiscal policy in the 1990s.

On Generational Accounts

The Kotlikoff critique of the traditional deficit measures can best be understood with a simple analogy. Suppose two parents with an eight-year-old child decide to reduce the child's allowance from $10 to $5 per week. Kotlikoff would argue that it is impossible to tell whether such a transaction would reduce the resources available to the child. First, he would note, the notion of an allowance is ill defined: we could view each $5 per week transfer as an interest-free loan from the parents to the child, to be settled as part of the parents' estate. The timing of these transfers should therefore not affect the child's behavior. Second, one might observe, not all intergenerational transfers are channeled through allowances. Periodically, the parents visit their lawyer and redraft their will, potentially changing the present discounted value of resources the child can expect to receive from them. Allowances, which fail to capture these changes, might be viewed as providing a quite unreliable measure of intergenerational resource flows.

There is obviously some validity to both of these critiques. Yet if we are trying to explain the spending decisions of the eight-year-old, I suspect that the current flow of allowance money would be a variable of central importance. There are many potential reasons for this. Our eight-year-old may face liquidity constraints that prevent him from borrowing against his future income or bequest. He may simply be myopic and focus primarily on his current resources rather than per-forming a complex present-value calculation reflecting all future en-dowments. Or he may simply recognize that future actions, such as his parents' bequest behavior, are quite uncertain and discount them in making consumption decisions.

I suspect that all three of these factors are operative for the eight-year-old, and that they apply to the behavior of a significant fraction of grown-ups, too.[1] The current level of taxes relative to government out-lays affects the level of consumption. It is therefore impossible to analyze the economic effects of fiscal policy without at least some reference to measures like the traditional budget deficit. This does not imply that the present definition of the government deficit is ideal: convincing arguments can be made for adjusting interest payments for inflationary premiums, for recognizing the expected present cost of some contingent liabilities, and for distinguishing between current and capital outlays. Nevertheless, a measure similar to the current deficit, and distinct from the generational accounts, is of some use.

Some difficulties are also associated with generational accounts as a benchmark for fiscal policy. First, they could lead to sizable changes in the measured fiscal stance for reasons unrelated to government be-havior. An increase in real interest rates due to a change in the an-nounced policy of a foreign central bank, for example, would change the present discounted value of liabilities for social security and a variety of other spending programs. It is not clear that this should be viewed as contractionary fiscal policy.

Second, generational accounts could record large changes in fiscal policy in response to preannounced tax or spending changes that have no effect on current government behavior, and that could be rescinded before taking effect. The very fact that policy makers are currently discussing how to treat the accumulating trust fund surpluses indicates the uncertainty surrounding the eventual implementation of the 1983 social security reforms. This is a pervasive problem. The substantial increases in the generosity of social security during the early 1970s have been partially rescinded by the actions of the 1980s. The Economic Recovery Tax Act of 1981, which is an important example of a tax policy transfer from one generation to another, was largely reversed by the Tax Reform Act of 1986.

Third, generational accounts would introduce new uncertainty and a new dimension for manipulation into fiscal analysis. Two analysts confronting the same data on current outlays, but making different assumptions about the future trajectories of mortality rates, interest rates, or even future legislation, would obtain different estimates of the generational accounts and therefore draw different conclusions about fiscal policy. Rather than encouraging consensus on the measurement of fiscal policy, generational accounts are likely to enhance the disagreement between analysts.

These considerations suggest that measures like the current deficit concept have at least some appeal as indexes of fiscal policy. Although they are not perfect and they could surely be enlightened by information like that contained in the generational accounts, it would be unwise to scrap them completely.

National Saving and the Trust Funds

While I disagree with some of Kotlikoff's analysis, I fully agree with his conclusion that the trust fund surpluses that will develop during the next decade should not be offset by loosening other aspects of fiscal policy. My more traditional view of public finance suggests that accumulating trust fund surpluses will reduce private consumption outlays. This is precisely what is needed to raise the anemic U.S. national saving rate. A central consideration in setting fiscal policy for the next decade should be the influence of government behavior on the national saving rate.

During the late 1980s the U.S. economy devoted a far higher share of national output to consumption than in any comparable period of this century. Total consumption (the sum of personal consumption and government purchases of goods and services) was 92.1 percent of net national product (NNP) in the 1970s. Spending by individuals accounted for 69.3 percent of NNP. For the period 1985–1987, however, total consumption was 97.9 percent of national income. The decline in national saving has potentially serious long-run consequences for the U.S. economy. Capital formation is widely recognized as an important determinant of long-run growth in living standards. The low saving rate in the United States exposes our economy to the cruel dilemma of low investment and slow growth in productivity and living standards or heavy reliance on capital inflows from foreign investors.

The United States would benefit from a program to reverse the alarming decline of national saving. The most direct method of achieving this end would be to reduce government spending, although the limited increase in such spending as a share of GNP during the past decade suggests that cuts will be difficult. Tax increases of various kinds could also reduce the deficit: a twenty-five-cent per gallon increase in the gasoline excise could raise roughly $25 billion per year, various "sin taxes" on alcohol and cigarettes could yield another $10 billion, and an increase in personal income tax rates to 16 percent and 30 percent would raise $42 billion per year by 1993. The political environment makes such tax increases unlikely, however. Programs to encourage private saving, such as extension of saving incentive plans for individual investors, would also be valuable additions to the program for raising national saving.

One device for encouraging deficit reduction would be exclusion of the social security trust fund surpluses from the deficit reduction targets. I believe this would pressure Congress and the president to forge a consensus on spending cuts and revenue increases. Raising national saving should be a central objective for government fiscal policy in the next decade, and the treatment of social security trust fund surpluses could have an important effect on policy choices regarding other items in the budget. If larger measured deficits promote deficit reduction, as I suspect they do, then the treatment of trust fund surpluses can be used to encourage government saving and hence increased national saving.

The Ineffectiveness of
Trust Fund Surpluses

A Commentary by John H. Makin

Laurence Kotlikoff addresses an issue that is gaining considerable attention—the effect of government policy on the intertemporal allocation of resources. He argues that the 1983 Social Security Amendments "were sound generational policy," transferring resources from older to younger generations and thus increasing national saving. Urging the adoption of "generational accounts" in lieu of official measures of the deficit, he suggests that we could thereby properly assess the impact of the social security surpluses and also reduce the likelihood of adverse fiscal policy decisions.

On the question of whether the federal government has accurate or misleading measures of the deficit, he rightly argues that cash flows are very poor measures of the discounted present values of stocks. We have been using a rather naïve income statement when discussing the posture of federal fiscal policy.

Kotlikoff sells the political process a bit short, however, in claiming that flawed government accounts are adversely affecting fiscal decisions, which are ultimately political decisions. The American Association of Retired Persons surely has a good set of intergenerational accounts—even if not written ones. Certainly the AARP responds predictably to potential alterations in the intergenerational allocation of resources. Further, the other end of the age spectrum is beginning to speak up. The Americans for Generational Equity, for example, focuses largely on generational issues from the other perspective. These groups do not need a sophisticated new measure to know whether they will benefit from some new policy.

Important economic policy questions, however, have been raised by the advance funding of social security. First, can the government alter the national saving rate by running surpluses in the social security trust funds? Second, if it can, should it? Kotlikoff's premise is that the answer to both questions is yes, although he does not discuss the necessary qualifications.

For both theoretical and empirical reasons we should question whether the social security surpluses will result in higher national saving. The theoretical reason derives from a long-standing debate about the effect of an unfunded social security system on private saving. If individuals expect a reduction in their take-home pay as a result of higher payroll taxes and they believe these taxes will be used to finance retirement benefits, will they not be inclined to reduce their saving?

For the higher payroll taxes to reduce consumption and thereby increase national saving, presumably either individuals must have decided to increase their total saving or they must doubt that the benefits promised under social security will be forthcoming at current tax rates and therefore save more to provide for expected increases in future taxes.

Viewed more broadly, the impact of social security on private saving is related to the degree of rationality of savers. The ultrationalist school argues that higher social security benefits not funded by higher taxes are seen merely as an indication of higher future taxes and therefore induce an offsetting rise in private saving to pay the higher expected future taxes. National saving is seen as unaffected. Others argue that taxpayers are not superrational and are therefore unable to foresee prospective tax increases that may be twenty or thirty years down the road; they believe that higher social security benefits not funded immediately by higher taxes do, to some extent, reduce national saving.

What do we know about the private saving rate, that is, the share of GNP saved by households and businesses? Empirically, the private saving rate has been remarkably stable for most of the postwar period at about 16 percent. Until 1980 the saving rate was so stable that the 16 percent level was enshrined as Denison's Law after Edward Denison who observed the stability in the private saving rate in the United States.

During the 1980s the personal saving rate dropped enough to depress the private saving rate. The drop in the personal saving rate was difficult to explain, although some have ascribed it to the way private pensions are funded,[1] to the lower saving propensities of the baby-boom generation,[2] or to the negative experiences of savers during the 1970s when high inflation rates lowered real rates of return.

Should the government alter the national saving rate if it is within its power to do so? As Kotlikoff says, the saving rate essentially determines the allocation of resources between generations. A higher saving rate means that the current generation forgoes consumption to provide more generously for future generations. A lower saving rate means that the increase in the living standard of future generations will occur more slowly than otherwise, not that future generations are being impoverished, as is often asserted. To argue that the federal government should affect the national saving rate is to argue that the federal government has a better idea about the intergenerational allocation of resources than do individuals. Alternatively, we would have to claim that greater provision for future goods through higher saving somehow confers benefits on the economy that ought to be encouraged.

One of the often-mentioned benefits of increased saving is greater growth for the economy and higher income per capita. Here again some careful consideration is necessary. If the rate of saving increases, thereby lowering market interest rates and encouraging capital formation, neoclassical growth theories suggest that real wages and output per capita will rise. What is often forgotten is that neoclassical growth theory also suggests "a golden rule of growth"—that is, a persistent saving ratio in excess of the optimal saving rate will increase gross national product per capita but will lower consumption per capita. The reason is that depreciation on a larger than optimal capital stock and diminishing returns from a higher capital labor ratio will leave less money available for consumption per capita.

Those arguing for higher saving and therefore higher capital formation are presuming that the saving rate is below the level consistent with the golden rule of accumulation that maximizes consumption per capita.

My own view is that if we want to tell people how to arrange their consumption over their life cycles, individually and collectively, then we should know what the optimal pattern of life cycle consumption is, and we do not. Economic theory suggest that individuals can save too much or can save too little; it is very difficult to determine when one gets beyond the point of having saved enough.

We can make other possible slips "'twixt cup and lip" when considering the benefits from increasing national saving. In an open economy higher national saving may spill out into world capital markets, thereby failing to depress the interest rate or to encourage capital formation. Further, for a large economy like the United States, even if the increase in the national saving rate is sufficient to depress interest rates and enhance capital formation, there is no guarantee that American consumers will capture all of the benefits. If American exports are produced with capital-intensive methods, an increase in the stock of American capital will lower the price of our exports relative to the price of our imports, thus eroding the American terms of trade and benefiting American trading partners.

The point is that much of the traditional analysis about the benefits of faster capital formation has been done in a closed-economy setting. This setting is inappropriate for the 1990s as the American economy becomes more and more open and we rely more on our ability to export in world markets.

In my view, the primary benefit of the highly publicized surpluses in the social security trust funds is that it has occasioned careful reexamination of social security. Such a reexamination will surely reveal that the system is poorly designed and will require further tax increases or benefit reductions if the sharp increases in payroll taxes already undertaken are to have their desired effect on the national saving rate. The intergenerational transfer from the working age to the retired population implicit in such changes may make social security the focus of political attacks based upon its intergenerational inequity.

PART TWO
Budgetary Politics of the Surpluses

3

The Budgetary Politics
of Social Security

James M. Buchanan

Social security is off limits for serious political discussion and debate. When crisis threatened in the early 1980s, both an independent commission and a genuinely bipartisan agreement were deemed necessary. But were the proposals that were developed and legally incorporated into the system exposed to sufficient scrutiny? Many are now concerned that the reforms failed to take into account important macroeconomic and macropolitical implications. This chapter addresses some of the rather obvious problems that emerge when political spillovers between social security and the comprehensive federal budget are acknowledged.

The second section presents a stylized model of social security financing as it is—was—supposed to work under the reforms enacted in 1983. In describing this model, I shall emphasize the restrictiveness of the conditions that must be satisfied to ensure the desired results. The third section then examines the difficulties raised by the interdependence of the revenues and the outlays of the social security account and non-social-security components in the comprehensive federal budget. The impact of the 1983 reforms on the budgetary politics of the late 1980s and the 1990s assumes center stage in this discussion. The fourth section examines the institutional sources of possible interdependence and analyzes the prospective effects of taking social security out of the comprehensive federal budget. In the fifth section, I try to place the system in the larger political context, and I make some predictions about future developments.

For convenience, I ignore the nontemporal redistributional elements in the social security tax and benefit formulas and make no efforts to analyze impacts on aggregate economic variables. My com-

I am indebted to my colleague, Richard E. Wagner, for helpful discussions.

ments refer only to the Old-Age, Survivors, and Disability Insurance (OASDI) part of the social security structure, which excludes Medicare.[1]

Sufficient unto Itself—The Idealized Postreform System

Assume that, in a stylized prereform setting, the social security account operated on a purely pay-as-you-go intergenerational transfer basis. There was no trust fund accumulation, but the participants were en-sured a return on tax-financed "investment" at least equal to the growth rate of the economy, which in turn was approximately equal to the real rate of return on private investment.

This fully operational pay-as-you-go system of intertemporal transfer is then shocked by a dramatic and unpredicted shift in demo-graphic patterns. An unanticipated surge occurs in the rate of increase in population over a limited period of years, which is then followed by a return to slower rates of increase. The projected impact of this demo-graphic shift on the operation of the pay-as-you-go transfer system comes to be widely recognized. As the baby-boom generation reaches retirement, the rate of tax on productive income earners must be in-creased sharply if, indeed, the implicit contract with members of the baby-boom generation is to be honored. Failing reform, the present value of future social security liabilities will exceed, and by a large order of magnitude, the present value of anticipated revenues.

At some point, the "crisis" could have been expected to provoke attempts at reform. To forestall the dire predictions about possible default on the implicit intergenerational contract in future decades, suppose an attempt was made—as in 1983—to shift from the purely pay-as-you-go system to one that embodies some elements of a funded system. Rates of tax on current income earners are increased beyond those rates that would have been dictated by strict pay-as-you-go ac-counting integrity. In the late 1980s, the trust fund accounts start to accumulate surpluses, and these surpluses are programmed to accel-erate dramatically over the decades of the 1990s, 2000s, and 2010s.[2] These surpluses, invested at interest in government debt claims, are designed to meet the pension commitments to the baby-boom genera-tion during the drawdown decades of the next century, without undu-ly onerous tax increases on the workers at that time. In a real sense, the members of the baby-boom generation are subjected to current taxes sufficient not only to finance the pensions of those who are now retired or who will retire in the 1990s but also to finance a portion of *their own* retirement in the third, fourth, and fifth decades of the next century. The period of trust fund accumulation is to be followed by an anticipated period of depletion, which is to be financed from the previously accumulated surpluses.

The central difference between a pay-as-you-go system of intergenerational transfers and a fully funded system lies in the fully funded system's investment of excess revenues in income-earning assets. These assets, in turn, generate returns sufficient to finance the future obligations that are currently incurred. For future income streams to be higher than they would be under the pay-as-you-go system, the rate of capital formation must increase. But social security trust fund surpluses are invested exclusively in claims against the U.S. government. These claims earn interest, which accrues to the account; but since the federal budget is in deficit, the funds collected from payroll taxes are used directly to finance current outlays by the federal government. Can we say, then, that the shift to a partially funded system increases the rate of capital formation in the economy?

The answer is affirmative, if we impose the economists' *ceteris paribus* and consider the social security account in isolation. The actual use of the tax revenues is irrelevant in this setting. The debt claims against the government earn interest, and the account, therefore, grows precisely as if the funds had been invested in private income-earning assets in the economy. But how can we be assured that the net result is an increase in the rate of aggregate capital formation? This result is ensured if social security, in fact, operates independently from the rest of the budget. If choices made outside the social security system are not themselves affected by the trust fund accumulations (a relationship to be discussed at length later), then the rate of capital formation in the economy must increase, because as the social security trust fund "purchases" debt claims from the Treasury, there is a dollar-for-dollar reduction in the private sector's purchase of Treasury obligations. This increases purchases of private sector securities, those issued by private borrowers who, in turn, use the funds to purchase income-earning assets that can provide returns sufficient to amortize the obligations.

As trust fund surpluses grow over the next three decades, the *ceteris paribus* scenario will ultimately require that social security "purchase" not only the debt claims issued by the government to finance Treasury deficits but also a portion of the outstanding debt claims held by the public. That is to say, some share of trust fund surpluses will go toward retiring privately held public debt. The effects of this operation, of course, are no different from those involved when the trust fund surpluses replace private purchases of Treasury securities to finance a Treasury deficit. In either case, private funds are freed for additional investment in income-yielding assets.

In the drawdown period (projected by the social security board of trustees to commence in the second third of the next century), the social security account will find it necessary to call its debt claims against the Treasury to meet its implicit obligations to the baby-boom retirees. To honor these calls against it, the Treasury will find it necessary to increase its sale of securities to purchasers other than the social security account. As lendable funds are shifted to the purchase of government debt instruments, the rate of investment in interest-earning assets in the economy will be reduced. The period of trust fund shrinkage will affect the aggregate rate of capital formation in precisely the opposite way from that generated during the period of trust fund accumulation.

Social Security Trust Funds and the Federal Budget

As many critics of Marshallian (partial equilibrium) economic method have noted, *cetera* are seldom, if ever, *paribus*. This criticism applies particularly to the stylized scenario of social security independence sketched earlier and which arguably served as the basis for the reforms enacted in 1983. As has been the case with many other ill-advised ventures into economic policy, however, the reforms failed to reckon with the elementary realities of democratic politics. A small dose of public choice theory might have dampened the enthusiasm of those who sought to ensure the integrity of the system.

The fact is that the social security fiscal account is not, and cannot be, *politically* independent of the income and outlays that describe the more inclusive fiscal operations of the federal government. There is no necessary economic interdependence here; there is no internal contradiction, in a general equilibrium sense, involved in treating the social security account as if it were separate and apart from remaining components of the comprehensive federal budget. The interdependence is political rather than economic, and it emerges from the predicted behavior of political decision makers who are ultimately responsive to the demands of voting constituencies.

Budgetary Complements to Social Security Independence. To understand the potential effects of the projected trust fund accumulations over the decades of the 1990s, 2000s, and 2010s, we should carefully define the budgetary discipline that political agents would have to follow to ensure full social security isolation. As noted, the operation of the system *as if* it were independent would require that the partial derivative of the reform-induced changes in non-social-security revenue and outlay streams over the half-century be zero. That is to say, the path through time of non-social-security revenues and outlays could not vary with shifts in social security financing from periods of pay-as-you-go, to trust fund accumulation, and later to trust fund depletion.

Note that the genuine independence here does not require specification of any particular relationship between non-social-security revenues and outlays, either early, middle, or late in the projected temporal sequence. The non-social-security portion of the budget may be in deficit, in balance, or in surplus, and shifts among these three possible sets of relationships may occur over time as dictated by political forces. All that is strictly required for independence is that this time path of the budget deficit (positive or negative) not be affected directly by what happens in the social security account itself.

How would the required invariance reveal itself in the comprehensive federal budget? The comprehensive budget deficit would be observed to move toward budget surplus during the period of social security trust fund accumulation and to move below the non-social-security time path toward budget deficit during anticipated periods of trust fund shrinkage. If we state this requirement more simply as part of the measured budget deficit, the comprehensive deficit must be reduced, dollar for dollar, with increases in social security trust fund balances and increased, dollar for dollar, with decreases in trust fund balances in later periods.

Interdependence Imposed by Aggregate Budgetary Targets. This requirement for social security independence and isolation will be violated under any and all policy regimes that involve aggregate targets for the revenue-outlay relationship in the comprehensive federal budget. Suppose, by way of a simple and unreal example, that there existed a rigidly enforced rule for comprehensive budget balance under the pay-as-you-go period for the social security account and later. In operation, this rule would prevent the necessary generation of a comprehensive budget surplus during the periods of social security trust fund accumulation. Conversely, it would facilitate an expansion in other outlays or a reduction in nonpayroll taxes, while at the same time allowing the budget balance target to be met. Alternatively, suppose that the comprehensive budget was in deficit during the period of pay-as-you-go social security financing but that medium-range legislative targets were established to reduce and then eliminate the comprehensive budget deficit; this is the setting under Gramm-Rudman-Hollings. In this case, surpluses in the social security account allow the deficit reduction targets to be satisfied, while still allowing for *increases* in the non-social-security deficit. Much the same results emerge under any scheme for deficit control that uses balance or imbalance in the comprehensive budget as a criterion for policy achievement. As a final example, suppose that a decision is made to keep the relationship between the measured comprehensive budget deficit and the gross national product constant. Again, satisfaction of this norm would allow non-social-security deficits to increase during the period of trust fund accumulation.

Social Security Surpluses and Budgetary Ease. What will be the effects of any of the predicted violations of the strict independence requirement? Suppose that social security, in fact, runs surpluses and that these surpluses serve merely to relieve pressures on politicians to reduce the deficit, in the rest of the budget. Outlays in the rest of the budget increase relative to tax revenues, and the non-social-security deficit increases despite the apparent decrease in the comprehensive budget deficit. This scenario, which is almost certain to be descriptive of fiscal and political reality in the 1990s, implies that the 1983 reforms will not accomplish their ultimate purpose, which was to relieve pressures upon income earners when the baby-boom generation reaches retirement age.

It may be useful to trace the steps in the analysis here. Suppose that the generation of a trust fund surplus (payroll tax revenues and other income in excess of current program payments) causes politicians to expand outlays on other government programs. This policy combination negates the funding purpose of the 1983 reforms, because no funds are released for an increase in private capital formation. No displacement of private lending to government takes place. As before, the social security account "purchases" claims against the Treasury with the enhanced payroll tax receipts; but the government now uses these revenues, *not* to replace funds previously borrowed from the private sector but to expand outlays on other government programs. There is no release of funds that can be made available to private investors in income-earning assets.

One feature of this politicized interdependence scenario deserves special notice. If the trust fund surpluses are used to expand other government spending, this will not be reflected in an increase in the measured comprehensive budget deficit because the added spending is financed by the payroll tax revenues that generate the surpluses in the first place. The deficit is simply higher than it otherwise would have been. But because surplus social security receipts are used directly to "purchase" claims against the Treasury, the measured national debt will increase, and, with it, interest obligations.[3] This apparently paradoxical feature stems, of course, from the accounting conventions that allow for the dual counting of payroll tax revenues, both as the source for the "purchase" of the internally held social security claims against the Treasury and as the revenue offset to general outlays in the comprehensive budget. Payroll taxpayers think of themselves as paying for the future benefits that the social security claims against the Treasury measure. But who then is paying for the expansion of other outlays? This payment must finally rest with future taxpayers, who must finance the amortization of the social security claims.

As noted, to the extent that the trust fund surpluses are offset by expansions in other spending, there will be no induced increase in the rate of private capital formation in the economy. There will be no direct or indirect "funding" of the future pension obligations. The social security account, treated as an administratively separate unit, will accumulate claims against the Treasury, and hence the general taxpayer, but there will be no increase in future income that will allow such claims to be more easily financed, either through taxation or debt issue.

Postsurplus Political Consequences. The independence and interdependence scenarios described above are dramatically different in their relevance to macroeconomic policy. The first embodies an increase in private capital formation as a result of the 1983 social security reforms, independently of the movements in the rest of the federal budget. The second, and more realistic, scenario involves a dissipation of the social security trust fund buildup through politicized profligacy in the rest of the budget. However, and this is a point worthy of some emphasis, the political consequences in the postsurplus period need not be so great as the economic differences in the two models might suggest.

In either case, at the beginning of the drawdown period, social security will call in its claims against the Treasury, and the Treasury will stand obligated to advance the funds that are required to meet the emerging social security deficits. This demand on the Treasury can be met by increases in the sale of government securities to the private sector, by taxation, or by a reduction in other government spending. The Treasury will face this fiscal choice regardless of whether it has maintained the discipline dictated by the independence scenario during periods of the trust fund buildup. And under either scenario social security advocates can argue that payroll taxes have indeed been sufficiently high to "finance" the drawdown of the trust fund accumulations, quite apart from the presence or absence of fiscal discipline in other sectors of the comprehensive budget. Conversely, under either scenario, social security critics can argue that program changes are necessary because of the large deficits in social security, regardless of fiscal policy in the predeficit period.

A fully symmetrical interdependent fiscal stance over the whole buildup and drawdown cycle might suggest that during the surplus period the non-social-security deficits would be higher than under the independence scenario but lower during the drawdown period because of the increased fiscal pressures. But there would seem to be no behavioral basis for predicting such symmetry. The social security surpluses can, as noted, facilitate a hidden increase in the deficit in the rest of the budget, an increase that is consistent with the natural proclivities of constituency-responsive politicians. The later social security deficits present politicians with much less desirable options. Unless otherwise constrained, they will finance the social security deficit with additional borrowing from the private sector, thereby producing explosive growth in the size of the comprehensive budget deficits over the entire drawdown period. This resort to the private sector for sale of bonds would, of course, be more appropriate under the independence model, since public borrowing from the private sector would have been reduced and possibly eliminated during the surplus period.

Sectoral Independence

Would the independent integrity of social security be more likely to be respected with accounting separation from the other revenue-outlay components of the comprehensive federal budget? That is to say, for purposes of Gramm-Rudman, should earmarked payroll taxes be excluded from federal budget revenues and should social security payments be excluded from federal expenditures? There exists a well-grounded public choice argument for sectoral separation among elements in the comprehensive budget, especially if revenues from particular sources are earmarked for and limited to spending on particular programs and, further, if the financing of such programs is limited to the defined sources of revenues. The rationality of the political decision-making process is enhanced if the costs and benefits of particular programs can be more readily identified and if the institutional structure is such that it encourages politicians to make choices on a program-by-program basis. If the social security structure could be removed from the comprehensive federal budget, there would seem to be less likelihood that the surpluses over the next three decades would facilitate increases in deficits in the rest of the budget, thereby reducing or eliminating the economic advantages of "funding."

There is an institutional difficulty of major proportions, however, in removing the social security account from the comprehensive federal budget, a difficulty that may negate the apparent advantages to be gained in overall fiscal responsibility. The payroll tax and the revenues therefrom finance both retirement and disability payments *and medical payments* under the Hospital Insurance (HI) account. It seems unlikely, therefore, that the social security account could be meaningfully separated from the HI account, or that one account could be removed from Gramm-Rudman without the other. And so long as the HI account faces prospective deficits, politicians would have a natural proclivity to use the buildup in the social security trust funds to finance the mounting deficits in the HI trust fund, rather than to increase net purchases of securities from the Treasury. Because the two accounts would seem likely to be included in any institutional or administrative sectoralization of the comprehensive budget, little would be gained by attempts to accomplish social security's independence by this route.

A somewhat different argument can be advanced against removing the social security account from the comprehensive federal budget, which relates to the politics of social security itself. Throughout most of the history of social security, benefits have increased well beyond the limits justified by actuarial standards. This suggests that surplus revenues in the account are politically vulnerable. If the social security and the HI accounts are removed from the comprehensive budget, political pressures to use emerging surpluses to fund increases in non-social-security deficits would tend to give way to comparable or greater pressures to fund unjustifiable increases in program benefits.[4]

Prospects, Politics, and Predictions

Application of elementary public choice theory to the current social security financing arrangement yields relatively straightforward predictions, especially over the medium term extending through the mid-1990s. The much-heralded reforms enacted in 1983 have commenced to generate the anticipated trust fund surpluses. These surpluses will not, however, be allowed to reduce the size of overall federal deficits, as would be required if the funding purpose of the revised tax structure were to be achieved. Instead, it seems almost certain that the trust fund accumulation will become one of the primary means through which the comprehensive budget deficit will be kept within the limits defined by deficit-reduction targets, such as those embodied in Gramm-Rudman. As I noted earlier, non-social-security deficits, including those in the HI account, will likely be increased rather than decreased over the interim. In particular, because of the political and accounting links between the various social security programs, the surpluses will provide the politically justifiable source of financing for the increasing deficits in the HI account. To the extent that the social security surpluses exceed the HI deficits, they will allow for still further increases in federal spending outside the social insurance system.

To appreciate the full impact of the reforms and the inclusive budgetary politics of the federal government, we should recall the fiscal setting of the early and mid-1980s. By 1983, it had become clear that some of the extremist supply-side projections were not within the realm of the possible; the tax changes of 1981, the unsuccessful attempts to reduce nondefense federal spending, and the increase in defense spending combined to ensure an explosion in the size of the comprehensive budget deficit. A constitutional amendment to require budget balance gained support, both in several states and in the Congress itself. Prospects for the adoption of such an amendment became very real in 1983. While this was taking place, Congress itself began to acknowledge that its own procedures were seriously flawed; there was an emerging recognition that the proclivity to generate ever-increasing and permanent deficits must, somehow, be curbed.

First in 1985 and again in 1987 after judicial rejection of some features of the 1985 legislation, Congress enacted the Gramm-Rudman-Hollings budgetary reforms that incorporated specific targets for deficit reduction over a five-year period, the first version dictating budget balance by 1991 and the second by 1993. This phase-in feature of the legislation was grounded, apparently, on the conviction that taxpayers and beneficiaries in the late 1980s were unwilling to accept the fiscal austerity that would be required to move more directly to budget balance.

The public did not recognize that the earlier-enacted "reforms" in social security would make the achievement of the Gramm-Rudman targets much easier than if pay-as-you-go financing had been maintained. The increases in the social security tax rates virtually guaranteed that there would be a substantial excess of social security revenues over payment obligations in the interim. From the standpoint of social security alone, these reforms did indeed incorporate the fiscal austerity that was deemed politically impossible if undertaken directly.

If we view all this cynically, the wage earners subjected to the increased payroll taxes were tricked by the illusion created by dual counting into financing the targeted reduction in the comprehensive budget deficit. Beneficiaries of other government programs and non-payroll taxpayers will enjoy unchanged, and even enhanced, benefit flows at the expense of payroll taxpayers. In a very real sense, the fiscal crisis that appeared on the way to resolution was simply postponed for up to three decades by the changes enacted in social security.

The social security account will, to be sure, accumulate very substantial nominal claims against the general taxpayers and beneficiaries of the federal government. There will have been no "funded" increase in the tax base, however, that will facilitate the financing of these claims when due. After the first two decades of the next century, when these social security claims are called, wage earners will be able to make a plausible case against further payroll tax hikes to help finance these system-held claims. But by that time, the events of the 1980s will be bygones, and the democratic politics of the 2020s will not respect the good intentions of the reformers of the 1990s.

What are the conclusions? Were the 1983 reforms a mistake? Did they foster fiscal illusions that will make ultimate reform in fiscal procedures more difficult? I shall not answer these questions directly here. But the analysis does allow me to identify the gainers and losers from the changes that were made. In any resource or commodity dimension, current payroll taxpayers lose; they are required to sacrifice current consumption and investment opportunities. These losses need not be matched in a subjective psychological dimension if payroll taxpayers think of themselves as "purchasing" a more secure funding of their own future retirement payments. Current nonpayroll taxpayers and non-social-security program beneficiaries gain in an opportunity cost sense. They are not required to reduce the benefits they get from the spending flows that generate the current deficit. Future taxpayers generally (payroll and other) along with future beneficiaries of other government programs lose relative to their positions under either a continuation of the pay-as-you-go system combined with non-program sources of comprehensive deficit reduction or the genuine "funding" of the surpluses. In either case, future taxpayers and beneficiaries would have available a larger income base from which to meet social security payment obligations. Alternatively, future social security claimants may themselves lose benefits if their claims are not honored.

The result seems clear. The pattern of gains and losses, among groups within the current generation and between groups in the current and future generations, is not what motivated the 1983 legislation. The National Commission on Social Security Reform (the Greenspan Commission) and its advocates may have produced a fiscal chain of events that was no part of their intention. Would they have been so enthusiastic in support of the changes and so self-satisfied with their apparent accomplishments if they had looked more realistically on the working of modern democratic politics?

The predictions made here have implications, on the one hand, for the playing of budgetary politics in post-Reagan Washington, and especially in the 1989–1993 term of the president. On the one hand, the "deficit issue," which is discussed almost exclusively in terms of the measured comprehensive budget, will be less acute because of the trust fund accumulations and will therefore be less acute politically unless major increases in domestic spending take place. There need be no major tax increase unless such spending increases do, in fact, occur. On the other hand, the machinations of politicians should never be neglected. Especially in the period 1990–1992, residues of the deficit issue from the mid-1980s may be used to justify broad-based tax increases and (non-revenue enhancing) increases in upper-bracket income taxes. This pattern of revenue enhancement, together with the social security tax increases underpinning the trust fund surpluses, would allow for a shift upward in the share of income returned to the government in taxes. Such a scenario will not, of course, embody genuine funding of social security. After Reagan, we may face a political reality that simultaneously embodies a continuing deep mistrust of both politicians and institutions and a return to the public sector growth pattern that has characterized almost the whole of this century.

4

In God We Trust—
The Political Economy of the
Social Security Reserves

Herman B. Leonard

In the 1980s, social security fell victim to a new form of financial crisis. The pattern for many years had been that social security slipped from solvency toward cash crisis, only to be rescued each time. Now, its rescue promises, and is delivering, a surplus of cash, swelling the trust funds' reserves. But this, too, is said to herald a crisis. What temptations will the buildup cause? What additional spending might be unleashed? What bankrupting benefit increases might come to seem affordable? How can the system be saved from the burden of having extra cash?

It was fairly clear in 1983 that as a consequence of the reform legislation reserves would begin to build up by the late 1980s if no intense recession occurred in mid-decade. Most observers, though, took a wait-and-see attitude born of many previous predictions of buildups-to-be that never were. With the strong performance of the economy over the course of the 1980s and the arrival of a reserve sufficiently large not to be missed without effort, two policy questions can no longer be kept from center stage. What impact will the reserves have? How should they be invested?

The task of identifying the most important impacts of the reserves can be simplified by keeping some other questions off the table.

For instance, as a matter of fiscal or social policy, should the nation build up its social security reserves? This is a worthy question, which has been pursued by Martin Feldstein, Alicia Munnell, Michael Boskin, and a number of other observers.[1] To many, it is still an open question. The reserve buildup has commenced, however, and will be taken as given so that we can explore its implications.

We will also set aside the closely related question of how the buildup of the reserves will influence citizens' saving behavior. The buildup has a direct influence on disposable incomes through the payroll tax withdrawal of resources from private hands. But if future beneficiaries believe that trust fund reserves make their benefit promises more secure, the existence of the trust fund may indirectly alter saving behavior. In what is now a famous debate, which underlies the question about the desirability of funding, Feldstein has argued that the social security system's promises of benefits reduce future beneficiaries' private saving; since the system is largely unfunded, this reduces national saving. Partial funding through the buildup of reserves may offset this effect—except that it may enhance the perception that benefits will really be paid and thus deepen the phenomenon it offsets. Robert Barro argues that citizens see through the veil, understanding both the liability and the asset sides of social security promises, and are thus unaffected by the promise or the reserves that back it. We will hold this issue aside, presuming that whatever influence social security has on individuals' saving behavior, that influence does not change markedly when the system has reserves.[2]

If we set aside the question of whether it is advisable to have reserves and also assume that the existence and investment of the reserves have minor (if any) impacts on private savings behavior, then what is left to be affected? The existence of sizable reserves—and the public and private perceptions of them, influenced by our choices about how they are invested—could profoundly affect our public behavior. The buildup of reserves could (and probably does) create "surplus illusion"—the sense that the federal government's budget balance problems are not as severe as they really are.

The decision to fund future benefits through higher payroll taxes now rather than later—a decision taken in the 1983 Social Security Amendments—should, in principle, be separable from any other decisions about federal taxes and spending. But the principle that these decisions should be separable has no enforcement clause. What matters is how these decisions come to be perceived as linked, or come unconsciously to be linked, through our system of political economy.

Seen against the backdrop of our political system, decisions about the long-term financing of social security could easily come to be linked to current spending in at least two ways. First, if some believe that current payroll taxpayers are overburdened by the requirement of building up a reserve, that buildup can be undone by financing more current spending through borrowing. Future taxpayers, who would have faced the burden of paying social security benefits, would then face the burden of paying off public debts for general expenditures instead. The intergenerational transfer of the social security financing burden toward present taxpayers (contained in the 1983 amendments) means nothing if it is simply offset through an increase in deficit spending in the rest of the budget.[3] If the shift of burden toward current taxpayers was regarded by some as unfair, then the political system could respond by explicitly attempting to redress the balance through the rest of the budget.

The second form of linkage is more subtle—and seems more likely. Rather that being an explicit reaction to the rearrangement of social security financing responsibility, it flows from the apparent availablity of spendable funds created by the social security surplus. Under pay-as-you-go financing, no large social security surplus would accumulate; the Treasury would have to borrow all necessary money directly from the public. With the 1983 amendments, a portion of that financing is provided by funds accumulating as surplus in the social security trust funds, automatically lent to the Treasury. If this automatic flow reduces the sense in Congress that the rest of the budget is seriously out of balance, it could easily—and unconsciously—result in greater current spending or in delays in increasing taxes.

The crucial issue, then, is how our system of political economy will respond to the existence and method of investing the reserves.

The Inexorable Logic of Righteous Entitlement

To understand the dynamics of the interaction between the social security surplus and how it is invested with the rest of the budget, we must first frame the backdrop against which that interaction will be played out. The central feature of that backdrop is the enviable—indeed, nearly unassailable—political support enjoyed by social security.

No program created in modern times has carved so wide a social and economic path across the fiscal landscape as social security. The program has withstood the onslaught of rival programs, fiscal austerity, a world war and two other major conflicts, rapid productivity and wage growth, stagflation, and a host of other changing political and economic circumstances—not to mention the attempts of armies of policy-oriented economists to get everyone to see the program as they see it, as a transfer rather than an insurance scheme. The program is not exactly unscathed, but it is surely intact. Its revenue source is relatively unchanged, its benefits and the size of its beneficiary groups have (with a few puts and takes here and there) only expanded, and the way it is perceived—as a contributory insurance program—is little altered after a half-century of intense discussion and budgetary pressure.

What is the (open) secret of this unassailable political logic? We might call it the logic of righteous entitlement. What sustains the program is the political fervor of millions of participants, a fervor born of their having made payments they view as contributions to an insurance program. Imagine the political support enjoyed by a program that sends nearly 40 million beneficiaries a check each month. Now imagine what support the future of that system could foster when over 125 million taxpayers pay into the system funds they view as contributions for future benefits. Never mind that the program pays out these contributions almost as quickly as it receives them. Never mind that it can, from the economist's perspective, be seen as a massive transfer program, with benefits vastly more generous than could reasonably have been financed with a funded system.

From the participant's perspective, contributions give rise to a right to receive benefits without embarrassment. Those contributions have extended over a considerable period, often spanning the individual's working life. With every paycheck, the worker has taken what we might call the "social security pledge of allegiance":

> I pledge allegiance to the social security system of the United States of America, and to the insurance program for which I suppose it to stand, one contributory trust, indivisible, with security and benefits for all.

Having taken that pledge in hard-earned dollars every payday of his or her working life, the payroll taxpayer is not about to stand idly by and watch the awaited benefits be swept away.

The program's central feature—that the benefits are a just return on contributions paid in—exists only in the mind of the beholder. But in politics, appearances are reality, and the perception is more than sufficient to sustain the program. The perception persists despite the fact that from the beginning it has been directly contradicted by the pay-as-you-go financing of the program and by the descriptions economists offer of the program. Most taxpayers and recipients apparently know that the system is not literally a contributory program; they simply feel righteously entitled to benefits from a system they have so long supported. Social security endures because of its intrinsic capacity to get each generation of financial contributors to support the program—and, also in turn, to demand their benefits.

The Evolution of Social Security with Reserves

The evolution of social security will continue to be guided by the politics of righteous entitlement. The immediate and salient implication is that the existence of reserves and the choice of how those reserves are invested will have relatively little to do with what happens to social security. More powerful influences are at work. The following propositions are therefore quite likely:

• *We will pay (at least approximately) the projected social security benefits.* The political logic will continue to work. The next generation will demand the benefits slated for them. We may not pay all those benefits; we may make some additional benefits taxable, we might trim cost-of-living adjustments and so on, but the political momentum of people's feeling of entitlement ensures that society will not substantially reduce benefits. Benefit payments are the defining characteristics of the system—both of its benefits and of its costs. This means that the choices that we make about the level of reserves or how they are invested will have at most a small impact on the level of benefits and the overall shape of the system.[4]

• *Congress will not directly divert the reserves.* Some observers are concerned that the social security reserves may be a tempting source of financing for other programs. Congress might divert payroll tax revenues to the general fund and use them to support other, non-social-security spending. According to this logic, it was a mistake to use the political support for social security in 1983 to win payroll tax increases beyond those necessary to pay for social security benefits. In a period of great pressure to hold down other tax increases while maintaining a wide array of spending programs, Congress may decide that these currently unneeded tax revenues are available for other purposes. It could, for example, reduce the social security portion of the payroll tax and institute a payroll tax to finance some other expenditure, so that the total is unchanged but the flow into social security is cut.

This scenario is quite unlikely. The payroll tax is strongly associated in the minds of most social security taxpayers and recipients with the social security system. The payroll tax increases were approved in 1983 on the basis of support for the social security system, not as general tax increases to be used for whatever Congress finds most important. The supporters of social security would see direct diversion as a severe challenge to the integrity of the program's financing and benefits. It is hard to imagine such a frontal assault on the system triumphing over the politics of righteous entitlement.

• *Congress may place new burdens on the system.* If Congress believes that the social security reserves indicate the program is unnecessarily flush—at least in comparison with other spending programs—it can move money out of the system more subtly. Non-social-security budget items that can be portrayed as part of social security could be funded by transferring the responsibility for them to the social security system. This has just as much effect on the balance in the rest of the budget as transferring the money out of the social security system—but is a good deal more subtle. Instead of being seen as raiding the reserves, Congress can present itself as creatively using funds that happen to be available to finance needed, related expenditures.

Congress has a number of natural opportunities it can exploit if it wants to proceed down this path. Over the years, many of the system's strongest supporters have sought to avoid transfers of general revenues to the system on the theory that it would come to be seen as a welfare program and that this would undercut its firm political support. In certain instances, though, Congress has avoided payroll tax increases either by providing such inflows to the system or by financing expenditures that could have been labeled "social security benefits" out of the general fund instead.

In 1983, for example, Congress changed the federal income tax status of social security benefits. Up to half of social security benefits are now taxable for beneficiaries with other income. Generally, payments by federal agencies for salaries, or any other expenditure, are taxable, and the tax proceeds are credited as general revenues to the Treasury. But under the 1983 amendments, taxes on social security benefits are credited to the social security trust funds.[5] No other agency enjoys the benefit of having the income taxes generated as a result of its spending treated as an offset to its budgetary cost. Social security currently receives about $5 billion annually from this unique provision.

Congress could choose to terminate this transfer to the trust funds. Given the large buildup of reserves, the extra credit from the Treasury would not be missed immediately by social security—and the revenues would be welcome in the rest of the budget. Moreover, retaining the income taxes in the general fund would encourage Congress to increase the taxability of social security benefits. Under the current arrangement, it would be politically costly to do so, and all the extra revenues would be credited to the social security system, merely increasing reserves already in surplus and providing no relief to the rest of the budget.[6]

Congress has likewise used general revenues to finance some expenditures that could be viewed as social security benefits. Currently, the hospitalization portion (of Medicare Part A) is funded through the social security payroll tax; about $25 billion each year in doctors' bills (Part B) is paid for out of general revenues.

Congress could transfer financing responsibility for all Medicare-related health benefits for the elderly to the social security system. If carried out under a reorganization and consolidation of the Medicare program, this transfer of responsibility would provide a more politically plausible way to use the resources of social security than simply diverting the funds—but the budget effect is the same. Plugging a $25 billion drain on the rest of the budget by offloading the payment responsibility to social security has just as much impact as diverting $25 billion in payroll tax revenues to the general fund. Needless to say, it would be much easier to move the costs into social security than to move the money out.

These realignments of revenues and costs would divert money from the social security trust funds. With the right polish and marketing, they are politically possible. What makes them plausible is that they can be presented as "corrections" to current arrangements. Why should only the hospitalization portions of health care costs for the elderly be paid by social security taxes? The distinction between hospital costs and doctors' costs is arbitrary and irrelevant. In fact, it arises largely as a historical accident of what social security could afford under an earlier payroll tax regime. The return of taxes on social security benefits to the system can likewise be presented as an anomaly. The IRS collects and credits to the general fund income taxes generated from every other source in the country—why should social security alone get them back? Again, the answer is that it was a device of convenience—the arrangement helped to close the cash deficit in the social security system when it neared cash bankruptcy in 1983. Today, as reserves build, that imperative no longer exists, and the mechanism could be made to fade away into richly deserved oblivion.

Possible technical fixes and appropriate rearrangements of responsibility between social security and the general fund, however, are intrinsically limited. Trying to present the star wars program, for example, as related to social security is simply implausible. Only a limited number of devices for moving money out of the trust funds or moving financing responsibilities in could be made to seem even remotely appropriate. In the end, Congress may pursue some of these alternatives, but no such scheme is likely to have a very sizable impact on the social security system.

• *Congress may choose to expand social security benefits.* If funds cannot be transferred out and if spending responsibilities not clearly germane to social security cannot be transferred in, then the money slated to flow into the social security reserves must be used for social security purposes. But if Congress finds that budget stringency in the rest of its spending programs forces it to be less generous in dispensing public benefits than it would like, it may find the social security reserves a tempting source with which it can afford to behave generously. The concept of social security could be enlarged. New beneficiaries could be added. New benefits could be offered or old benefits expanded.

History suggests that this is not an unlikely path. On a number of occasions over the fifty-year history, Congress has found itself in the happy position of having surpluses developing from payroll taxes enacted at rates that had been predicted merely to keep the system solvent. Each time, it could have reacted by cutting taxes. Projections always indicated that the surpluses were temporary, however, and that the rates that were creating surpluses would be necessary to keep the system solvent later on. On occasion, Congress responded by deferring scheduled tax increases. It also often found it convenient to expand benefits or beneficiaries.

There are many attractive ways to spend the accumulating reserves under the social security rubric. Any number of legitimately deserving groups for whom society could be doing more have nominated themselves, including those who seem arbitrarily disadvantaged by some peculiarity of the system (like the "notch babies"), those about whom we made poor projections (like the very aged elderly, who are the fastest growing population group), and those whose frailty is a newly discovered social concern (like the mildly incapacitated who need additional help to continue living independently).[7] The apparent capacity of the social security trust may make it hard to resist developing spending programs to meet the very real needs of these and other groups.

The peril here is again to future taxpayers. The seeming capacity of the reserves to bear additional burdens from expanded benefits or beneficiaries is an illusion. The reserves contain "spent" money, already committed to meet slated benefits; it is simply being held for timely disbursement. Having been spent already, it cannot be spent again. Any expansion of benefits or beneficiaries is new spending, which will require new financing—either now or later. Expansions of benefits may be justified, but they are not free; uncommitted resources do not exist to fund them.

Congress could also eliminate the reserves by granting a payroll tax reduction. If the perceived perils of having reserves—together with the perceived political benefits of legislating a tax cut—come to be seen as greater than the virtues of having the social security system operate in reasonably close actuarial balance, a tax cut could easily result.[8]

This proposal is not without its own dangers, however. In particular, it implies increases in payroll taxes starting between 2010 and 2020 and continuing thereafter to fund benefits for the retiring baby-boom generation. At the same time, it implies a substantial reduction in the fraction of those retirement costs that the baby-boom generation actually pays, transferring that burden to later taxpayers. In short, it would undo the intergenerational transfer of financing responsibility embodied in the 1983 amendments, which more closely balanced what each generation pays in with what it gets back.[9] Given the political economy of righteous entitlement, the problems under this scenario accrue largely to future taxpayers.

• *The existence and investment policies of the reserves will have relatively small direct effects on benefits or on real economic costs.* Theoretically, investment policies could affect benefit levels, but this feedback effect is probably so small as to be irrelevant. If (by virtue of the choices made about investment vehicles for the reserves), for example, the level or composition of interest rates across financial assets is significantly changed, the level or pattern of real investment in the economy would shift as well. This, in turn, could have an impact on productivity growth and thus on real wages and social security benefits. Thus, at least in theory, the social security reserve investment policies could affect the actuarial balance of the system not simply on the income (interest earned) side of the ledger but on the outflow side as well. The likely magnitude of these effects, however, is small. While global financial markets can hardly be said to function perfectly, even the scale of investments contemplated by the social security system seems unlikely to disrupt the pattern of interest rates determined by other forces in the financial markets.[10]

Two quite thorough simulation models developed by Brookings and ICF both suggest that the pattern of interest rates in the economy is not very sensitive to the pattern of social security investments. Few observers expect the outstanding debt as a fraction of GNP to decline appreciably. Thus, there will continue to be federal debt for the social security system to buy, and it will almost surely continue to hold a substantial portion of its assets in that form. Even if the system moves some holdings out of "special obligations" to other forms, such a shift is unlikely to disrupt financial markets unless it is made precipitously or narrowly.

The social security program is not imperiled by its reserves. The threats, for the most part, are to other taxpayers. If the existence or investment of the social security reserves is to make a material difference, it will be through its impact on the conduct of federal spending policy.

The Effect of Social Security Reserves on Other Spending

The importance of social security's reserves to the rest of federal spending is made manifest by a simple but startling observation: the accumulated reserves can be spent in practice without touching them in principle or on paper. It is relatively easy for Congress, under the current pressure to reduce budget deficits, to adopt a posture of reducing only the "unified" budget deficit rather than the deficit in the non-social-security portion of the budget. This would treat payroll-tax financed purchases of Treasury debt as freely spendable inflows to the Treasury. Such a policy amounts to unraveling in the aggregate budget the partial funding of the social security system.

For the short run, Congress appears already to have adopted just that posture. Budget limitation targets under Gramm-Rudman-Hollings were set on the basis of the unified budget including the current surplus in the social security accounts. What target would have been set in the absence of the social security surplus? If, in the absence of a social security surplus, Congress would have tightened spending or raised revenues more than it did, then it took the existence of the surplus as an excuse not to have to balance the remaining budget as closely and in effect spent the social security surplus. If, in contrast, it would have left other spending unchanged and accepted the impact of larger net borrowing by the federal government, then the social security surplus actually reduced net federal borrowing from the public and increased government saving. Given that most of the economic effects that Congress seems concerned with—interest rates, international capital flows, the strength of the dollar, inflationary pressures, and so on—are influenced by net federal borrowing, it seems reasonable to suppose that there would be more pressure to balance the remaining budget it there were not a surplus in social security. If so, this suggests that the surplus is, at least in part, not being saved. In any case, the surplus may tempt Congress to be less vigorous in its attempt to balance the non-social-security budget.

The temptation to spend the funds borrowed from social security accounts in the form of special obligations exists whether or not they constitute net national savings. Whether the reserves were built up from reductions in government consumption, personal consumption, or private investment, or were offset by the actions of foresighted taxpayers—that is, whether or not they came from or constituted savings—they can be turned into current government consumption. They may or may not be real savings, but they can surely become real spending.

If we follow this path, what will the endgame look like? Some observers are worried that if the reserves are borrowed and used to finance spending now, the torque applied to the federal budget later will be all the more severe, and that programs—including social security—will be trimmed indiscriminately. It is not hard to see where that worry comes from. What is available to Congress to spend is the annual increment to the reserve—the current surplus. While the reserves are projected, under moderate assumptions, to peak around 2030, the annual surplus will first grow in the 1990s and then shrink to zero between 2010 and 2020. At that point social security will switch from providing net lendable funds (and budgetary flexibility) to demanding net redemption. The Treasury will then be required not only to meet the full demands of the non-social-security portion of the budget without the accustomed helpful lending from social security but also to procure additional resources to be transferred to social security. Thus, if Congress is using the reserves by borrowing and then spending them, it is sending the federal budget on a fiscal roller coaster. Sometime in the first quarter of the next century, social security will produce an apparent severe drain on federal resources.

How will the conflicting pressures be resolved? One possibility, raised by some social security supporters as a good reason to avoid building reserves in the first place, is that social security benefits will be threatened. According to this logic the slated benefits, with their resulting squeeze on the budget, will look too generous to a generation of Americans beleaguered by other spending cuts, tax increases, and stagnation in real wages resulting from foreign competition. Why should we cut still farther in already lean programs to redeem too-generous social security promises?

Some of the gap might, indeed, be closed under this scenario by trimming social security benefits. It seems unlikely that benefits would be fully paid if our children would then lead less comfortable lives than we have lived. Moreover, since there will be a particularly high ratio of retirees to workers during this period, any shortfall in real income growth for workers will be felt acutely.

This scenario poses the only potentially serious peril to recipients. Still, if there is any program that can withstand this pressure, it is social security. As has been true from the beginning, the beneficiaries are and will seem deserving, having paid their dues. Their children, even if beleaguered, should still hesitate to attack too forcefully a system in which they themselves have already begun to pay membership fees. They will be, as others before them have been, worried about what would happen to their parents if benefits from the government are cut—will the family be able to support them from its own resources? The power of the politics of righteous entitlement has been underestimated many times before.

The current system produces a strong temptation to spend the money raised for social security twice. Spending the money twice will ultimately require raising it twice. If we contrive to spend the reserves (by borrowing them and allowing that to relax the pressures to balance the rest of the budget), we will not subsequently close the gap by severely reducing social security benefits. When social security beneficiaries present their claims, there will be no real choice but to pay them. Taxpayers, who first put up the money to fund the social security benefits through the reserves and then watched as that money was siphoned off to permit more current government spending, would then be forced either to abrogate the political commitments of the social security system—a virtual impossibility—or, reluctantly, to fund social security again.[11] What is stunning about this possible—indeed, apparently continuing—sequence of events is that the powerful political logic and demands of social security create legitimate spending claims twice.

Questions about the impact of reserve investment policies on social security and the economy, while potentially important, are likely to be very small relative to the consequences of saving or spending the reserves. Both the Brookings and the ICF models indicate relatively minor impacts from altering investment policies, once federal fiscal policy has been set. But both find that it makes a great deal of difference whether federal fiscal policy validates or, instead, offsets the buildup of social security reserves. The major differences are not to social security, although there are some impacts on productivity, wage growth, and so on, with material consequences for the size of benefit payments, interest rates earned by the reserves, and other matters of some importance to the system. Rather, the major differences are in the scale of the national debt, the amount of other federal spending, and the corresponding economic indexes—for example, interest rates influenced by the amount of net borrowing.

Controlling the impulse to exploit the fiscal freedom granted by the trust fund surpluses to the non-social-security budget will not be easy amid the climate of political foment against tax increases, against further borrowing, and for further spending. Under the current institutional arrangements, such a maneuver leaves no definitive trace, there is every incentive to do it, and there is no particular political constituency against it. Future social security recipients are not really threatened—they will get their benefits. While future taxpayers are threatened—they will simply have to pay—they are notoriously difficult to organize as a political constituency.

Those concerned with social security tend to worry about what the federal budget can do for social security; the time has come to worry about what social security can do for the federal budget. Although the social security system cannot control federal budget spending, it may be able to influence it. It may be able to influence the degree to which the system's reserves are insulated from federal budget pressures, are regarded as separate, distinct, and unavailable by Congress, and are perceived by current and prospective social security beneficiaries as importantly involved in whether they will be paid. If Congress and beneficiaries come to see the reserves as inviolable and we find a mechanism to broadcast when defunding is taking place, the impulse to defund the reserves may be partly countered.

In short, since the direct effects of investment policies on social security appear to be small, the most important impacts of reserve investment policies may be on the evolution of the rest of federal spending, taxation, and borrowing—that is, on the degree to which the reserves are validated. There are relatively few instruments through which the degree of validation can be influenced, and the reserve investment policy may be among the most important of them.

Using Reserve Investment Policies to Reduce Surplus Illusion

What can be done to increase the insulation of the reserves from the federal budget? First, social security can be removed from the budget, so that we focus separately on the non-social-security and the social security budgets. Congress has already approved this change, but in a time-honored tradition deferred its implementation until after 1992: better late than not at all, but better still if even sooner.

Second, the reserve investment policies can be designed to increase the apparent distance between social security and the rest of the budget. A large fraction of the reserve could be invested in nongovernment or, at a minimum, non-Treasury securities.[12] Treasury borrowing (not Treasury borrowing net of social security lending) would then be a focus of discussion, and this would redirect attention to the net deficit in the rest of the budget. The idea is to reduce the unintentional or hidden cross-financing between social security and the rest of the budget. Forcing that cross-financing to flow through the hands of the public, and thus to show up in the accounts as Treasury borrowing from the public, at least shines a brighter spotlight on the relevant magnitudes. Attention may not be a very powerful resource for altering political decisions, but it is one of the few resources available.

A further argument supports investing at least a significant part of the surplus in securities other than special obligations of the Treasury. If there is a threat to social security, it will arrive during the redemption phase of the reserve, as the funds built up in earlier years are drawn down to pay for benefits to the swelling ranks of the baby-boom retirees. If those investments are held in special obligation form, the act of redemption itself will put pressure on the federal Treasury, which will have to borrow or tax to raise the cash to meet the obligation. This is not the case if the investments are made elsewhere. When social security needs to draw down its reserve, it will be calling in its debt from a broad portfolio of businesses.

To see this, suppose a corporation had borrowed $10 million on fifteen-year terms from the fund in 1995. (The funds it borrowed arrived in the form of payroll tax revenues and interest payments on trust fund investments in 1995 beyond what was required to pay benefits in that year.) The corporation paid interest each year, which was used to pay benefits or was reinvested in other assets. As 2010 approached, the corporation made preparations to pay off the note, either out of its own available funds or perhaps through borrowing. It had always known that that particular debt would be due in 2010; those were the terms to which it voluntarily agreed when it borrowed the funds in 1995. The redemption is thus completely unexceptional. It is simply a voluntary debt contract, being redeemed as agreed and, if the corporation is wise, as planned by both parties. The fact that many other corporations have notes coming due to the social security system at about the same time is of little direct consequence to any particular borrower. And the fact that the social security system is increasingly using these repayments to finance benefits rather than for reinvestment is also of little concern to particular borrowers. The redemption of each particular debt contract—the generation of funds by the corporation and the payment to the social security system—is entirely ordinary, not unlike thousands of other financial obligations being met each day.

Now suppose that the social security reserves continue to be reinvested in special Treasury obligations, so that in 1995 social security lends its available funds on fifteen-year terms to the Treasury. Unlike the many small transactions with individual corporations, each of which faces the obligation to repay a relatively small debt, social security lending to the Treasury is in one large lump sum. For the sake of example, let us suppose that $10 billion of the 1995 surplus were placed with the Treasury for repayment in 2010. What happens when the obligation must be redeemed? Treasury has no large stock of excess cash available; it must raise funds from tax increases, spending reductions, or new borrowing at that time. Assuming that between now and 2010 the non-social-security budget has not come into balance, Treasury will already be borrowing to fund current expenditures. The requirement to pay off the social security debt will be in addition to this. Thus, the $10 billion repayment obligation due from the 1995 transaction, together with other billions of obligations due from investments of reserves from other surplus years between 1990 and 2010, present a demand for funds from the Treasury in 2010. This demand is, from the perspective of what is affordable in the budget of 2010, indistinguishable from any other demand for a dollar of spending. Thus, it will be encountered as a large, concentrated pressure on the budget created by the social security system. And it will be followed by a next year in which an even larger social security drain of otherwise spendable funds has to be confronted.

The dynamics of these cash flows is thus fundamentally different under the two alternative reserve investment policies. If the reserves are invested in a broad array of corporations, the redemption will be encountered as a vast number of small obligations to repay, each voluntarily entered and long planned upon. If the reserves are invested in special obligations of the Treasury, then as the social security system slips from surplus into deficit, the system will produce a sizable, concentrated pressure on the rest of the budget—all in order to pay large retirement benefits to a distressingly numerous generation. Even if funds are lent to private corporations, though, the drawdown of social security reserves may have aggregate credit market effects that are felt by Treasury.

As social security stops its accustomed lending, the aggregate liquidity it is providing to financial markets will decrease. To meet the obligations to social security, corporations may seek to borrow elsewhere, or may in turn call in debts owed them. One of the major debts they are owed is the public debt, owed by the Treasury.

Thus, either way, Treasury will feel pressure. But if the reserves are invested outside of Treasury, the pressure applied will not be directly by social security. Treasury will be finding a less liquid public attending its weekly auctions of debt, through which it will be refinancing, rolling over, and perhaps adding to its outstanding debt. It may be forced to pay higher interest rates, and Congress may find it prudent to trim spending or raise taxes to reduce the requirement for borrowing. No one, however, will be able to say that Congress is having to raise taxes to pay social security benefits. Treasury will not be redeeming debt to pay social security benefits. GM, IBM, Bank of America, and other borrowers will.

The advantage of investing funds outside of Treasury comes from the diffusion of what will otherwise be perceived as a concentrated burden from social security benefits competing with other spending programs for available public cash. The advantage becomes larger as the distance from Treasury becomes greater. The redemption process is likely to be even less conspicuous if the obligations being redeemed are those of a wide array of domestic and foreign corporations. If Mitsubishi enters a voluntary financial agreement in 1995 and promises to pay $50 million to the social security system in 2010, few will propose cutting social security benefits to reduce its burden when it comes due. By contrast, if Treasury makes the same promise, some may wish in

2010 to relieve some of the burden on Treasury that will appear to be being generated by social security benefit payments.

By virtue of the power of the politics of righteous entitlement, social security probably does not need much protection, even during the period when it is drawing down reserves. If the threat of blame for exerting pressure on the federal budget during the drawdown period looks ominous, then having the public intermediate the loans of social security reserves to the Treasury puts a large and diverse group of noncaptive third parties between social security and the budget. From the perspective of the social security system, political insulation is desirable; a change in the investment policy can produce it.

Managing Non-Treasury Assets

If social security reserves were invested outside the Treasury, Congress would immediately face the problem of deciding which investments to make, with what borrowers, at what rates of return. One of the great attractions of the Treasury as a borrower is that the credit rating of the debtor is not in question. The reserves could be invested in the securities of other federal agencies. This, however, would constitute only an elaborate paper shuffle; it could as easily be accomplished by relabeling some of the existing special obligations. The virtues of diffusing the investments are obtained only by truly diffusing them. This approach confronts the system with the prospect of managing a high volume of small, private financial contracts. It would have to guard against fraud and against simple mismanagement. It would have to resist being used as a means of providing hidden subsidies to politically favored constituencies. Can a management process be devised whose liabilities are smaller than the virtues that investment of reserves outside the Treasury can confer?

There are several models that suggest the management problems need not be fatal. Pension funds face similar problems of potential fraud and mismanagement, and some face similar problems of political abuse. The federal government has recently joined the ranks of public sector enterprises managing private investments through its new federal employee retirement system. There is no intrinsic reason why social security reserves could not be managed similarly. One important characteristic of successful public pension funds is that the funds invested are treated as belonging to private beneficiaries, not to the public sector. A similar cultural orientation would have to be developed within social security, but there is no reason to think it could not be.

Conclusion

Social security is a brilliant political design. That it will pay benefits for the foreseeable future is not in doubt. That it will temporarily have significant, though not enormous, reserves seems reasonably clear. The existence of the reserves may lead to some minor changes in the social security system, but the basic components of the system are robust. How the reserves are invested will also have only minor, if any, direct consequences for social security.

In contrast, the existence and chosen investment policies of the social security reserves may have a substantial effect on federal spending on other programs. The 1983 amendments shifted financing responsibility for social security benefits to current taxpayers. That shift can easily be undone through shifting financing responsibility for other spending away from current taxpayers. The 1983 amendments only assert fiscal responsibility in a portion of federal spending; like a dam across half of the harbor, they cannot alone hold back the tide.

Under the arrangements now in place, the social security system's financing produces confusing signals in the overall federal fiscal system. Making those signals clearer should be a high priority of federal fiscal policy. Changing the investment mechanism of the accumulating reserves provides one of the few meaningful ways to filter out the noise and focus attention on the realities of federal fiscal performance.

Fiscal Policy and Politics

A Commentary by David G. Mathiasen

The central issue before us is how to make society better off in the next century when the baby-boom generation retires. The economic well-being of individuals at that time will be determined by how much total output there is and how it is divided between workers and retirees. The amount of total output will be influenced by national savings rates and investment between now and then. The way that output is divided will depend on, among other things, how benefits for future retirees are credited under the social security system. Ultimately the credits are no more than records on computer tape; they represent a claim on resources but do not create any resources. The answer to the questions "how much" and "who gets it" will depend in part on government policies in the coming decades, which in turn, will be influenced by two things: the way we account for government programs and politics, which is the focus of this discussion.

It is fascinating to me, as someone who has worked in budgeting for many years, that this discussion of budget accounting takes place at all. Budget decisions are profoundly political. Accounting matters, of course, but politics is the driving force.

Having said that, I will offer a slightly different perspective, which is based on my experience with fourteen businessmen and politicians who made up the National Economic Commission.

First, fiscal illusion, to the extent it still exists, is likely to be a thing of the past within a year. People are catching on quickly to the fact that the social security surpluses are being spent on financing the current operations of the government, partly because of the large number of policy forums bringing attention to the issue. Certainly, the General Accounting Office has stressed the degree to which the social security surplus masks the government's operating deficit.

The Committee for a Responsible Federal Budget runs workshops on budgets all over the country. These workshops are like focus groups in which citizens spend an afternoon working on budgets. I am told that, *without exception*, people are incensed over the notion that social security payroll taxes are being used to fund other government programs. Some and perhaps a majority of the members of the National Economic Commission would have agreed that if this practice continues, as a political matter, the payroll tax will be reduced.

There is a lot of truth in James Buchanan's argument that if more resources are available to be spent, they will be spent. I suggest, however, that social security may be different. For the reasons that Herman Leonard stated, social security has a special political status. Because it does, it is not a foregone conclusion that through a 1967 device called the "unified budget" the public can continue to be fooled into believing the surpluses are being saved. If there is confusion, I suspect a number of politicians will try to clarify the issue, and the public reaction—already very negative—could spread. An effective political campaign could be waged around the charge that the payroll taxes are being used to fund the current operating expenses of government. This potential was recognized in the majority and minority reports of the National Economic Commission. The majority spoke of procedures to require a balance in the non-social-security budget, including safeguards against the use of social security's reserves for other purposes. The minority report, in which Senator Moynihan was heavily involved, recommended that the social security surpluses be "insulated," which basically means keeping the rest of the budget in balance.

On the particular question of how the social security surpluses are invested—in special-issue government bonds or in private securities—it is not obvious to me that the overall economic effects will be substantially different. Either way, enormous resources will have to be withdrawn from earned income in the economy to meet anticipated benefits for baby-boom retirees. Either way, there will be major effects on monetary and fiscal policy and on aggregate economic activity.

I agree with Leonard's proposition, however, that the way these funds are treated in the federal budget does matter. This is not just a vague academic issue. Consider, for example, the Federal Life Insurance System. Under this program, the federal government as employer makes payments directly to a private insurer. Whether that insurer invests in Treasury securities or in private securities, I do not know, and indeed I do not care. But the way the program is handled in the federal budget is very important. The premium is treated as payment to the public just like salary. It is gone from the government's point of view and creates a privately owned asset for the employee—almost as "private" as a house. In contrast, the accounting treatment of the old civil service retirement system, which still covers a substantial portion of the federal work force, is quite different. Under this program the government's payments are made directly to a government trust fund. The funds are not considered privately owned and they do not leave the government or appear as deficit-increasing outlays until the (much later) benefit payments are made to the (retired) workers. In a crude way, the difference between including social security in the official budget or excluding it may be thought of as comparable to the difference between these two accounting techniques.

I have one serious political concern with investing a large social security reserve—say, $500 billion—in the private sector. It is not difficult to imagine a member of Congress in 1994 saying, "Mr. President, I rise to offer an amendment to the debt limit bill, which is that no social security funds can be invested in a company that. . . ." You can fill in your own ending; for example, "practices animal testing of cosmetics," "produces automobiles with average fuel economy below forty miles per gallon," or "trades with South Africa." Some state and local governments have already imposed these types of restrictions on allowable investments. The labor unions take a very practical view: why should we spend our pension funds financing nonunionized companies? I can imagine a majority in Congress asking the same type of questions and imposing the same type of restrictions. The return on invested funds would necessarily suffer if investment decisions were politically based.

Political Effects of the Social Security Surpluses

A Commentary by Alan S. Blinder

The purpose of the chapters by James Buchanan and Herman Leonard is to divine—I use the term advisedly—the political effects of the social security (Old-Age, Survivors, and Disability Insurance) surpluses on the federal budget. Before addressing their analysis of this subject, however, I feel compelled to issue two warnings. First, forecasting the political consequences of an unprecedented sequence of events is an inexact art, certainly not a science. So we should get nervous if we hear too many experts agreeing too readily. Remember, for example, what the political pundits said would come of the social security reform commission in 1983 and tax reform in 1986. Second, I confess that I am in broad agreement with both authors—who mostly agree with one another. Forewarned is forearmed; so I shall proceed with my discussion.

I said we mostly agree. What do we agree about? One could imagine that the current and impending surpluses in the social security part of the budget might tempt Congress to:

- raid the trust funds to pay for other things
- raise social security benefits
- cut social security payroll taxes
- take a more relaxed attitude toward reducing the deficit in the non-social-security portion of the budget

Amazingly, when Buchanan, Leonard, and I think about these possibilities, we all find the first three possibilities—the ones that imperil the projected trust fund buildup—unlikely and worry about the last.[1] Furthermore, we all seem to agree that taking social security truly off budget would probably reduce the extent to which the trust fund surpluses will lead to larger deficits in the rest of the budget.

I will concentrate on developing shades of difference within this broad area of agreement. Then I will enter one objection to Buchanan's paper and one to Leonard's.

Both authors point out that, since Gramm-Rudman-Hollings sets targets for the unified budget, every $1 increase in the social security surplus "allows" an additional $1 deficit in the rest of the budget. That is certainly true at the margin. But it does not mean that the fiscal stance at the end of the Gramm-Rudman horizon will be looser because of the social security surpluses, as both authors suggest. Why? Congress, or at least those members most closely involved in budgeting, knew about the projected social security surpluses when Gramm-Rudman was revised in 1987. So, for example, when it set a target of a balanced *unified* budget by fiscal 1993, it knew that this implied an approximately $100 billion deficit in the non-social-security budget. And it knew it could get away with calling that a "balanced budget" because of the social security fig leaf.

If we accept the hypothesis that Congress knew what it was doing in 1987—and how else can we explain its seemingly curious decision to take social security "off budget" and yet count it in Gramm-Rudman calculations?—then there are three ways in which the social security surpluses might lead to bigger deficits in the rest of the budget between now and 1993.

First, perhaps Congress would have set tougher targets for the non-social-security deficit were it not for the social security surpluses. Buchanan and Leonard seem to think so—and maybe they are right. But let us remember that Congress was loosening its corset at the time. Having suffered the indignity of abandoning the first version of Gramm-Rudman, adopted in 1985, it could have set whatever new targets it wanted. Maybe it did what it thought right, balancing economic and political merits as usual. Furthermore, the deficit-reduction targets adopted in 1987 are, in my judgment, quite reasonable. A $100 billion non-social-security deficit in 1993 would amount to roughly 1½ percent of gross national product, which is in line with historical norms. So maybe Congress actually did the right thing.

Second, perhaps the coming social security surpluses will weaken congressional resolve to abide by Gramm-Rudman. But I do not see why.

Third, maybe social security will make achievement of the Gramm-Rudman targets easier because payroll tax receipts grow more rapidly or benefit outlays rise more slowly than Congress thought they would in 1987. On the other hand, however, social security might make the targets tougher to achieve because flows into the trust funds do not live up to expectations. Between these two scenarios, I frankly find the latter more likely.

What all this implies to me is that there is unlikely to be any sense in which the social security surpluses lead to larger non-social-security deficits between now and the Gramm-Rudman horizon.

To me, the real issue arises after that point. For concreteness, suppose we end fiscal 1993 (and the Gramm-Rudman era) with a balanced unified budget composed of a $100 billion social security surplus and a $100 billion deficit in the rest of the budget. If social security remains on budget de facto, even though off budget de jure, as at present, then it seems to me that Congress will be tempted to declare victory and go home. By contrast, if social security is truly taken off budget in 1993, the official budget deficit will revert to $100 billion and there will be continuing pressure on Congress to reduce the non-social-security deficit. The two situations may be identical economically; but I do not think they are identical politically, where symbols *are* reality.

The political difference between the two scenarios grows in subsequent years as the annual social security surpluses mount. If Congress is focusing on a unified budget, which is moving into increasing surplus year after year, less budget discipline seems likely in comparison with a situation in which Congress is focusing on the non-social-security budget, which is chronically in deficit. I take it that both Buchanan and Leonard agree with me on this point, but neither one gives it much emphasis. I think they should. The social security surpluses give us a golden opportunity to shift the policy mixture in the direction it should have moved years ago: toward tighter budgets and looser monetary policy. This is important in its own right as a way to speed the pace of capital formation and also as a way to ease the future burdens on the social security system, for a more capital-intensive society has higher labor productivity and hence requires a lower payroll tax rate to finance any given level of social security benefits. So I attach more importance to the accounting separation of social security than either author seems to.

At this point, a serious question, mentioned by both authors, arises. Is it just social security or social security and Medicare (hospital insurance) that we should take off budget? The difference is no small matter, either economically or politically. Politically, as Buchanan points out, Medicare and social security are natural bedfellows; they are the two main ways we support the elderly. So, if the retirement system is roped off from the rest of the budget, it seems likely that Medicare would go with it. Economically, the projected Medicare deficits early in the next century are approximately one-third the size of the projected social security surpluses. So if the two are taken off budget together, we could wind up spending about a third of the social security surpluses on Medicare, rather than squirreling it away. It will take some creative political thinking and tinkering to prevent this from happening. Perhaps a bipartisan blue-ribbon commission could do for Hospital Insurance today what the Greenspan Commission did for social security in 1983. The demise of the National Economic Commission, however, gives little reason for optimism on this score.

I now raise one major objection about each chapter.

Leonard downplays the accounting separation that I have just promoted and suggests instead using another economically meaningless political symbol—investing the social security surpluses in corporate, rather than Treasury, bonds. It is hard for me to imagine that this symbol would galvanize Congress or even have the limited political power that the accounting deficit has; but my criticism lies elsewhere. Corporate bond issues run about ¼ percent of GNP these days. According to current projections, the annual social security surpluses will rise to about 1¼ percent of GNP within a few years and stay in that range for about two decades. Under his plan the social security trust fund would therefore become a huge leviathan gobbling up a large share of the corporate bond market. In such an environment, the danger that the trust fund's investment policy would become politicized is, I think, greater than he admits.

The mention of leviathan brings me to my criticism of Buchanan's chapter. Buchanan asserts that the social security *surpluses* of the next thirty years or so will make the government prone to do more non-social-security spending than it otherwise would have done. As I have already made clear, I suspect he is right. But he also asserts that the social security *deficits* of the following thirty years or so will exert no comparable downward pressure on spending. Thus his leviathan grows fat on social security surpluses but fails to slim down when fed a regimen of unending social security deficits. Here I part company and see a more symmetric political biology.

As evidence for my position, I offer a pair of numbers and a pair of rhetorical questions. Between 1986 and 1988, the share of noninterest federal government spending in GNP fell from 21.2 percent to 19.8 percent. Was this not the result of pressure on spending created by the desire to reduce the budget deficit? Why should we not expect similar budgetary pressures when the social security trust funds are being drawn down after 2020?

PART THREE

The Effects on Government Budgets and National Savings— Evidence from the United States and Abroad

5

Foreign Experience with Public Pension Surpluses and National Saving

Alicia H. Munnell and C. Nicole Ernsberger

Under the U.S. Old-Age, Survivors, and Disability Insurance (OASDI) program, receipts are projected to exceed outlays for the next thirty years, resulting in an accumulation of assets equal to nearly 30 percent of gross national product (GNP) by the year 2018.[1] Although current law provides that these accumulated reserves be drawn down in later years, proposals are already emerging to raise taxes and maintain the amassed reserves. Hence, the United States has a convenient mechanism for augmenting its low level of national saving. By accumulating assets in the social security trust funds, the federal government can create government saving and thereby raise the national saving rate. This will not happen automatically, however.

Whether government saving actually occurs depends on how Congress reacts to the buildup in the social security trust funds. If Congress substitutes the increase in reserves for a tax increase or spending reduction to finance current consumption—that is, to pay for current outlays in the rest of the budget—no real saving will occur. But if the government alters its spending and taxing patterns to produce surpluses in its unified budget accounts—not just in the social security trust funds—the nation will enjoy higher saving and investment.

While saving through the trust funds may be the most desirable action, its importance for either the OASDI program or future generations should be kept in perspective. If the economic assumptions underlying the intermediate cost projections of the social security board of trustees prove to be roughly correct, social security will function perfectly well regardless of whether reserves are accumulated in advance or financing is returned to pay-as-you-go. If reserves are not accumulated between now and 2018, then social security taxes will have to be raised between one and two percentage points each for employees and employers in 2018, rather than 2046, to finance annual deficits on a current cost basis. This tax increase is not insignificant but completely manageable. Likewise, if the productivity growth underlying the intermediate cost projections materializes, the difference between how well-off people would be with and without the additional saving is fairly small. Recent estimates indicate that in 2020 the net real wage for the average earner after paying social security taxes will be 199 percent of today's level without the additional saving, 211 percent with it.[2]

The necessity of prefunding may be open to debate, but almost all commentators agree that the reserves amassed in the social security trust funds should not be spent on current consumption. This outcome would have the undesirable distributional consequence of financing general government activities by the more regressive payroll tax. Hence, if reserves are to be accumulated, it is important to translate public pension accumulations into national saving.

The United States is not the first country to attempt to prefund, at least partially, its public pension system. Canada, Japan, and Sweden in particular have accumulated large public pension trust fund reserves in an effort to ease the burden of future pension costs. This chapter explores the experiences of those countries to see if they suggest any policies or procedures that might help ensure that pension fund surpluses are used to augment national saving and investment rather than merely to replace current taxes and pay for current general government outlays.

Relevant Considerations

Before looking at the experiences of the individual countries, it is useful to consider the major concerns regarding the ability of the federal government to increase national saving through trust fund surpluses and to identify those factors that might influence the likelihood that these surpluses raise future output and national income.

Since the origins of the social security program in the 1930s, opponents of funding have argued that Congress will use the assets in the trust funds to pay for current consumption. This potential problem is typically, albeit imprecisely, characterized as using surpluses in the social security trust funds to cover deficits in the rest of the budget. The real concern, however, is not one of deficits but rather one of behavioral response. That is, critics worry that the surpluses in the social security trust funds will encourage Congress either to spend more money or to raise less tax revenue than it would have otherwise. Thus, the issue is one of fiscal discipline. By removing pressure to scrutinize the merits of alternative spending proposals, the social security reserves could allow Congress either to liberalize social security benefits or to finance marginal projects in the non-social-security portion of the budget, producing higher government spending than would otherwise occur. Alternatively, by appearing to be available to cover general government outlays, the social security surpluses could reduce incentives to raise additional taxes.

The likelihood of producing this type of behavioral response would seem to vary inversely with the availability of trust fund revenues for general budget or deficit reduction purposes. One factor in this regard is the treatment of the social security programs in the unified budget. If trust fund activity is integrated with other federal functions and the total reported as a single figure—as in the United States since 1969[3]—Congress and the public would be encouraged to think that the trust fund reserves are available to cover general government outlays. This tendency is reinforced if social security is included in deficit reduction targets, as with the Gramm-Rudman-Hollings legislation. Hence, the buildup of assets in public pension programs would be expected to have the least effect on other government tax and spending decisions when budget totals and budget targets exclude social security.

Another closely related factor is the ease with which the Treasury can borrow from the trust funds. This depends on the extent to which the administration and the finances of the social security trust funds and the rest of the government are intertwined. In the United States the secretary of the Treasury is also the managing trustee of the trust funds. Although the secretaries of labor and of health and human services and two public members also serve as trustees, the Treasury secretary has the authority to make decisions that affect the financing of the trust funds without involving other members of the board. In 1985, for example, when the Treasury was constrained by a statutory debt ceiling from issuing any new securities, the secretary made the decision to convert $28 billion in long-term specially issued bonds held by the trust funds into non-interest-bearing cash balances without notifying the two public trustees.[4] The use of payroll taxes, in effect, to underwrite temporarily general government expenses occurred because the secretary of the Treasury was forced to choose between forgoing interest earnings on the funds or defaulting on government obligations.

Moreover, in the United States the finances of the social security trust funds and the rest of the budget are closely intermingled.[5] The Treasury Department, rather than the Social Security Administration, collects the earmarked payroll taxes and deposits them in a general account with other revenues it receives. The trust funds are then issued special federal securities in a compensating amount. While the balances of the securities reflect the resources available to social security, they more closely resemble spending limitations than control over resources. One would expect less use of trust fund revenues for general government expenditures in situations where the trust funds are more than a bookkeeping activity on the part of the Treasury Department.

In the same vein, the extent to which the trust funds are a captive market of the Treasury might also affect the extent to which social security surpluses produce additional investment. An investment mechanism that diverted reserves directly to the private sector might discourage Congress from spending the social security balances. Of course, the amount of investment is not directly affected by whether social security reserves are invested initially in Treasury securities or private securities. The potential impact is only indirect; forcing the government to go to the private sector to finance all of its debt might highlight, and thereby create pressure to control, the size of the deficit in the non-social-security portion of the budget. Hence, one would expect less use of social security revenues to cover general government outlays in those countries where the fund trustees have more discretion over investment options.

The discussion so far has assumed that reserves in the trust funds are translated into national investment in the private sector: that is, the trust funds buy government debt, thereby freeing private investors to increase their purchase of private sector securities. In fact it is also possible for investment to take place directly through the public sector. Not all government spending is consumption; the building of roads, bridges, and other types of physical infrastructure by the government is just as much an investment as the construction of any factory in the private sector. Equally important is government investment in human capital; increases in future output will require a healthy and educated work force. Money spent on programs such as Head Start may contribute just as much as physical investment to ensuring higher future incomes. In both cases the spending initiatives would have to be over and above what would have occurred without the trust fund accumulation; otherwise the buildup of trust fund reserves would simply have substituted for tax increases and no additional investment would have taken place.

Because of the potential role for government investment, the evaluation of whether trust fund accumulations produce greater investment may sometimes entail a two-step process. The first step is an assessment of whether the existence of the surpluses generated greater expenditure or lower taxes in the rest of the budget. If the overall government budget deficit remains unchanged, probably no additional saving has occurred. An exception would be those instances in which the government increases expenditures in the form of investment in physical or human capital rather than consumption. Thus, a second step in gauging a nation's success in translating social security reserves into higher future incomes requires an appraisal of the composition of government spending after the trust fund accumulation. While generally such an appraisal would be quite difficult and require a detailed analysis of spending patterns, some information on government investments in physical capital may be readily available when capital outlays are treated separately in the national accounts.

The following sections explore the experiences of Sweden, Japan, and Canada to learn what might be useful for the United States about effectively prefunding public pension plans. These countries have accumulated substantial amounts of money in their public pension plans; pension reserves currently amount to 30 percent of gross domestic product (GDP) in Sweden, 18 percent of GDP in Japan, and 8 percent of GDP in Canada. The individual countries, however, have had varying degrees of success in translating pension fund accumulation into national saving. Part of this variation in outcomes may be attributable to differences in political climates.

All three countries have parliamentary forms of government in which the prime minister is also the leader of the majority party. This arrangement eliminates much of the conflict between the executive and legislative branches and produces a stable political environment as long as one party remains in power; otherwise the results can be extremely unstable. As discussed below, Sweden has been governed almost continuously by the same party since 1932 and Japan has been controlled by the same party since 1955, while control of the Canadian government has alternated on a regular basis between the Liberals and the Conservatives. Because one would expect more success using the government to increase saving in a stable and disciplined political environment, the discussion of each country begins with a brief political overview.

The bulk of the discussion of each country consists of three parts. The first is a summary of the developments that led to the prefunding of the public pension program. The second is a preliminary assessment of the impact of the pension fund buildup on national saving, based on government accounts data prepared by the Organization for Economic Cooperation and Development (OECD). These data are particularly valuable since they standardize for differences in accounting and they include separate figures for government deficits (revenues less outlays) and for government saving (revenues less outlays plus net capital investment).[6] The third is an assessment of the factors, such as budgetary procedures or investment policies, that may have contributed to each country's apparent success or failure. The necessarily tentative conclusions are presented in a final section.

Sweden

Sweden is a constitutional monarchy with a parliamentary form of government. Since World War II, the same five political parties—the Moderates, the Centerists, the Liberals, the Social Democrats, and the Left Party Communists—have been represented in Parliament. The Social Democrats were in power, either alone or in coalition, from 1932 to 1976, and they returned to power in 1982. From 1976 to 1982 the Moderate, Center, and Liberal parties—typically referred to as the bourgeois parties—ruled in coalition. The Social Democrats are closely aligned with the workers' trade union movement, which has been the motivating force behind most of the social security reforms.[7]

Development of a Funded Pension Program. Sweden has two public pension programs: (1) the basic social security pension and (2) the Swedish national pension, Allman Tillaggspension (ATP).[8] The basic social security program dates from 1913 and pays old-age benefits to all persons sixty-five and older (sixty-seven before July 1976) regardless of their labor force status. The ATP pays an earnings-related pension to those with a substantial number of years in the labor force and their dependents. The basic social security program is financed on a pay-as-you-go basis, with 75 percent of the revenues from payroll taxes levied on employers and 25 percent from general revenues. The ATP program is financed on a partially funded basis with contributions derived completely from employer payroll taxes. Employees do not make direct contributions to either pension.

In the early 1950s the workers' trade union movement began pushing for reform of the public pension system, and its efforts led to the establishment in 1957 of a commission to study ways of improving public pension benefits. As a result of the commission's report, in 1958, by a one-vote margin, Parliament passed legislation that raised benefits under the existing social security program and introduced the new ATP supplementary earnings-related pension program.

Policy makers were concerned that the substantial increase in benefits might reduce private saving incentives. They also worried that, with the ratio of old-age beneficiaries to workers scheduled to rise rapidly (table 5–1), ATP benefits would absorb an increasing share of

TABLE 5–1

TRENDS IN DEPENDENCY RATIOS IN CANADA, JAPAN, SWEDEN,
AND THE UNITED STATES, SELECTED YEARS, 1960–2030

Country	1960	1980	2000	2010	2030
	Elderly Dependency Ratio[a]				
Canada	13.0[b]	14.1	19.0	21.3	37.2
Japan	8.9	13.4	22.4	27.5	31.8
Sweden	18.1	25.4	25.1	26.6	35.5
United States	15.5	17.1	18.3	18.5	31.7
	Total Dependency Ratio[c]				
Canada	71.2[b]	48.1	47.8	46.6	65.7
Japan	55.7	48.4	48.4	56.4	58.5
Sweden	51.4	56.0	51.6	52.5	62.5
United States	67.6	51.1	49.9	46.7	61.7

a. Ratio of population age 65 and over to population age 15 through 64.
b. 1961.
c. Ratio of population under age 15 or over 64 to population age 15 through 64.
SOURCE: United Nations, *Demographic Yearbook, 1962* (New York: UN, 1962), table 5; Organization for Economic Cooperation and Development, "Aging Populations: Implications for Public Finance and the Macroeconomy" (Paris: OECD, 1988), tables 4 and 5.

the nation's resources. To meet both concerns, the program's architects established the National Pension Insurance Fund (Allmanna Pensionfoden or AP fund) in 1959. The legislation refers to both of these motivations. Regarding the intergenerational issue, the drafters stated:

> The fund to be created in accordance with the proposed legislation of ATP would facilitate an equalization [over time] of the costs of supplementary pensions so that future contributions needed to cover the benefit payments could be less than they would otherwise be if contributions were not made to a fund.[9]

The comments in the legislation about the impact on national saving must be viewed against the persistent capital shortage experienced in Sweden after World War II. Shortages and restrictions during the war had created an investment demand that far outstripped the country's gross saving. Because of the country's precarious trade position and the general scarcity of international capital during reconstruction, importing foreign capital was not a possible solution.[10] In view of Sweden's continuing capital shortage, the goal of the fund was not merely to

91

counteract the expected decline in the private saving rate but also to increase national saving:

> The flow of income into private pension funds, which is often used to finance business expansion, will not continue [upon the introduction of a public pension scheme]. This saving, which is used for capital investment, must be replaced by [public] saving in the form of a fund. Moreover, a rate of saving in excess [of the private rate] will permit a faster expansion of productive capacity and thus an increase in the rate of future production, which will benefit all.[11]

To build up the AP fund, the program gradually phased in the payment of benefits, not awarding full benefits until 1979.[12] This delay meant that ATP provided mainly for the future retirement of persons with a substantial number of working years under the program.

The Growth of AP Reserves and National Saving. OECD data (summarized in table 5–2) seem to indicate that Sweden's effort to use the AP fund to increase national saving has been successful, at least through the mid-1970s. Large annual surpluses in the social security programs—frequently exceeding 4 percent of GDP—were augmented by somewhat smaller surpluses in the central accounts to produce significant saving at the federal level. (The difference between the saving and the deficit figures in the table is explained by net government expenditures on capital items.)

Since the mid-1970s, two adverse developments have affected Swedish government saving. First, productivity growth slowed in Sweden after 1973 as it did in other developed countries during the widespread recession of 1974–1975. Like other oil-importing countries, Sweden was also faced with the need to spend more of its domestic output to pay the higher costs of imported energy. In an effort to stave off unemployment, the Swedish government continued a high level of public spending that far exceeded the growth in tax revenues and led to large deficits in the central accounts.[13] These deficits dwarfed the continuing surpluses in the social security trust fund and produced overall deficits at the federal level.

The maturation of the ATP system also limited the Swedish government's ability to contribute to saving and capital formation. Paying promised benefits to the rapidly increasing number of beneficiaries has required the use of investment earnings on fund assets in addition to the receipts from annual ATP premiums.[14] Despite an increase in the premium rate from 10.2 percent of wages to 10.6 percent in 1987, the proportion of pension disbursement covered by interest income is expected to grow.[15] Thus the annual increase in AP reserves as a percentage of GDP will continue to decline.

A return to balance in the non-social-security portion of the budget has been an important goal of economic policy in Sweden since 1982, and significant progress has been made. The estimated deficit for the 1988 fiscal year is only 1.1 percent of GDP, compared to 11.1 percent in 1982.[16] A balance in the central accounts combined with declining annual surpluses in the social security account implies, however, that the federal government will not be a major source of national saving in the future.

Although the experiment may well be over, the Swedish effort to increase national saving by accumulating assets in the AP fund appears to have been quite successful. In large part this success may be attributable to the separateness of the ATP system.

The ATP and the Budget. The ATP system is treated separately from other activities in the Swedish budget process and in the budget documents. Budget proposals are first submitted to Parliament at the start of every calendar year; the Ministry of Finance then presents its economic forecast, and budget projections are revised. The final budget for the July fiscal year is presented to Parliament and voted on in April. The budget document and the deficit targets exclude the ATP system, and in almost all Swedish statistical publications government spending is defined as that of the central government excluding social security. While ATP benefits are mandated by law and therefore not subject to annual parliamentary approval, proposals for ATP premium increases are submitted to Parliament in the spring. For this reason, the ministers of health and social affairs discuss these pensions in their section of the budget document. In addition some government documents present a category of public spending that includes both social security and local spending.

Although it is impossible to state with certainty, the surpluses in the social security funds do not seem to have encouraged additional spending in the rest of the budget or to have reduced the incentive to raise non-social-security taxes. The large deficits in the central account during the late 1970s and early 1980s are best explained by an inability to adapt quickly to slower growth and apparently are unrelated to the buildup of trust fund reserves. Moreover, as noted, once the deleterious effects of the persistent deficits were recognized, the resolution to restore balance was stated in terms of the central account without reference to the ATP system. Likewise the Parliament appears to set ATP premiums without reference to deficits in the central accounts. The decision to increase the ATP premium in 1987 from 10.2 percent to

TABLE 5-2
Swedish Government Saving and Deficit (−) or Surplus as a Percentage of GDP, 1960–1986

Year	General Saving	General Deficit or surplus	Central and Social Security Saving	Central and Social Security Deficit or surplus	Central Saving	Central Deficit or surplus	Social Security Saving	Social Security Deficit or surplus	Local Saving	Local Deficit or surplus
1960	5.25	2.01	3.39	2.01	2.62	1.24	0.77	0.77	1.86	0.00
1961	6.72	3.47	5.37	4.03	4.34	3.01	1.03	1.02	1.36	-0.56
1962	7.63	4.04	5.78	4.41	3.97	2.61	1.81	1.80	1.86	-0.37
1963	7.27	2.93	5.42	3.76	3.07	1.42	2.35	2.35	1.84	-0.83
1964	7.68	2.92	5.87	4.09	3.21	1.43	2.66	2.66	1.81	-1.17
1965	9.22	4.53	7.34	5.49	4.43	2.59	2.91	2.90	1.89	-0.96
1966	9.11	4.20	6.49	4.73	3.27	1.51	3.23	3.22	2.62	-0.53
1967	9.07	3.68	5.77	3.95	2.18	0.36	3.59	3.59	3.30	-0.27
1968	9.64	3.97	6.26	4.52	2.08	0.34	4.18	4.18	3.38	-0.55
1969	9.86	4.63	6.80	5.14	2.52	0.86	4.28	4.28	3.07	-0.50
1970	9.77	4.42	7.96	6.05	3.83	1.91	4.14	4.14	1.80	-1.63
1971	10.08	5.20	8.88	7.02	4.40	2.54	4.48	4.48	1.20	-1.82

1972	9.14	4.42	6.77	4.66	2.10	-0.02	4.68	4.67	2.37	-0.24
1973	7.87	4.08	6.03	4.21	1.61	-0.21	4.42	4.42	1.84	-0.13
1974	5.43	1.96	4.09	2.41	-0.13	-1.81	4.22	4.22	1.34	-0.45
1975	5.79	2.75	5.39	3.93	1.49	0.03	3.90	3.90	0.40	-1.18
1976	7.57	4.54	7.28	5.64	3.12	1.49	4.16	4.15	0.29	-1.10
1977	5.38	1.68	4.53	2.53	0.46	-1.54	4.08	4.07	0.85	-0.85
1978	3.46	-0.47	0.95	-1.37	-2.84	-5.16	3.80	3.79	2.50	0.90
1979	1.43	-2.95	-0.58	-3.43	-3.99	-6.84	3.41	3.40	2.01	0.49
1980	-0.22	-3.74	-1.84	-3.78	-5.05	-7.00	3.22	3.21	1.62	0.04
1981	-1.27	-4.91	-2.89	-4.90	-6.14	-8.14	3.24	3.24	1.62	0.00
1982	-2.51	-6.35	-4.07	-6.50	-7.05	-9.47	2.97	2.97	1.57	0.15
1983	-1.39	-4.98	-2.81	-5.07	-5.51	-7.77	2.70	2.70	1.42	0.09
1984	-0.07	-2.60	-1.23	-2.63	-4.08	-5.48	2.85	2.85	1.16	0.03
1985	-1.28	-3.76	-1.91	-3.29	-4.42	-5.80	2.51	2.51	0.63	-0.47
1986	1.53	-0.72	1.21	-0.14	-1.33	-2.68	2.54	2.54	0.32	-0.58

NOTE: The general budget consolidates the activities at the federal level (central plus social security) with those at the local level.
SOURCES: 1974–1986: Organization for Economic Cooperation and Development, Department of Economics and Statistics, *National Accounts: 1974–1986*, vol. 2, *Detailed Tables* (Paris: OECD, 1988), Swedish tables 1, 6.1, 6.3, 6.4; 1970–1973: OECD, unpublished data; 1960–1969: OECD, *National Accounts of OECD Countries: 1960–1977*, vol. 2, *Detailed Tables* (Paris: OECD, 1979), Swedish tables 1, 10, 11, 12.

TABLE 5-3
COMPOSITION OF BOARDS FOR SWEDEN'S FIRST, SECOND, AND THIRD FUNDS

Constituency	First Fund	Second Fund	Third Fund
Government	3	1	1
Unions	3	4	4
Private employers	—	3	1
Public employers	3	—	—
Cooperative employers	—	1	—
Self-employed, small business	—	—	3

SOURCE: Jonas Pontusson, *Public Pension Funds and the Politics of Capital Formation* (Goteborg, Sweden: Tryckt av Graphic Systems AB, 1984), p. 21.

10.6 percent, for instance, seems to have been a response to the ATP boards' projection that the trust funds would decline in real terms at existing premium rates.[17] In short, by keeping social security and the rest of the budget quite separate in Sweden, the activities of one sector do not seem to influence those of the other.

Structure and Investment Policy of the AP Funds. Aware that the projected accumulation of reserves might become very large relative to the capital markets, the 1959 legislation built in safeguards to prevent the fund's dominance by special interests and interference in the capital markets. To this end the National Pension Insurance Fund was divided into three separate subfunds, each presided over by a nine-member board representing government, employers, and employees.[18] The First Fund receives its receipts from public employers, the Second Fund from large private sector employers, and the Third Fund from the self-employed and firms with fewer than 50 (20 before 1980) employees; the composition of each of the three boards reflects its fund's orientation (table 5-3). These boards are totally responsible for the investment decisions undertaken by each fund.[19]

The investment regulations governing the AP funds grow out of the principle that the boards should not make discretionary decisions about the allocation of credit to a large number of final borrowers.[20] Hence, while the National Pension Fund may lend directly to the public sector, it may engage only in indirect lending to the private sector. The AP fund can purchase corporate bonds and promissory notes of intermediary credit institutions, but it cannot extend credit directly to a private company. Through commercial banks the fund can also provide retroverse loans to employers by allowing them to borrow as

TABLE 5-4

INVESTMENTS AT YEAR END OF SWEDEN'S FIRST, SECOND,
AND THIRD FUNDS, 1985

Instrument and Borrower	Percentage of Total Assets
Bonds	76
Central government	29
Local government	2
Public companies	3
Private companies	5
Housing finances	35
Financial intermediaries	2
Debentures	1
Promissory notes	18
Local government	3
Public companies	3
Housing finances	4
Financial intermediaries	8
Retroverse loans	4
Money market investments	1

SOURCE: Swedish National Pension Fund, *Annual Report* (Stockholm: Swedish National Pension Fund, First, Second, and Third Boards, 1985), table 2, p. 29.

much as 50 percent of the contributions that they paid into the social security program during the previous year. Table 5-4 summarizes the 1985 investments of the First, Second, and Third Funds.

The extent to which the AP fund can be viewed as a captive market for government securities or as an instrument of government policy in Sweden is a complex issue. Until 1986, the potential for independent investment decisions by the ATP boards had been largely preempted by the central bank's regulation of the credit markets—that is, the central bank determined what instruments were available and at what rates and thereby established what a large supplier of credit, such as the ATP fund, could buy.[21] Because the central bank was primarily interested in keeping interest rates low, the priorities of the AP managers were frequently at odds with the goals of the central bank.[22]

Despite the inherent conflict, from 1960 to 1974 the funds in the ATP system enjoyed special status among the suppliers of credit: their lending was not subject to quantitative regulation by the central bank. The managing director of the AP fund defended this status on the grounds that the fund was already accountable to the public through the broad representation of interests on the boards and therefore did not require direct regulation.

The boards recognized from the beginning that a large amount of the fund's capital would necessarily be allocated to investments prioritized by the government, and they did not stray far from central bank policies for fear of tighter regulation. They also, however, viewed investment in the private sector as an important objective, reflecting their belief that private investment was somehow more productive than public investment and that productive investment of fund assets was the most effective way to guarantee the payment of future pension benefits. Investment in the private sector was also consistent with the objective of maximizing the return on assets since corporate bonds always had a higher yield than securities prioritized by the government.

Tensions between the AP boards and the central bank, which had always existed, worsened in the 1970s. In 1973 the fund circumvented the constraints of the central bank's control of bond issues, by providing export credit to individual private firms through promissory-note loans to commercial banks. Moreover, the fund's efforts to maximize returns on investments by anticipating interest rate changes were viewed by the central bank as a threat to its interest rate policy.

It is unclear whether this increasing conflict led to the change, but beginning in 1974 the amounts that the AP fund invested in government and housing bonds were determined by annual agreement of the fund and the central bank. Central bank control over AP lending became increasingly important after 1976 when the central government began running annual budget deficits. Although the bourgeois governments of 1976–1982 were less committed to low interest rates in principle, they were interested in financing the budget deficits at the lowest possible costs. Furthermore, they wanted to finance them outside the banking sector to curb the growth of liquidity.

The additional constraints imposed by the central bank probably did not significantly alter ATP investment policies. Indeed the fund actually purchased more prioritized bonds in 1975 than the central bank recommended. But when the central bank's 1980 recommendation meant that 75 percent of all AP lending would have to be invested in government and housing bonds, the boards protested. They indicated that they would do their best to carry out the central bank's directive but affirmed that in the event of a shortage of capital for private productive investments "the boards consider it their obligation to finance such productive investments in order to assure future pension payments."[23] The conflict eventually petered out since the business sector's demand for capital was so low that the fund could find few alternatives to prioritized investments. The dramatic decline in the central budget deficits during the 1980s also reduced the need for mandatory purchases by the AP fund. Thus the direct investment regulations for the National Pension Fund and the other credit controls were eliminated in November 1986; currently neither the fund nor any other institution is under any explicit obligation to favor government borrowing.[24]

Assessment of the Swedish Experience. The fact that the Swedish public pension funds have been forced to purchase government bonds does not negate the effectiveness of trust fund accumulation as a mechanism to increase national saving. As discussed in the first section, it matters little—from the perspective of national saving and investment—whether the trust funds are invested in government or private securities. The only concern is that easy access to financing might encourage larger central government deficits, and this does not appear to have been the case in Sweden.

Moreover, the current decline of the trust fund surpluses as a percentage of GDP should not have adverse implications. The decision was made to accumulate a reserve to help pay benefits as the population aged, and the time has come to use the interest on the reserves for that purpose.[25] Because the fund's reserves appear to have been invested productively, rather than spent on consumption, the Swedish people probably have higher levels of income from which to finance today's pension benefits.

Japan

The Japanese Diet (parliament) consists of the House of Representatives, with 512 members, and the House of Councillors, with 252 members. The Liberal Democratic party, founded in 1955 when two conservative parties united, has continuously controlled the Diet. The more liberal Japan Socialist party, founded in 1945, became the second most important party in Japan when left-wing and right-wing factions reunited in 1955. By 1960 opposition parties had once again begun to emerge. Japan has eight parties plus a group of independents represented in the Diet.[26] Nevertheless, the Liberal Democratic party maintains an overwhelming majority, with 302 members of the House of Representatives and 144 members of the House of Councillors.

Development of Funded Pension Programs. A totally different approach from Sweden's to increasing national investment through pension fund accumulation also appears to have produced measured success. Japan has two partially funded public pension schemes. The

National Pension (NP) covers all residents of working age (twenty to fifty-nine) and provides a universal basic benefit at age sixty-five regardless of employment status. This program is financed by employer and employee contributions as well as a general revenue subsidy equal to one-third of benefit costs. Retired workers also receive an additional wage-related pension, which for most private sector employees is provided by the Employees' Pension Insurance (EPI) plan.[27] EPI is now financed entirely by an earmarked payroll tax, although before reforms in 1985 it also received a general revenue subsidy.[28]

From the beginning the Japanese government intended that both the NP and EPI systems would be backed by substantial funds. The motives behind the plans to accumulate reserves, however, cannot be traced as easily to deliberate decisions to increase saving or to equalize burdens across generations as they can in Sweden.

When the Employees' Pension Program was introduced in 1941, it was charged with raising funds for the war effort as well as providing security for workers in their old age. In fact some observers contend that it was established "less for welfare purposes than to mobilize employers' and workers' contributions into a government-controlled capital fund for the war industry."[29] This interest in accumulating immediate funds may explain why the payment of full benefits was delayed until forty years after the program was inaugurated.

The buildup of assets in the NP fund is probably attributable to its founders' recognition that the ratio of elderly to working-age population would increase sharply. In 1960 the number of persons sixty-five and over amounted to less than 9 percent of the population aged fifteen to sixty-four—a dramatically lower percentage than any other developed country. That percentage is projected to rise to 27 percent by the year 2010. Because of this concern over the prospect of dramatically rising costs, payment of the contributory portion of the pension did not start until 1971, twelve years after the plan was established.[30]

By 1985 the EPI reserve fund had reached 7.9 times 1984 expenditures; the NP fund had reached 1.1 times expenditures. Despite this substantial accumulation of assets, the financial health of these programs was threatened by the sharp projected increase in costs as the population aged. In response the Japanese government implemented a series of reforms in 1985 that dramatically restructured the EPI and NP programs.[31] The legislation also addressed major nonfinancial problems, such as the patchwork nature of Japan's existing social insurance system.[32]

In an effort to reduce pension costs, the Japanese government sharply scaled back benefits. These reductions will become fully effective in 2006, after a twenty-year phase-in period.[33] The magnitude of the benefit reductions can be measured by the projected reduction in future contribution rates. Japan's Ministry of Health and Welfare had estimated that under the prereform EPI the combined employer-employee contribution rate would have risen from 10.6 percent in 1985 to 38.8 percent in the year 2030—the year when the beneficiary-to-worker ratio reaches its highest point. With the benefit reductions, the EPI contribution rate is projected to reach a peak of 28.9 percent in 2030 and will not require any government subsidies.[34]

Although the reasons for the initial funding decision are difficult to determine, many Japanese officials and commentators now view the lack of full funding of the public pension plans as a failing.[35] In conversations with the authors, representatives of international organizations indicated that the Japanese are frequently reluctant to provide data on the reserves in the EPI and NP funds; the Japanese believe these monies provide a misleading picture of the financial health of the government since these public pension programs face commitments for future benefits that dwarf the magnitude of the assets on hand.

Nevertheless, the combined EPI and NP reserves exceed 18 percent of GDP, placing Japan far ahead of the United States in terms of the relative size of public pension reserves. Therefore, it is useful to explore how these assets have been invested and try to ascertain the extent to which they have increased national saving and investment.

Impact of Public Pension Surpluses on National Saving. The OECD data presented in table 5–5 show that the social security funds (primarily EPI and NP) consistently experienced large annual surpluses over the period for which information is available. From 1970 through 1974, increases in trust fund reserves augmented surpluses of similar size in the central accounts to produce central government surpluses in excess of 4 percent of GDP. Beginning in 1975, however, total federal government saving fell to less than 1 percent.

The key question is whether the existence of surpluses in the public pension trust funds has encouraged larger deficits in the rest of the budget. The answer seems to be probably not; the source of the deficits appears to be fiscal policy initiatives undertaken to stimulate the economy. A brief look at the Japanese budget and budget processes and at Japanese fiscal policy will help buttress this conclusion.

The EPI and NP Programs and the Budget. While the Japanese budget is extremely complicated, the budget process is fairly simple and orderly. Each summer the cabinet sets forth guidelines for all the ministry and agency budget requests. The ministries and agencies then present their requests to the Ministry of Finance by early autumn. Following

101

negotiation, the Ministry of Finance prepares drafts of fifty-one separate budgets for the cabinet to present to the Diet in January. Deliberations in the Diet usually take about five weeks.

Although opposition parties may not like the budget proposals, they are rarely able to change the budget or significantly delay its progress.[36] In 1989, for example, the budget went into effect on April 8, eight days after the start of the fiscal year, in the same form that it had been presented to the Diet in January.

The Japanese budget consists of four parts: the general budget, thirty-eight special accounts, eleven government-affiliated agencies, and the Fiscal Investment Loan Program (FILP), which has been characterized as the Japanese capital budget even though it makes only loans rather than direct investments in capital projects. Typically references to the budget mean the general budget, which accounts for less than half of total federal government expenditures. The general budget receives all nonearmarked taxes, which are then used to meet on-budget expenses, to provide money to government-affiliated agencies, to pay subsidies to local governments, and in some cases to provide additional funding for special accounts. Government subsidies to the EPI and NP programs, for example, show up as an expenditure in the general budget. In addition to receiving money from the general budget, special accounts also receive designated taxes directly and in some cases may issue debt.[37]

The EPI and NP programs each maintain special accounts. As noted, the EPI account receives contributions from employers and employees and a payment from the general budget for one-third of the amount transferred from the EPI to the NP account. The NP account receives contributions from participants not covered under EPI in addition to transfers from the EPI account on behalf of persons covered by both programs. The government also provides a subsidy from the general budget equal to one-third of NP benefit costs less transfers from EPI.

After paying out benefits, EPI and NP deposit any surpluses with the Trust Fund Bureau, which also maintains a special account. Two other accounts, loan repayments and postal savings, also deposit their assets into this fund. The assets of the Trust Fund Bureau, along with those of the Industrial Investment Special Account and the Postal Life Insurance Fund, and bonds and borrowings guaranteed by the central government are made available to the Fiscal Investment Loan Program. FILP then provides funds for housing, hospitals, power plants, and other public endeavors by purchasing bonds from a variety of special accounts, government-affiliated agencies, local governments, and public corporations. One public corporation of special note is the

Pension Welfare Agency, which receives roughly one-third of the assets produced by the EPI and NP programs and funds projects exclusively for the beneficiaries of these programs. The primary mandate governing the capital budget agenda, however, is that the funds be used on a sound and profitable basis to meet public needs. In this manner the Japanese government manages to direct a large portion of the reserves of the EPI and NP programs toward productive investments.

Japanese Fiscal Policy. While it appears that the Japanese government, through FILP, invests the EPI and NP surpluses productively, the net impact of these surpluses on national saving and investment could be eroded if they caused larger deficits in the general budget. The evidence from the discussions of fiscal policy indicates that this has probably not been the case.

Fiscal policy in Japan is framed almost exclusively in terms of the general account. This conceptualization is hardly satisfactory as the general account expenditures amount to only half of total government outlays and exclude the various forms of government investment. Simply adding all the budgets together, however, would vastly overstate the fiscal thrust of the government since there is considerable overlap. Because it is impossible to infer fiscal policy from any set of Japanese budget figures, the government and most observers concentrate on the general account, with some attention to FILP.[38]

Until 1965, fiscal policy in Japan was constrained by a balanced budget rule established by the U.S. occupational forces. This rule was interpreted to mean that the central government should neither borrow from the Bank of Japan nor issue marketable securities to finance general budget expenditures. The government strictly maintained this posture until 1965, when it revoked the rule as part of a strategy for recovering from a recession.[39]

Central government deficits remained quite small until 1974, when Japan, like other oil-importing countries, experienced the shock of the oil crisis. The ensuing inflation and slower growth sharply reduced tax revenues, especially from corporations, and receipts did not return to their pre-oil-shock levels until 1978.[40] By that time two major changes had occurred on the expenditure side. First, the accumulated government liabilities were creating noticeable debt-servicing costs. Second, general budget expenditures for health, public welfare, and public pensions had grown enormously.

Ever since the deficit first increased in 1974, public documents have emphasized the need for a reexamination of expenditure policy to restore balance to the budget. This process was postponed several

TABLE 5-5
Japanese Government Saving and Deficit (–) or Surplus as a Percentage of GDP, 1960–1986

Year	General		Central and Social Security		Central		Social Security[a]		Local	
	Saving	Deficit or surplus	Saving	Deficit or surplus	Saving	Deficit or surplus	Saving	Deficit or surplus	Saving	Deficit or surplus
1960	5.73	1.75	n.a.	n.a.	n.a.	n.a.	n.a.	n.a.	n.a.	n.a.
1961	6.62	2.44	n.a.	n.a.	n.a.	n.a.	n.a.	n.a.	n.a.	n.a.
1962	6.43	1.41	n.a.	n.a.	n.a.	n.a.	n.a.	n.a.	n.a.	n.a.
1963	5.94	1.03	n.a.	n.a.	n.a.	n.a.	n.a.	n.a.	n.a.	n.a.
1964	5.72	0.81	n.a.	n.a.	n.a.	n.a.	n.a.	n.a.	n.a.	n.a.
1965	5.25	0.45	n.a.	n.a.	n.a.	n.a.	n.a.	n.a.	n.a.	n.a.
1966	4.85	–0.32	n.a.	n.a.	n.a.	n.a.	n.a.	n.a.	n.a.	n.a.
1967	5.51	0.76	n.a.	n.a.	n.a.	n.a.	n.a.	n.a.	n.a.	n.a.
1968	5.64	0.83	n.a.	n.a.	n.a.	n.a.	n.a.	n.a.	n.a.	n.a.
1969	5.96	1.19	n.a.	n.a.	n.a.	n.a.	n.a.	n.a.	n.a.	n.a.
1970	7.06	1.81	4.62	2.24	2.30	–0.03	2.32	2.27	2.44	–0.43
1971	6.62	0.51	4.34	1.59	1.71	–0.99	2.63	2.58	2.28	–1.08

Year										
1972	6.82	0.18	4.55	1.36	1.99	-1.14	2.55	2.50	2.27	-1.18
1973	8.14	2.07	5.72	3.09	2.98	0.41	2.74	2.68	2.42	-1.02
1974	6.33	-0.04	4.12	1.25	1.33	-1.47	2.79	2.72	2.21	-1.29
1975	2.25	-3.81	1.39	-1.61	-1.18	-4.11	2.57	2.50	0.87	-2.20
1976	2.15	-3.67	0.95	-2.05	-1.51	-4.43	2.46	2.38	1.20	-1.62
1977	2.18	-4.25	0.85	-2.40	-1.95	-5.12	2.80	2.72	1.33	-1.86
1978	2.93	-4.28	1.15	-2.52	-1.36	-4.94	2.50	2.42	1.78	-1.76
1979	2.68	-4.52	0.57	-3.15	-2.13	-5.76	2.70	2.62	2.12	-1.38
1980	3.01	-4.13	0.83	-2.82	-1.95	-5.52	2.78	2.70	2.18	-1.31
1981	3.02	-3.76	0.86	-2.50	-2.04	-5.31	2.90	2.81	2.16	-1.26
1982	2.94	-3.46	0.60	-2.51	-2.21	-5.24	2.82	2.73	2.34	-0.95
1983	2.86	-2.99	0.60	-2.22	-2.22	-4.94	2.82	2.73	2.26	-0.77
1984	3.47	-1.87	1.26	-1.26	-1.70	-4.12	2.97	2.85	2.21	-0.61
1985	4.43	-0.79	1.88	-0.51	-1.46	-3.74	3.34	3.23	2.55	-0.28
1986	4.58	-0.54	2.09	-0.12	-1.01	-3.11	3.10	2.99	2.49	-0.41

n.a.=not available.

NOTE: Government data for 1970–1986 are on a fiscal year basis, while GDP remains on a calendar year basis. The general budget consolidates the activities at the federal level (central plus social security) with those at the local level.

a. Includes health insurance provided by local governments.

SOURCES: 1974–1986: Organization for Economic Cooperation and Development, Department of Economics and Statistics, *National Accounts: 1974–1986*, Vol. 2, *Detailed Tables* (Paris: OECD, 1988), Japanese tables 1, 6.1, 6.3, 6.4; 1960–1973: OECD, unpublished data.

times, however, since the Ministry of Finance intended to reduce the deficits by introducing a new tax. Once it became clear that a new tax was politically unacceptable, serious efforts were made to restore balance to the general budget through austerity on the expenditure side.

For the entire period, fiscal policy is described by commentators in terms of the general budget; the surpluses in the EPI and NP accounts are never mentioned. The two are not totally unrelated, however, and the EPI and NP programs have occasionally been affected by actions taken in the general budget. Responding to the central government's call for a restrictive fiscal stance, for example, the Ministry of Finance and the Ministry of Welfare negotiated a postponement of general revenue transfers to the EPI from 1982 to 1985.[41] Additionally, as noted, one of the intents of the 1985 reform was to eliminate the EPI's subsidy through increased reliance on participant contributions. The government's behavior in these two instances shows that even when fiscal goals are stated totally in terms of the general budget, the trust funds cannot be completely isolated from general fiscal policy initiatives.

Assessment of the Japanese Experience. The Japanese appear to have been successful in their efforts to prefund at least partially their public pension system. The accumulated surpluses do not seem to have promoted either greater deficits or less saving in the general account. The primary reason, as in Sweden, appears to be that except for the subsidy, the pension programs are not part of the general budget. Fiscal policy objectives are set without consideration of the EPI and NP accounts. This separation makes it difficult, although not impossible as long as general revenue subsidies exist, for the government to use the increase in reserves in the special accounts as part of its effort to balance the budget.

The investment of public pension reserves follows a different pattern in Japan from that in Sweden. The EPI and NP reserves are directed by the capital budget into government-sponsored companies and other investments that serve public purposes. Some observers have expressed concern that the interest paid to the EPI and NP programs on their loans was at one time fixed by the government at rates that were often below market.[42] First, this practice no longer occurs.[43] Second, while this implicit tax will make the trust funds worse off in the future, it need not have an adverse impact on the well-being of future beneficiaries as long as the projects are yielding returns commensurate with those undertaken in the private sector. In short, through their capital budgeting mechanism, the Japanese appear to be turning their accumulated public pension reserves into increased saving and investment.

Canada

Canada, a federal state consisting of ten provinces and two territories, is a member of the British Commonwealth. The queen and her representative in Canada, the governor general, are the formal heads of state. The governor general summons and dissolves Parliament, signs state documents, and gives assent to parliamentary bills but in almost all cases must carry out these duties in accordance with the advice of the responsible ministers.

Parliament consists of two houses: the Senate, where representation, as in the United States, is determined on the basis of a fixed number of representatives from each region, and the House of Commons, where representation is based on population. Three political parties have significant representation in the Canadian Parliament: the Progressive Conservatives, the Liberals, and the New Democrats. The Progressive Conservatives are currently in power. Since 1930, parliamentary control has alternated fairly regularly between the Liberals and the Conservatives; the New Democrats have never been the ruling party.

Development of a Funded Pension Program. The Canada and Quebec Pension Plans (CPP and QPP) were developed in the 1960s by the Liberal government in response to growing inadequacies of the existing federal universal pension system. Parliamentary debate began in 1963 over the establishment of an earnings-related old-age, survivors, and disability public insurance system to supplement the flat benefit provided to all persons sixty-five and over by the old-age security program.[44]

The federal government originally proposed a pay-as-you-go financing scheme, but the provincial governments objected.[45] Feeling the effects of almost a decade of deficits and facing the prospect of massive investment in schools to meet the educational needs of Canada's baby-boom generation, the provinces were determined that the system be substantially funded, with annual surpluses made available to them for investment.[46] The current financing of the CPP represents a compromise between the federal and provincial government positions; the program has run annual surpluses since its inception and, by 1988, had accumulated $35 billion (Canadian dollars) in assets, or 6 percent of GDP.

Rather than participate in the CPP, Quebec elected to create its own public pension, the QPP. Because contribution rates and benefit levels have always been the same under the two programs and the buildup of assets in relation to outgo is identical, the two programs are

107

often referred to together. QPP assets amount to 2 percent of GDP. As noted below, however, the investment practices for the $13 billion (Canadian dollars) held by the QPP differ from those of the CPP.

The founders of the CPP felt that reserves equal to two times annual outlays would be sufficient for their purposes. To hasten the buildup of reserves, tax rates were originally set at 1.8 percent each for employers and employees and 3.6 percent for the self-employed, and the payment of full benefits was delayed until 1976. From the outset, however, the CPP's designers recognized that the initial rate schedule would not be sufficient indefinitely and recommended a future review of the reserve fund's status. In 1985 the federal and provincial ministers of finance conducted a series of meetings aimed at setting a rate schedule for the next twenty-five years. Despite the fact that the reserve fund then held assets in excess of six times annual outlays, the original intent of a reserve fund equal to two times outlays was reaffirmed at the meetings.[47] A new rate schedule, recommended by the ministers of finance, was passed by Parliament in 1986 and enacted in 1987. The revised schedule called for the 3.6 percent payroll tax to rise 0.2 percent annually from 1987 through 1991 and 0.15 percent annually from 1992 through 2011. As benefits are expected to increase sharply, this schedule should result in a decline in the ratio of reserves to outlays from 6.0 to 2.0, while the absolute size of the fund remains constant.

Additionally the 1986 reform provided that the CPP system be subject to actuarial reviews at five-year intervals. Should it be found that alterations in taxes are necessary to meet the ultimate goal of a reserve fund equal to two times outlays, the actuaries will so advise the Ministry of Finance, which in turn will submit a bill to Parliament.

The CPP, QPP, and National Saving. Table 5–6 presents the OECD budget data for Canada. CPP and QPP have consistently produced annual surpluses equal to roughly 1 percent of GDP. Since 1974, however, these surpluses have been swamped by large annual deficits in the central accounts, producing substantial deficits at the federal level. As discussed, deficits in the non-social-security portion of the budget do not indicate, in and of themselves, that the effort to increase national saving and investment has failed. What must be evaluated is whether the existence of the pension fund surpluses caused general government expenditures to be higher, or taxes lower, than they otherwise would have been. To a large extent this may depend on how social security is treated in the budget.

The CPP and the Budget. CPP financing is entirely off-budget, and there is no discussion of the system's finances in the budget document.

The CPP's annual report is an independent publication, prepared by the chief actuary of the Office of the Superintendent of Financial Institutions. (The Office of the Superintendent of Financial Institutions is an arms-length department of the Ministry of Finance.) While there is no legislated schedule for these annual reports, Health and Welfare Canada is required to submit its *Main Estimates* to Parliament each February; part III of this report focuses on the CPP. Parliamentary tradition dictates that the federal budget be presented in February as well.[48]

It is unlikely that members of Parliament take any comfort from the buildup in the CPP. Not only are the reserves not included in budget totals or deficit targets, but also the fund is in no way a captive market for Treasury securities. The vast majority of CPP reserves are loaned to the provinces, and only a small residual may be used by the central government. Because the provinces have such easy access to the accumulated pension reserves, it is necessary for Canada to worry about a behavioral response not only from the members of Parliament but also from the provincial governments.

Investments of the CPP. The provinces are allowed to borrow from the CPP in proportion to their contributions, with any leftover funds used to purchase federal twenty-year bonds. Table 5–7 shows how the $35 billion (Canadian dollars) held by the CPP were divided as of April 1988; less than 8 percent has been loaned to the central government.

The provinces might increase their expenditures in response to the CPP commitment to purchase their bonds for several reasons. First, the average (and marginal) interest rates that the provinces have to pay on this debt is below market. Interest rates charged by the CPP are weighted averages of all federal twenty-year bonds outstanding, which are typically below those of provincial debt. Hence, provinces can borrow from the CPP at lower rates than they would have to pay on the open market. They may also be able to lower their own open market rates by reducing the supply of provincial bonds sold to the general public. The Atlantic provinces, which tend to be poorer, have the most to gain from the CPP lending provisions since they face the largest gap between the rate that they are charged by the CPP and the rate that they must pay on the open market. If the provincial deficits are large, the implicit reduction in marginal costs may be substantial. Lower interest costs may thus induce more current consumption of government goods and services.

An even greater increase in government expenditures might occur if the provinces felt that they would never have to pay back the loans from the CPP fund.[49] A number of Canadian observers originally

TABLE 5-6
CANADIAN GOVERNMENT SAVING AND DEFICIT (−) OR SURPLUS AS A PERCENTAGE OF GDP, 1960–1986

Year	General Saving	General Deficit or surplus	Central and Social Security Saving	Central and Social Security Deficit or surplus	Central Saving	Central Deficit or surplus	Social Security[a] Saving	Social Security[a] Deficit or surplus	Local[b] Saving	Local[b] Deficit or surplus	Provincial Saving	Provincial Deficit or surplus	Municipal[b] Saving	Municipal[b] Deficit or surplus
1960	0.60	−1.71	−0.49	−0.58	−0.49	−0.58	c	c	1.09	−1.13	0.47	−0.54	0.62	−0.58
1961	0.47	−2.06	−0.70	−1.01	−0.70	−1.01	c	c	1.17	−1.05	0.11	−0.69	1.05	−0.35
1962	1.12	−1.60	−0.94	−1.15	−0.94	−1.15	c	c	2.07	−0.45	0.74	−0.13	1.32	−0.32
1963	1.32	−1.32	−0.42	−0.60	−0.42	−0.60	c	c	1.74	−0.71	0.61	−0.21	1.13	−0.50
1964	2.51	0.19	0.80	0.67	0.80	0.67	c	c	1.72	−0.47	0.77	−0.16	0.95	−0.32
1965	3.06	0.36	1.28	0.95	1.28	0.95	c	c	1.78	−0.59	0.90	0.00	0.88	−0.59
1966	3.52	0.66	1.81	1.47	0.70	0.36	1.11	1.11	1.71	−0.80	0.65	−0.27	1.06	−0.53
1967	3.05	0.22	1.55	1.17	0.26	−0.12	1.29	1.29	1.50	−0.95	0.47	−0.49	1.03	−0.47
1968	3.20	0.67	1.69	1.33	0.35	−0.01	1.34	1.34	1.51	−0.65	0.65	−0.07	0.86	−0.58
1969	4.53	2.32	2.90	2.59	1.55	1.24	1.35	1.35	1.63	−0.27	1.06	0.39	0.57	−0.65
1970	2.91	0.80	1.93	1.63	0.58	0.28	1.35	1.35	0.98	−0.82	0.30	−0.29	0.67	−0.53
1971	2.46	0.03	1.52	1.18	0.20	−0.14	1.32	1.32	0.94	−1.15	0.42	−0.50	0.52	−0.64

1972	2.32	-0.04	1.24	0.78	-0.03	-0.49	1.27	1.27	1.08	-0.83	0.25	-0.67	0.83	-0.16
1973	3.05	0.89	2.01	1.51	0.85	0.34	1.16	1.16	1.04	-0.62	0.70	-0.09	0.34	-0.53
1974	4.22	1.89	2.54	2.01	1.37	0.84	1.17	1.17	1.68	-0.12	1.32	0.47	0.36	-0.60
1975	-0.07	-2.52	-0.52	-1.07	-1.70	-2.25	1.18	1.18	0.44	-1.45	-0.07	-1.00	0.51	-0.45
1976	0.22	-1.81	-0.07	-0.59	-1.18	-1.70	1.11	1.11	0.29	-1.22	-0.08	-0.74	0.37	-0.48
1977	-0.58	-2.53	-1.86	-2.36	-2.89	-3.40	1.04	1.04	1.28	-0.16	0.37	-0.27	0.92	0.10
1978	-1.40	-3.19	-3.03	-3.51	-4.06	-4.53	1.02	1.02	1.63	0.32	1.05	0.42	0.58	-0.10
1979	-0.52	-2.02	-2.17	-2.44	-3.15	-3.42	0.98	0.98	1.64	0.42	0.61	0.00	1.03	0.42
1980	-1.26	-2.80	-2.18	-2.49	-3.15	-3.47	0.98	0.98	0.92	-0.31	0.40	-0.18	0.52	-0.13
1981	-0.03	-1.48	-0.89	-1.15	-1.81	-2.07	0.92	0.92	0.86	-0.33	0.27	-0.30	0.59	-0.02
1982	-3.86	-5.96	-3.68	-4.44	-4.69	-5.45	1.02	1.02	-0.18	-1.53	-0.84	-1.53	0.66	0.00
1983	-4.82	-6.97	-4.41	-5.42	-5.21	-6.21	0.79	0.79	-0.41	-1.55	-0.96	-1.56	0.56	0.01
1984	-4.73	-6.70	-5.07	-6.15	-5.81	-6.88	0.73	0.73	0.34	-0.55	-0.12	-0.56	0.46	0.00
1985	-5.13	-7.06	-5.24	-6.05	-5.91	-6.72	0.67	0.67	0.11	-1.01	-0.47	-1.07	0.58	0.06
1986	-3.80	-5.51	-3.64	-4.29	-4.26	-4.91	0.62	0.62	-0.16	-1.22	-0.68	-1.27	0.52	0.05

NOTE: The general budget consolidates the activities at the federal level (central plus social security) with those at the local level.
a. Canada and Quebec Pension Plans only.
b. Includes hospitals.
c. The Canada and Quebec Pension Plans were not instituted until 1966.
SOURCES: 1974–1986: Organization for Economic Cooperation and Development, Department of Economics and Statistics, *National Accounts: 1974–1986*, vol. 2, *Detailed Tables* (Paris: OECD, 1988), Canadian tables 1, 6.1, 6.2, 6.3, 6.4; 1960–1973: OECD, unpublished data.

TABLE 5–7
DISTRIBUTION OF CPP LOANS, APRIL 1988

Province	Percentage of Total Loans
Atlantic provinces	
Newfoundland	2.1
Prince Edward Island	0.4
Nova Scotia	3.9
New Brunswick	2.9
Central provinces	
Quebec[a]	0.4
Ontario	47.1
Manitoba	5.5
Western provinces	
Saskatchewan	4.5
Alberta	11.8
British Columbia	14.0
Yukon Territory	b
Northwest Territories	b
Federal	7.4

a. Quebec is allowed to borrow from the CPP because some Quebec citizens work in Ontario and because the Royal Canadian Mounted Police who reside in Quebec still contribute to the CPP.
b. Less than 0.1 percent.
SOURCE: Health and Welfare Canada, Income Security Programs, *Canada Pension Plan Account Monthly Report* (Ottawa: Health and Welfare Canada, April 1988), schedule F.

thought that this might be the case.[50] Early statements by the government of Ontario implied that CPP-owned debt was treated differently than publicly owned debt.[51] In fact the provinces have taken this borrowing seriously; they have never missed an interest payment and in some instances have already repaid the loans.

Some commentators simply assume that the availability of ready credit encouraged more spending by the provincial governments;[52] no one appears to have made strong arguments to the contrary. The only effort to document increased expenditures was a 1981 study prepared for the Economic Council of Canada. This study found that the borrowings from the CPP induced the Atlantic provinces to reduce their revenues from their own sources and to increase expenditures, thereby increasing their total borrowings; the results for the other provinces were ambiguous.[53] Although it is difficult to say with certainty, it appears that the CPP money loaned to the provinces induced greater provincial spending.

The issue remains, however, as to whether this increased spending produced additional consumption or greater investment. The data in table 5–7 tend to indicate that provincial spending on investment did not increase in response to the ability of the provinces to borrow from the CPP. Provincial saving was 0.6 percent of GDP from 1960 through 1965; it increased only slightly from the inception of the CPP through 1974; thereafter it became negative. This pattern is also evident in the figures for provincial expenditures on gross capital formation, which have declined steadily since the inception of the plan from a high of 14 percent of total provincial expenditures in 1964 to less than 4 percent in 1986.[54] Thus it appears that the provincial governments have allocated a large share of the CPP surpluses to current consumption.

Investments of the QPP. The QPP, which as of June 1989 held $13 billion (Canadian dollars) in assets, does not lend to other provinces. Instead the assets, along with the assets of other Quebec public employee pensions, are supplied to the Caisse des Dépôts (a deposit fund). The Caisse des Dépôts invests its assets in regional businesses and crown corporations, with an eye toward the highest possible return. The fund is even allowed to purchase private corporate equities, although it may not hold more than 40 percent of the voting stock in any one firm. Directors of the Caisse des Dépôts are often taken from the private sector, despite some concern over conflicts of interest. By placing its funds directly into regional businesses, the investment patterns of the QPP contrast sharply with those of the CPP. In short the QPP appears to have increased national saving and investment while the CPP probably has not.

Assessment of the Canadian Experience. Except with Quebec, the Canadian government apparently has failed to prefund its pension system in a meaningful way. On balance the buildup in the trust funds seems to have stimulated additional consumption spending at the provincial level and to have reduced the incentive to raise provincial taxes. Would the same thing happen in the United States if the social security funds invested their reserves in state and local bonds? A partial answer may rest on the functions for which the two entities— provinces and states—can borrow.

It appears to be much easier for provinces in Canada to borrow for consumption expenditures than it is for states in the United States. Although New Brunswick, Newfoundland, and Nova Scotia maintain capital accounts, all borrowing is considered revenue, so debt may be used to meet deficits in their general accounts. Alberta has several off-budget special accounts for capital investments and crown corporations, and borrowing for the general budget is not encouraged. Because Alberta is so dependent upon oil prices for its revenues, however, it is occasionally forced to borrow for current consumption. Ontario, British Columbia, Manitoba, and Saskatchewan do not even maintain capital accounts. Therefore borrowing for current consumption is in no way differentiated from borrowing for capital investments. Only Prince Edward Island has legislative restrictions on current consumption borrowing; deficits in the general account may be met only by short-term debt issues. On balance, however, the lack of legal prohibitions and the negative saving in the OECD accounts indicate that the provinces are certainly able to borrow and probably have been borrowing for current consumption.

In the United States forty-nine of the states (Vermont being the exception) have balanced budget laws. This means that any borrowed general consumption funds must be repaid within a legislated time frame, typically under one year.[55] The OECD data for the United States (table 5–8) show consistent surpluses at the local level since 1972 (1975 is the only exception), which tend to confirm that the states and localities have not engaged in deficit financing for their general accounts. Hence, as long as the social security funds limited their state bond purchases to those with long-term maturities, the states could not use social security funds to cover general account deficits. This constraint would help ensure that trust fund loans to state and local governments would result in productive investment.

Conclusions and Policy Implications

Before drawing any conclusions, we must emphasize the speculative nature of this entire exercise. This is a preliminary analysis and involves hypothesizing, on the basis of limited information, about what would have happened without trust fund accumulations in foreign countries with different cultures and institutions. With this important caveat some tentative conclusions are possible.

The key concern in the United States is that Congress will increase its spending or reduce its tax-raising efforts in response to the buildup of large reserves in the social security trust funds. Such a response would mean that no saving would occur, and future incomes would be no higher than they would have been otherwise. It would also have the undesirable distributional consequence of financing current general government activities by the more regressive payroll tax.

The likelihood of the members of Congress responding to the

social security surpluses probably depends to a considerable extent on their ability to count the surpluses toward overall deficit reduction. All three countries studied keep their social security accounts separate from the rest of the budget, and this appears to have discouraged their legislatures from incorporating social security surpluses in their general budget decisions or their deficit reduction efforts. As long as the United States retains a unified budget and frames its deficit targets in these terms, Congress will be tempted to keep one eye on the surpluses when voting on tax and expenditure proposals. Hence, ensuring that social security does indeed go off-budget when the Gramm-Rudman-Hollings legislation expires in 1993 is an important first step.

The separateness of the social security program as an institution seems to be another important dimension, although separate institutional arrangements do not guarantee complete control. The Swedish fund has total independence, but the nature of its investments was strongly influenced by the central bank's credit market regulations. Nevertheless more separateness may be desirable than currently exists in the United States. As described in the introduction, the U.S. program is really only a Treasury Department account with the secretary of the Treasury as managing trustee. This arrangement probably would not be desirable if the social security trust funds were to be used to increase national saving. The secretary of the Treasury should not have easy access to social security funds in a debt ceiling crisis such as occurred in 1985 or consider the trust funds available as a captive market for purchasing federal debt.

The solution may rest in part in resurrecting a proposal to make social security an independent agency. This change, which has long been advocated for the integrity of the program and administrative effectiveness,[56] may become essential in an era of reserve accumulation. Control over revenues and investment decisions should reside with a board that is totally separate from the Treasury.

The lessons so far have come primarily from Sweden and Canada; Japan, of course, has taken an entirely different approach to translating pension fund reserves into productive investment. It does not have a separate agency; instead the federal government tightly controls the allocation of the EPI and NP reserves through the capital budget. Although this approach does not seem to fit well with our institutional arrangement and political environment, it may be useful to take a new look at the capital budgeting process.

Investing the accumulated trust fund reserves, which might at first appear difficult, in fact seems to create few problems. The Swedish experience illustrates that purchasing of debt instruments and investing through financial intermediaries avoid any interference in private

115

TABLE 5-8
U.S. GOVERNMENT SAVING AND DEFICIT (−) OR SURPLUS AS A PERCENTAGE OF GDP, 1960–1986

Year	General		Central and Social Security		Central		Social Security		Local	
	Saving	Deficit or surplus	Saving	Deficit or surplus	Saving	Deficit or surplus	Saving	Deficit or surplus	Saving	Deficit or surplus
1960	1.67	0.58	0.81	0.96	0.68	0.84	0.12	0.12	0.86	-0.38
1961	0.28	-0.86	-0.57	-0.41	-0.18	-0.02	-0.39	-0.39	0.85	-0.45
1962	0.38	-0.57	-0.59	-0.28	-0.54	-0.22	-0.05	-0.05	0.97	-0.29
1963	1.11	-0.11	0.08	0.25	-0.11	0.06	0.19	0.19	1.03	-0.36
1964	0.61	-0.62	-0.51	-0.37	-0.76	-0.62	0.25	0.25	1.12	-0.25
1965	1.05	-0.21	0.04	0.19	-0.09	0.06	0.13	0.13	1.01	-0.39
1966	0.67	-0.63	-0.47	-0.26	-1.32	-1.11	0.84	0.84	1.14	-0.37
1967	-0.80	-2.16	-1.84	-1.58	-2.46	-2.20	0.62	0.62	1.04	-0.58
1968	0.42	-0.72	-0.79	-0.36	-1.24	-0.82	0.45	0.45	1.20	-0.35
1969	1.78	0.79	0.64	1.04	-0.04	0.36	0.68	0.68	1.15	-0.25
1970	-0.74	-1.39	-1.67	-1.06	-1.81	-1.20	0.14	0.14	0.93	-0.33

Year										
1971	-1.40	-2.03	-2.25	-1.72	-2.06	-1.53	-0.19	-0.19	0.85	-0.31
1972	-0.39	-0.65	-1.90	-1.19	-1.93	-1.23	0.03	0.03	1.51	0.54
1973	0.44	0.36	-0.82	-0.10	-1.35	-0.63	0.53	0.53	1.26	0.46
1974	-0.24	-0.35	-1.15	-0.41	-1.45	-0.71	0.30	0.30	0.91	0.06
1975	-3.97	-4.30	-4.45	-4.10	-3.51	-3.15	-0.94	-0.94	0.48	-0.20
1976	-2.48	-2.44	-3.24	-2.75	-2.45	-1.96	-0.78	-0.78	0.76	0.31
1977	-1.33	-1.14	-2.30	-1.90	-1.70	-1.31	-0.60	-0.60	0.97	0.77
1978	-0.22	-0.30	-1.25	-1.11	-1.16	-1.02	-0.08	-0.08	1.03	0.81
1979	0.04	0.17	-0.71	-0.40	-0.85	-0.53	0.14	0.14	0.76	0.57
1980	-1.60	-1.46	-2.23	-1.88	-1.76	-1.40	-0.48	-0.48	0.63	0.42
1981	-1.32	-1.13	-1.90	-1.63	-1.51	-1.25	-0.38	-0.38	0.58	0.49
1982	-4.15	-3.97	-4.38	-4.16	-3.36	-3.14	-1.02	-1.02	0.23	0.19
1983	-4.95	-4.86	-5.32	-5.15	-4.30	-4.13	-1.02	-1.02	0.36	0.29
1984	-3.92	-3.84	-4.70	-4.51	-4.61	-4.42	-0.09	-0.09	0.79	0.66
1985	-4.01	-4.13	-4.71	-4.63	-4.82	-4.74	0.11	0.11	0.70	0.50
1986	-4.31	-4.37	-4.91	-4.69	-5.12	-4.90	0.21	0.21	0.60	0.32

NOTE: The general budget consolidates the activities at the federal level (central plus social security) with those at the local levels.
SOURCES: 1974–1986: Organization for Economic Cooperation and Development, Department of Economics and Statistics, *National Accounts: 1974–1986*, vol. 2, *Detailed Tables* (Paris: OECD, 1988), United States tables 1, 6.1, 6.3, 6.4; 1960–1973: OECD, unpublished data.

sector decisions. Also, the United States should be able to invest in state and local securities without running into any of the problems experienced in Canada since states are restricted from long-term borrowing except for capital projects.

In short, we can learn much from Sweden's, Japan's, and Canada's efforts to prefund some of their future pension liabilities. These countries have already accumulated reserves equal to 30 percent, 18 percent, and 8 percent of their respective GDPs and have attempted to funnel them into productive investment, with varying degrees of success. A somewhat discouraging result, for those committed to increasing national saving through accumulating reserves in the social security trust funds, is that the greatest success has occurred in countries with stable and disciplined political environments, where one party has been in power almost continuously since the experiment began.

6

The Causal Relationship between Social Security and the Federal Budget

W. Mark Crain and Michael L. Marlow

As the 1990s begin, social security is once again at the center of public debate. Under current projections social security is expected to post substantial surpluses during the next two or three decades and a string of ever-increasing deficits thereafter. In the meantime the social security trust funds are projected to accumulate large reserves. At the heart of the current controversy is the question of how politicians will behave when the trust funds are temporarily flush with cash. Will the surplus funds actually be saved for future years, or will they be spent—either directly through social security expansion or indirectly through an expansion of the rest of the budget?

No binding rules on politicians dictate how surplus monies will be used. Under current law any excess revenues in the trust funds must be used to purchase new special-issue government bonds, but that does not reveal what is done with the revenues the Treasury has thus been lent. Excess social security revenues, like any other federal revenues, are available to finance the general operations of the government. They may be used to retire outstanding government debt or to finance an increase in federal spending or a reduction in federal taxes.

How political discretion determines this fiscal choice is the subject of this chapter. If tax and spending decisions in the rest of the budget are independent of social security, then any excess social security revenues reduce the federal budget deficit and allow the Treasury to retire outstanding privately held public debt. If politicians respond to the surplus social security revenues by increasing federal spending (or reducing federal taxes), then some or all of the surpluses translate into a higher deficit in the rest of the budget, with little or no reduction in the overall deficit or national debt.

The question of how politicians will use the surpluses in the coming years cannot be settled by force of conviction or ideals about political behavior. It is fundamentally an empirical question about the interrelationship between social security and other fiscal decisions.

This chapter attempts to provide an empirical analysis of several key fiscal relationships and, in so doing, to inform the debate over the advance funding of social security. In particular an empirical technique known as causality testing is used to examine the relationships between social security revenues, trust fund balances, and aggregate federal spending and between social security revenues and other federal revenues. Some understanding about the actual historical relationships between these variables can help to make informed judgments about the likely effects of the social security surpluses.

The remainder of the chapter first reviews previous empirical studies on the causal relationship between government taxation and spending, and the importance of testing the dynamic nature of political responses involving social security. Second, an empirical model is formulated and empirical findings evaluated. Finally, results are analyzed in the context of current policy deliberations.

The Importance of Dynamic Analysis

Almost all solutions to fiscal problems follow from some prescribed change in spending or taxes under a static, or independent, framework. Economists have long argued for advance funding of social security under the assumption that doing so would not trigger behavior by politicians that would undermine the attainment of the stated goal: an increase in national saving.

Economic or political behavior is seldom so simple. A dynamic framework of budgetary behavior—whether in the area of social security spending or aggregate federal spending—recognizes at least four possibilities in a world of political discretion: tax decisions are influenced by expenditure decisions, expenditure decisions are influenced by tax decisions, expenditure and tax decisions are unrelated, or expenditure and tax decisions are jointly determined. Static analysis of dynamic relationships can lead to an incorrect understanding of behavior and therefore to inappropriate policy recommendations.

Only recently have economists recognized the importance of analyzing fiscal policy in a dynamic framework. Using a common method of determining causal relationships referred to as Granger causality testing, more than nine studies have attempted to establish the tax-spend relationship at the federal, state, and local levels of government. While the results are not totally in agreement, the available studies suggest that a dynamic analysis of governmental budget behavior is appropriate and that in an examination of the historical relationship between taxes and spending, the hypothesis that expenditures will rise whenever taxes rise cannot be reasonably rejected, and vice versa.[1]

In this chapter this dynamic analysis is extended to social security. Before one can evaluate the likely effects of the trust fund surpluses or offer appropriate solutions, one must understand the political dynamics behind social security and other federal revenue and spending decisions. The interrelationships between the primary policy parameters—social security revenues, trust fund balances, and aggregate federal spending, as well as between social security revenues and other federal revenues—are analyzed. The more one understands about the politics of federal fiscal behavior, the less ambiguous are the effects of proposed solutions, and the higher is the likelihood that policy goals are attained.

The Budget Constraint Hypothesis and Social Security

The early research on causality, which was motivated primarily by political debate on the federal budget, focused on the question, Does a tax increase *unambiguously* lower the deficit?[2] On one side of the issue were those who argued that budget deficits were a symptom of fiscal irresponsibility and that tax increases were the appropriate solution. The other side, which was taken by many in the Reagan administration, agreed that the growth in federal budget deficits was a symptom of fiscal irresponsibility but argued that the appropriate solution was to lower spending.[3]

The latter view is consistent with the budget constraint hypothesis discussed extensively by Milton Friedman.[4] On the assumption that there always exists a worthwhile program that someone wishes to enact, the budget constraint model of government hypothesizes that revenues determine spending levels. This follows from standard microeconomic theory of the consumer: consumers operate with scarce resources and thus are limited in the amount they can consume. The limits of current consumption are determined by accumulated wealth, current income, and the ability to borrow on future resources, which together define the budget constraint. An expanded budget constraint allows for expanded consumption opportunities.

The budget constraint hypothesis implies that the government, like individual consumers, is subject to scarce resources. (Were it not, we would have no difficulty removing poverty, hunger, homelessness, and many other problems from our broad and growing list of policy concerns.) The budget constraint facing government consists of the

121

means by which expenditures are funded: tax receipts and debt. Taxes are levied either directly through legislation or indirectly through inflation. The deficit is the residual between collected taxes and current spending and determines new borrowing. Although only the central government has the power to create money, the government's ability to consume is constrained by the same factors that confront private citizens.

The budget constraint analogy offers an organizing framework for relevant policy questions. One obvious question concerns the expected impact on government spending of a deficit reduction policy that includes raising taxes. With the budget constraint approach, raising taxes, by itself, serves to expand the spending opportunity set of government. This is really nothing new: Friedman has often repeated his famous maxim that "governments spend what governments receive plus whatever they can get away with."[5] The relevant question, then, becomes an empirical one: What does the evidence indicate about the effect of past tax increases on government expenditures?

John Cogan presents an interesting variant of the budget constraint model that focuses on the dependence of budgetary decisions on the method of finance.[6] His argument is developed in two parts. First, he likens the institutional arrangements in the congressional budget process to a common property resource. The common resource is the general revenue fund. The problem is that when many congressional committees draw on the general revenues, no single committee has an incentive to restrain its spending commitments. Even worse, since no single committee has any residual claim to unspent general funds, there is competition to outspend other committees. Consequently expenditures financed from general fund revenues increase much faster than the revenues themselves.

Second, he argues that the creation of tax-financed trust funds, the first of which was social security, transferred spending authority from the appropriations committees to the tax-writing committees and thereby created a revenue bias in favor of trust fund taxes and against general fund taxes. Since the tax-writing committees have exclusive jurisdiction over trust fund expenditures (and taxes), it is easier for them to capture the political benefits of spending on these programs. In addition the proceeds of trust fund taxes (for example, the social security payroll tax) are tied more closely than general fund revenues to the interests of the tax-writing committees. This analytical framework suggests a substitution of trust fund revenues for general fund revenues, with social security taxes funding a larger share of government over time.

The opposing view to the budget constraint hypothesis argues that politicians are not self-serving spenders (or tax substituters) but rather are committed to living within their means. Here the possibility that tax increases could fund additional spending rather than reduce the deficit is either highly discounted or believed to be false as there is assumed to be no innate proclivity among politicians to use higher taxes to fund larger expenditures or new programs. This view therefore implies either that there is no causal relation between increased taxes and increased spending or that the true causal relation runs from spending to taxes.

One's view of the budget constraint hypothesis greatly influences policy recommendations regarding the social security surpluses. The budget constraint hypothesis suggests that social security surpluses will lead to increases (decreases)—within and outside of social security—in federal spending (taxes). That is, since social security surpluses are really excess social security revenues, and there is no prohibition on the spending of these revenues, politicians will be inclined to increase other spending programs or trim other taxes rather than enjoy a lower federal budget deficit and national debt. If the budget constraint view of political behavior is correct, today's excess payroll taxes will not be saved for payouts of future social security benefits but will promote the relaxation of the budget constraint facing politicians.

The major alternative hypothesis is that political behavior in the area of non-social-security spending and taxation is independent of social security spending and taxation. That is, social security surpluses, or excess taxes, will have no effect on the rest of the budget, leading instead to a reduction in the overall federal deficit and the amount of federal debt held by the public. This is the usual argument for running surpluses in the first place, and it assumes that politicians resist all temptations to spend the new resources at their command.

The Granger causality test is one way to test which hypothesis regarding political decisions is correct.[7] Based on the predictability of a variable over time, Granger causality attempts to determine whether the forecasts of a variable Y, such as government spending, using both past values of itself and that of another variable X, such as social security surpluses, are better than forecasts based solely on lagged values of Y. If so, then X is said to one-way cause Y. If it is found that X causes Y and that Y causes X, then two-way causality exists between X and Y. Finally, if one-way causality does not exist in either direction, the fourth possibility exists: the variables bear no causal relation to one another and are truly independent.

Empirical Evidence of Tax-Spend Causality

The available empirical evidence generally supports the view that government tax and spending decisions are causally related. Of the nine or more studies that directly test for causality, the majority find evidence of dependence between revenue and spending decisions. Neela Manage and Michael L. Marlow tested for causality in federal finances over the period 1929 to 1982.[8] In seven of the twelve cases studied (or 58 percent) they found bidirectional causality; in the remaining cases (42 percent) they found one-way causality running from budget receipts to budget outlays. This study concludes that even in the case of bidirectionality, one cannot reject the hypothesis that tax increases will be associated with subsequent spending increases. Using a similar framework, Rati Ram offers additional support for these results.[9] David Joulfaian provides evidence of two-way, or simultaneous, causality between federal taxes and spending.[10]

Paul R. Blackley uses causality tests on the federal tax-spend relation over the period 1929–1982.[11] He concludes that while it is not possible to reject the hypothesis that the tax-spend relationship is simultaneous, revenue growth appears to bear a much stronger causal link to spending growth than vice versa.

Marlow and Manage address the issue of whether the many different legislative and constitutional constraints at the state and local levels of government affect the causal relation between revenues and expenditures.[12] At the state level the evidence supports the budget constraint hypothesis. At the local level the evidence suggests no causality. Further testing of the same data by Abdur R. Chowdhry provides evidence that supports the budget constraint hypothesis at the local level.[13] Evidence of similar causality at the local level is also found by Douglas Holtz-Eakin.[14]

To date, only two studies do not support the budget constraint hypothesis. William Anderson, Myles S. Wallace, and John T. Warner find one-way causality running from real federal spending to real federal tax revenues.[15] In a study of quarterly federal tax and spending data, George M. von Furstenburg, Jeffrey R. Green, and Jin-Ho Jeogn find no significant relationship between spending and taxes.[16] Budgetary decisions, however, are made on an annual basis, so the use of quarterly data introduces many potential trouble spots concerning revenue and expenditure flows that have little, or possibly nothing, to do with annual political budgetary decisions.[17]

In sum, while the empirical evidence is somewhat mixed, most studies indicate one-way causality running from taxes to spending and therefore yield strong support for the budget constraint hypothesis.

Only one study shows causality in the other direction. The possibility that causality is complex, or bidirectional, should not be dismissed, however. While the budget constraint hypothesis appears to be at least partially correct, the alternative hypothesis may contain some validity as well.[18] The advantage of causality testing is that it does not impose any assumptions on behavior or causality; rather it tests for causal relations. This empirical approach allows both proponents and skeptics of the budget constraint hypothesis their day in court.

The important similarity between the federal tax and spending relation and the relation between social security and the federal budget is the existence of political discretion. Both relationships are unconstrained by rules. Therefore one cannot make a priori assumptions that are known to be correct about how a surplus of social security funds will be used. This chapter attempts to shed light on how politicians are likely to respond to social security's looming surpluses.

Empirical Tests. The data used in the causality tests are drawn from the 1989 U.S. budget. For the period 1940 to 1987, data are used for total (on- and off-budget) federal revenues and expenditures, and on social security revenues, expenditures, and reserves.[19] Social security is defined to include all four programs or trust funds: Old-Age and Survivors Insurance, Disability Insurance, Hospital Insurance, and Supplemental Medical Insurance. The reserve in any particular year is equal to the accumulated assets of the four trust funds as of the end of the fiscal year. These data are used to compute non-social-security expenditures (revenues), which are simply aggregate federal spending (revenues) less social security spending (revenues). The annual surplus or deficit in social security, referred to as the trust fund balance, is computed from the one-year change in trust fund reserves. The trust fund balances (rather than reserves) are emphasized here because they closely indicate, at the margin, the potential for changes in political discretionary spending opportunities.

Three technical issues should be considered before evaluating the empirical estimations. First, there are serial correlation problems in data on levels, such as annual federal expenditures, that must be corrected before using the Granger test. (The Granger test requires that each time series be stationary. The relationship between any two observations depends only on the time interval between them and not on time itself; most time series of level data contain some type of trend.) To handle this problem, the data were first-differenced: the value of the previous observation was subtracted from each observation. All the data were then transformed into annual growth rates, with additional first-differences taken until the time trend was eliminated.[20] The data

125

TABLE 6–1

TRIVARIATE CAUSALITY TESTS BETWEEN SOCIAL SECURITY REVENUES, FEDERAL SPENDING, AND SOCIAL SECURITY BALANCES

	Hypothesis					
	$FS = f(FS, SR)$ (SB causes FS)		$SR = f(SR, FS)$ (SB causes SR)		$SB = f(SB, FS)$ (SR causes SB)	
Lag	F	ΣSB	F	ΣSB	F	ΣSR
1	0.96	0.15	1.85	0.11	1.14	−0.13
		0.98		1.36		1.07
2	4.01[a]	−1.15[a]	1.64	−0.41	3.71[a]	−0.25
		2.12		1.51		1.17
3	4.93[b]	−2.13[a]	2.37[c]	−1.01[a]	0.93	−0.40
		2.43		2.07		1.10
4	2.13[c]	−2.63[a]	1.36	−1.00	0.30	−0.45
		2.10		1.29		0.78
5	3.23[a]	−3.03[c]	1.28	−1.49	0.45	−0.72
		1.98		1.24		0.83

	$FS = f(FS, SB)$ (SR causes FS)		$SR = f(SR, SB)$ (FS causes SR)		$SB = f(SB, SR)$ (FS causes SB)	
	F	ΣSR	F	ΣFS	F	ΣFS
1	2.83[c]	0.47[c]	0.01	−0.01	0.17	−0.03
		1.68		0.09		0.41
2	3.79[a]	1.33[a]	1.48	0.15	1.40	0.59
		2.41		1.65		0.82
3	5.38[b]	2.22[c]	2.98[a]	0.18	0.73	0.11
		2.80		1.39		1.04
4	4.90[b]	3.37[b]	1.99	0.12	0.25	0.06
		3.24		0.61		0.35
5	4.46[b]	2.39[c]	1.58	0.25	0.19	0.08
		1.72		0.75		0.30

	$FS = f(FS)$ (SR&SB cause FS)	$SR = f(SR)$ (FS&SB cause SR)	$SB = f(SB)$ (FS&SR cause SB)
	F	F	F
1	3.21[c]	1.03	0.73
2	3.13[a]	1.46	2.19[c]
3	4.28[b]	2.31[c]	0.61
4	2.74[a]	1.67	0.27
5	3.18[b]	1.58	0.30

SR = social security revenues
FS = total federal spending
SB = social security trust fund balances
a. Significant at the .05 level (absolute value of t-statistic below Σ).
b. Significant at the .01 level (absolute value of t-statistic below Σ).
c. Significant at the .10 level (absolute value of t-statistic below Σ).

on trust fund reserves required third-differencing; all other data required second-differencing.

The transformed data can be interpreted as follows. Social security revenues, non-social-security revenues, total federal expenditures, and non-social-security expenditures are measured as changes in annual growth rates. Since the first-difference of social security trust fund reserves is the current period's trust fund balance (surplus or deficit), the second-difference is the growth rate of the trust fund balance and the third-difference is the change in the growth rate of the trust fund balance. Therefore, causality tests will identify the causal relationships between changes in the growth rate of social security revenues, trust fund balances, and federal spending.

Second, there are differing views regarding the appropriate lag length to use in a causality test. Symmetric lags, ranging from one to five years, were used here.[21]

Third, two statistics of interest in this application of Granger causality tests are provided. One is the F-statistic, which is used to test the null hypothesis that all coefficients on the independent variables are zero.[22] Failure to reject the null hypothesis indicates that at least some subset of independent variables exerts a statistically significant effect on the dependent variable. The other statistic is the sum of the coefficients (Σ).[23] A t-test on the sum of the coefficients indicates whether the causal effects on the dependent variable are permanent or transitory in nature and in what direction as evidenced by the sign on the sum of coefficients.

Table 6–1 presents the results of a trivariate causality test between total federal spending (FS), social security revenues (SR), and trust fund balances (SB). Since there are three variables of interest, a trivariate causality approach is used here to understand how their past values are related to one another. Three causal orderings are possible: one or more variables one-way cause one or more variables, all variables experience tridirectional causality (that is, they are simultaneously related), or none of the variables are causally related to another.

The F-scores displayed in the first column are associated with the null hypothesis that social security revenues or trust fund balances are significantly related to aggregate federal spending. The number 0.96, for example, in the first column and first row is the F-score associated with the hypothesis that SB is significantly related to FS. It is obtained by comparing the sum of squared residuals ($SSRs$) of the two equations: $FS = f(FS, SR, SB)$ and $FS = f(FS, SR)$. The displayed F-score is obtained from the usual calculation that determines whether the change in SSRs is statistically different from zero. If the F-score exceeds the appropriate F-statistic, then SB is significantly related to FS. The

127

F-scores in the middle of the first column refer to the comparison between $FS = f(FS, SR, SB)$ and $FS = f(FS, SB)$; it is associated with the null hypothesis that *SR* is not statistically related to *FS*.

Next to the *F*-scores are the sums of coefficients (Σ) relating to the previous test of significance. As mentioned, the *F*-test is appropriate for testing whether all independent variables exert statistically significant effects on a dependent variable. The *t*-test on the sum of coefficients is appropriate for testing whether the independent variable exerts a permanent effect. The sum of coefficients is displayed along with its associated *t*-score below it. If the *t*-score exceeds its critical level, then the independent variable exerts a permanent effect on the dependent variable. Failure to exceed its critical level indicates that any effects are transitory in nature.

The results indicate that neither social security revenues nor trust fund balances are significantly explained by past values of any three of the variables. That is, with the equation of *SR* as the dependent variable, the *F*-scores associated with the influence of past values of *FS* and *SB* are generally not statistically different from zero. The only exceptions occur when three-year lags are used; even here, though, the *F*-scores are only marginally significant at the 10 percent level for the tests involving *SB* by itself and *FS* and *SB* together. Moreover, the only permanent effect from *SB* on *SR* is when it is by itself with the three-year lag specification; in this case it is a negative effect implying that past increases in *SB* have exerted an inverse influence on *SR*. When *SB* is the dependent variable, *SR* exerts a negative effect only with the two-year lag specification; the effect, however, is not permanent.

The equations with aggregate federal spending as the dependent variable indicate that both social security revenues and trust fund balances exert significant influences. Moreover, in most cases those effects are permanent. The results indicate that while past increases in *SB* exert negative effects on *FS*, past increases in *SR* exert positive effects. That is, the positive permanent coefficient on *SR* is empirical support for the tax-and-spend hypothesis. Here it is interpreted as indicating that past increases in social security revenues have exerted positive effects on total federal spending. In addition the permanent negative coefficient on *SB* indicates that past increases in trust fund balances have exerted inverse effects on total federal spending.

The implications for causality are as follows. There appears to be little evidence that social security revenues and trust fund balances are related to (or cause) past changes in themselves or to past changes in total federal spending. Past changes in social security revenues and trust fund balances, however, explain (or cause) significant movements in aggregate federal spending. The evidence thus suggests that over the period examined, causation runs from social security revenues and trust fund balances to aggregate federal spending. That is, past movements in trust fund balances and revenues explain current aggregate federal spending and not vice versa. Therefore tax and spending decisions are causal in nature, with changes in social security revenues and trust fund balances leading to (causing) changes in federal spending.

Table 6–2 is similar to table 6–1 except that total federal spending is disaggregated into its social security and non-social-security components. This allows an additional test within the causality framework. Comparison of tables 6–1 and 6–2 indicates that as before, past movements in social security revenues and trust fund balances have led to, or caused, non-social-security spending. Moreover, past increases in social security revenues have caused increases in non-social-security spending.

Additional Tests of Causality

While there is support for the budget constraint hypothesis in the case of the prospending effects of past increases in social security revenues, there is also evidence that past changes in the growth of trust fund balances have exerted negative and statistically significant effects on federal spending. One possible explanation for this latter result is that surplus monies in the trust funds are actually being saved, thus reducing the amount that the federal government must borrow and the amount of spending that is needed to service the government's debt. This explanation, however, conflicts with the above empirical support for the budget constraint hypothesis regarding past social security revenues and federal spending. In addition it conflicts with the finding that trust fund surpluses are not causally related to social security revenues or federal spending. Therefore the evidence in support of the argument that excess social security trust fund balances are saved and not spent is weak or nonexistent.

The results reported in tables 6–1 and 6–2 also indicate that neither federal spending nor trust fund balances are causally related to social security revenues. As such, the empirical relationship between trust fund balances and federal spending does not appear to be related in any causal fashion to increased social security revenues. Rather the relationship appears to be associated with the other determinant of trust fund balances: social security spending.

Table 6–3 contains the results of various bivariate causality tests that seek to determine why there exists an inverse causal relationship running from social security trust fund balances to federal spending.

TABLE 6–2
TRIVARIATE CAUSALITY TESTS BETWEEN SOCIAL SECURITY REVENUES, NON-SOCIAL-SECURITY SPENDING, AND SOCIAL SECURITY BALANCES

	Hypothesis					
	NFS = f(FS, SR) (SB causes NFS)		SR = f(SR, NFS) (SB causes SR)		SB = f(SB, NFS) (SR causes SB)	
Lag	F	ΣSB	F	ΣSB	F	ΣSR
1	0.82	0.14	1.82	0.11	1.14	−0.13
		0.91		1.35		1.07
2	3.87^a	−1.18^a	1.66	−0.42	3.74^a	−0.25
		2.12		1.53		1.15
3	4.82^b	−2.09^a	2.34^c	−1.02^a	0.90	−0.38
		2.32		2.08		1.05
4	2.09	−2.64^a	1.34	−1.04	0.31	−0.45
		2.08		1.35		0.77
5	3.22^a	−1.98^a	1.30	−1.61	0.46	−0.81
		3.13		1.34		0.69
	NFS = f(FS, SB) (SR causes NFS)		SR = f(SR, SB) (NFS causes SR)		SB = f(SB, SR) (NFS causes SB)	
	F	ΣSR	F	ΣNFS	F	ΣNFS
1	3.47^b	0.52^c	0.03	−0.01	0.28	−0.33
		1.86		0.02		0.53
2	4.14^a	1.37^a	1.42	0.14	1.37	0.05
		2.44		1.60		0.71
3	5.68^b	2.35^b	2.83^c	0.18	0.65	0.10
		2.91		1.39		0.98
4	5.06^b	3.96^b	1.90	0.12	0.27	0.05
		3.25		0.60		0.32
5	4.44^b	2.49^c	1.51	0.24	0.21	0.07
		1.74		0.73		0.27
	NFS = f(NFS) (SR&SB cause NFS)		SR = f(SR) (NFS&SB cause SR)		SB = f(SB) (NFS&SR cause SB)	
	F		F		F	
1	3.52^a		1.04		0.79	
2	3.26^a		1.43		2.17^c	
3	4.40^b		2.23^c		0.56	
4	2.86^a		1.62		0.28	
5	3.32^b		1.54		0.32	

SR = social security revenues
NFS = net federal spending (total federal spending minus social security spending)
SB = social security trust fund balances
a. Significant at the .05 level (absolute value of t-statistic below Σ).
b. Significant at the .01 level (absolute value of t-statistic below Σ).
c. Significant at the .10 level (absolute value of t-statistic below Σ).

TABLE 6–3
BIVARIATE CAUSALITY TESTS OF ALTERNATIVE HYPOTHESES

	Hypothesis	
Lag	SB causes SS F	SS causes SB F
2	6.57[a]	0.49
3	6.29[a]	0.20
4	1.89	0.38
5	0.98	0.23
	SB causes NI F	NI causes SB F
2	0.21	1.55
3	0.34	1.35
4	0.16	2.61[b]
5	2.19[b]	1.87
	SB causes NNI F	NNI causes SB F
2	0.23	6.88[a]
3	1.16	2.33[b]
4	1.87	1.40
5	0.55	1.63
	SB causes DEF F	DEF causes SB F
2	0.01	0.19
3	0.38	1.60
4	0.68	1.09
5	0.74	1.07
	SB causes NDEF F	NDEF causes SB F
2	0.03	0.52
3	0.30	1.39
4	0.75	1.01
5	0.73	0.88

SB = social security trust fund balances
NI = net interest (on- and off-budget) of U.S. government
NNI = NI – intragovernmental interest receipts of social security trust funds
DEF = federal budget deficit (on- and off-budget)
NDEF = DEF – intragovernmental interest receipts of social security trust funds
SS = social security outlays
a. Significant at the .01 level.
b. Significant at the .10 level.

The first set of causality tests are between the trust fund balances (SB) and social security spending (SS). After second-differencing the data on spending, there is evidence of a permanent inverse one-way causal relationship running from the trust fund balances to social security spending for the first two lag configurations. In other words the negative effect of the trust fund balances on federal spending appears to be related in part to their influence on social security spending.

While this may appear to run counter to the budget constraint hypothesis, the inverse relationship between federal spending and trust fund balances may be spurious, stemming from a mechanical problem that is unrelated to political behavior.[24] When an independent variable is jointly determined, as is clearly the case with trust fund balances, its coefficient can be difficult to interpret.

This problem does not arise in the causality tests using non-social-security spending, so one might argue that the evidence indicates that the budget constraint theory of political behavior is not supported by the past relationship between trust fund balances and non-social-security federal spending. This possibility deserves further testing since, if it is valid, it may place in doubt the earlier result concerning the positive one-way causal relationship running from social security revenues to federal spending.

To submit the data to further scrutiny, the counter hypothesis—that trust fund surpluses reduce interest payments to the public by reducing the amount of outstanding debt—is tested. Stated another way, past social security surpluses have not relaxed fiscal restraint in the rest of the budget. To test this, a bivariate causality test is performed between the net interest payments (on- and off-budget) of the U.S. government (NI) and the trust fund balances (SB).[25] The results are reported in table 6–3. After first-differencing the data on net interest, there is no permanent causal relationship between the two variables, suggesting that this hypothesis does not appear to have any empirical basis. As an additional test of the same hypothesis, net interest less interest receipts of the social security trust funds (NNI) was also considered. After first-differencing this data, the results of the causality test did not change. Social security trust fund balances bear no causal relationship to this adjusted measure of net interest.

Finally, the counter hypothesis—that social security surpluses cause, or lead to, federal government savings—is tested. Rather than a look at the effect of trust fund balances on the interest payment portion of the federal budget, their effect on the overall budget deficit is directly examined.

Two measures of the total (on- and off-budget) federal deficit are considered: DEF and NDEF. DEF is simply the difference between total federal spending and total federal revenues.[26] *NDEF* is defined as *DEF* less the interest receipts of the trust funds. After first-differencing both measures of federal deficits, the results in table 6–3 indicate that there exists no causal relationship between social security trust fund balances and either measure of the federal budget deficit. Therefore, the past relationship between these variables appears to be one of independence. This finding is not supportive of the counterhypothesis that the social security surpluses are saved.

Summary of the Empirical Evidence

The evidence in tables 6–1 and 6–2 provides support for the budget constraint hypothesis that past increases in social security revenues have led to an increase in federal spending. The evidence also indicates that there has been a historical one-way inverse causal relationship running from social security trust fund balances to federal spending. While the latter may appear inconsistent with the budget constraint hypothesis, however, it may stem from an empirical problem of including social security balances and social security spending in the same equation. Moreover, while some may wish to suggest that this inverse causal relation serves to invalidate the budget constraint hypothesis, the empirical evidence in table 6–3 does not contain any verification of the usual counterarguments to the budget constraint hypothesis. Specifically there is no evidence to support the view that social security surpluses lead to lower federal spending, interest payments, or deficits.[27]

Conclusions

The primary purpose of this chapter is to determine whether there should be concern that the projected surpluses of the social security trust funds might be spent rather than saved. Since there exist no written, or binding, constraints on the behavior of politicians concerning this issue, the answer to this important question cannot be projected with great certainty. At best, predictions can be based on the assumption that past political behavior is a good guide to the future, and to do so, causality tests between the primary policy variables can be employed.

The empirical evidence provides support for the budget constraint theory of political behavior: increased revenues will be treated as a general loosening of the budget constraint facing politicians. In periods when social security revenues have grown, there is a causal link to expansions in federal spending—both aggregate federal spending and non-social-security spending. This suggests that the decision to raise revenues in the 1983 Social Security Amendments will lead to an expansion in federal spending.

There is also evidence that both social security taxes and non-social-security taxes fund non-social-security programs. While taxpayers may operate on the assumption that social security taxes fund only social security spending, it appears that "a tax is a tax," when it comes to the tendency to expand government spending.

Notwithstanding the attempt to make predictions based on actual historical relations, there remains great uncertainty over future political behavior. This is merely a restatement of the fact that political decisions involving the use of social security surpluses are not subject to binding constraints. Given the importance that many place on social security, the replacement of political discretion with rules of conduct is suggested for the future relationships between social security taxes, trust fund balances, and aggregate federal spending and taxation. Absent such rules, guesses will continue about the future relationships between these important policy variables.

Securing the Benefits
of Advance Funding

A Commentary by John B. Shoven

There is much I agree with in the chapter by Alicia Munnell and Nicole Ernsberger, which deals with one of the most important public finance issues of the next twenty years. I will emphasize where I differ, however. At one level it is a matter of emphasis. The choice between allowing social security surpluses to accumulate as planned and returning to pay-as-you-go financing is terribly important. I do not agree with the authors that "the OASDI program will function perfectly well regardless of whether reserves are accumulated in advance or financing is returned to pay-as-you-go." This is the first of two major choices we face. The second is whether to allow the social security surpluses to affect our resolve to balance the rest of the federal budget. I am among those who consider the low level of net national saving to be among the most serious long-run problems we face. The choices we make about prefunding social security and accumulating a separate budgetary surplus for it can make a large difference in the level of our national saving and in future economic welfare.

Using the same source as the authors in advising us to relax about these matters, which is the Brookings study by Henry Aaron, Barry Bosworth, and Gary Burtless,[1] consider the stakes. Aaron, Bosworth, and Burtless predict that in 2020 the U.S. capital stock would be 23.7 percent higher if we allow the surpluses to accumulate and we do not offset them elsewhere in the government than if we were to return to pay-as-you-go financing. That strikes me as a big effect. I cannot think of many other decisions for which the stakes are so high. Let us not relax; let us do it right. The Brookings team goes on to forecast that net national product (NNP) would be 4.2 percent higher, consumption 2.6 percent higher, and wages 7.1 percent higher. The higher real wages would increase social security benefits 5.0 percent.

These higher levels of NNP, wages, and social security benefits do not occur for just one year. They are relatively permanent increases in the levels of these flow variables. These effects are large enough to be taken seriously. All of them are made even more dramatic when one includes the hospital insurance trust fund in the analysis; then the real wage effect in 2020 is 9.5 percent. Real wages have not gone up that much in many years. Munnell and Ernsberger state that the differences between how well-off people would be with and without the additional saving is fairly small. This was not the conclusion of the authors of the study they rely on for their projections. Aaron, Bosworth, and Burtless found that if productivity increases are the same over the next thirty years as they have been for the last fifteen, then the growth of net compensation by 2020 would be 41 percent faster if national saving were increased by the amount of social security reserves than if it were not. This was the case for which the effect was most dramatic, but it is not an unreasonable one. To a veteran analyst of the economic effects of the corporate income tax, the impacts of the social security trust fund accumulation are the sort of dramatic ones that we always find appealing.

Relative to current law, a return to pay-as-you-go financing would lower payroll tax rates about 25 percent for the current generation of workers (between now and, say, 2015) and raise them about 25 percent for those who work after 2020. Again, these magnitudes seem great. One generation of workers would face tax rates fully 50 percent higher than the previous one.

The chapter by Munnell and Ernsberger often mentions the regressive nature of the payroll tax. It is unfortunate that the connection between an individual's benefits and contributions is so weak that the proper way to look at social security is as a tax and transfer system. If the connection were strengthened, without reducing the built-in progressivity, then contributions would be more like deferred payments and would not be accurately construed as distortionary taxes. As it is, social security payroll taxes probably more than double the distortions in labor markets caused by the personal income tax. This unfortunate situation will only be exacerbated if rates are allowed to rise to the level necessary to run a pay-as-you-go system after 2020.

As for the foreign experiences, and the question of whether social security surpluses really add to government and national saving, the evidence presented by the authors is interesting, but anecdotal, and loosely supportive of my position that social security surpluses can make a large difference in national saving. The authors conclude that both Sweden and Japan have apparently increased government saving by building up social security reserves, while Canada has not. My own view is that it is difficult, if not impossible, to isolate the effect of the trust fund accumulation on other saving in these economies. Even Canada, for whatever reason, has a rate of national saving to which we can only aspire.

What do I take from all of this? Aaron, Bosworth, and Burtless conclude that "the accumulation of large social security surpluses presents a unique opportunity to increase the depressed saving rate of the United States.[2] We think it important to use this opportunity." I say, "Amen." The Gramm-Rudman-Hollings deficit targets should be redefined to exclude the social security trust funds. My goal would be a full employment balanced budget plus a social security surplus so that the government becomes a net contributor to national saving.

Testing for Economic and Political Effects of Social Security Funding

A Commentary by Arthur T. Denzau

The two chapters by W. Mark Crain and Michael L. Marlow and by Alicia H. Munnell and C. Nicole Ernsberger address a critical question for evaluating public policies toward the social security trust fund surpluses: What is the empirical link between social security and the federal budget? And thus what is the effect of social security on national saving? While others have been content to speculate on this, these economists have pored through the data to try to develop a way of quantifying the answers. Crain and Marlow examine the historical experience in the United States, while Munnell and Ernsberger examine the historical experience in Japan, Sweden, and Canada. Because the empirical work is not definitive, the findings must be viewed as preliminary; they warrant our careful attention nonetheless.

The two chapters arrive at quite different policy conclusions, and at this point I am not sure which one is more convincing. In the elaborate statistical approach used in chapter 6, powerful technique almost substitutes for good argumentation. In the simpler presentation-of-the-data approach used in chapter 5, three cases are discussed, and lessons are drawn for the United States. The strength of the latter argument, however, is clouded by the implicit assumptions used. In both cases the empirical arguments are not well developed. Before getting to the specifics, I first suggest a general framework for analyzing differences that are found in empirical data, whether in the results of different studies or in the observations of a single study.

Inconsistencies in empirical work can be caused by differences of two sorts. First, the underlying realities being studied can themselves differ. This is the case in any comparative study such as Munnell-Ernsberger. There may be different social institutions, for example, that establish the rules of the game, such as the constitutional framework within which year-by-year government decisions are made. Canada,

Sweden, and Japan have parliamentary governments, unlike the United States, and this may be a reason for the difference between the results they report and those reported by Crain and Marlow.

There may also be different government and private organizations that are directly involved in the determination of the variables. Three key factors may be relevant for interpreting the Munnell-Ernsberger results. One, which the authors highlight, is the separation of responsibilities between the government finance minister and the administration of the pension fund. Generally there is more separation in the countries studied than in the United States. Another is the degree of discipline or responsibility of legislative parties, which is considerably greater in the countries studied than in the United States. Finally, there is the degree of control that pension fund managers have over the investment of the funds. Some countries have few constraints on allowable investments, while in the United States the social security trust funds are invested wholly in U.S. federal bonds.

The underlying realities may also differ because of cultural differences that affect voters' tastes. Munnell and Ernsberger did not consider this possibility although it is likely to be important given the countries studied, particularly in relation to the United States. The tastes of voters affect what is politically possible and what is politically rewarded—in other words, the cost/benefit ratio for career politicians.

All of these factors may be important in generating the different results reported by Munnell and Ernsberger. Isolating them empirically is the key to understanding but may be almost impossible to accomplish. A larger set of countries, with greater variation in the key factors, would help. Even in the larger sample, however, there may be so much collinearity in the variables that it is impossible to distinguish causal factors.

Inconsistencies in empirical results, such as those noted by Crain and Marlow in previous studies on taxing and spending, can also be caused by differences in the variables used, the statistical technique used, or the specification of the statistical model. Slight differences in highly collinear variables, for example, can generate drastically different results. As time series variables are usually very collinear, one must take great care in examining the choice of variables. In addition the period or the jurisdictions analyzed can differ. Adding or removing a single year from a data series, for example, may be the cause of a significant shift in results, especially if there has been a structural change in the underlying reality.

Specific to chapter 6 by Crain and Marlow my first concern is that the period chosen is inadequately discussed. Fiscal year data for the period 1940 to 1987 is used. There are several problems with this sample. First, structural changes during the sample period would make the time series nonstationary. Disability insurance, for example, was introduced in the 1950s, and Medicare was introduced in the 1960s. The 1970s brought indexation of benefits. Finally, the early 1980s ushered in the beginning of an attempt to run substantial trust fund surpluses. How can the data on social security tax revenues be stationary with such large changes in the nature of the programs? Also, any statistical analysis is affected greatly by data points that contain more information than others: these are the outliers. In this regard, there was World War II, along with two other wars. Surely these events affected federal revenue and spending patterns enormously and may well dominate the results.

A second problem is the specification of the time series used. Three of four possible aggregates were used: social security spending, non-social-security spending, and non-social-security revenue. Why not use social security revenues? Perhaps this is an identity given the definition of the other variables, but this was unclear in the essay. Possibly more important, why not use separate variables for each of the three social security trust funds? Each could be analyzed separately by intervention analysis, a method that would also deal with some of the other problems mentioned above.

Third, although time trend problems in the data were corrected, one remaining problem was the business cycle. Cyclicality is not a time trend phenomenon and could not be removed by the techniques employed. Without further study one cannot tell whether the results are merely the spurious result of cyclical phenomena.

Fourth, logs of the variables were used. This raises the question of how negative changes in spending and taxes were handled, which would affect the results.

Finally, Crain and Marlow discuss only the statistical significance of their results, not the importance or relative size of these results. We do not know, for example, whether a measured effect amounts to .0001 percent or 50 percent of federal spending, only that the effect is statistically significant. We are told about two apparently contradictory findings pertaining to the effect of social security revenues and fund balances on non-social-security spending: increasing rates of growth of balances reduces the rate of growth of spending, while increasing rates of growth of social security revenues increases it. What is the net effect? Is it positive or negative? How important is it?

Regarding the Munnell and Ernsberger chapter, the primary difficulty with a study of this type is that it is not possible to assess the relative contribution of key institutional factors, such as accounting conventions or the administrative separation of the trust funds from the general revenues, to the results reported, let alone the contribution of acknowledged differences between countries. Would a different sample of countries with the same institutions have produced the same results? Can these results be applied to the United States?

Answers to these questions require tests on a statistical sample of countries, based on an underlying theory. Comparative work on only three jurisdictions does not allow one to draw policy conclusions for one's own country. The results reported by Munnell and Ernsberger are consistent with a number of alternative hypotheses.

What is needed to advance this empirical effort is not just better statistical tests but some serious attention to developing a theory of the relationship between spending and taxation decisions. The literature on the decision making of Congress is well developed and can support this type of effort. This literature is not in economics, however; it is in political science. In addition, the political scientists contributing to this literature espouse rational choice, which is the essence of economic models.

A new branch of this analysis of congressional decision making is due to research by a colleague at Washington University, John Gilmour. He is analyzing framing effects in politics. Economists generally attempt to look beyond the way policy questions are framed by politicians to analyze the actual impacts of policies. This generates a sometimes cynical view of politicians and ignores an important point: how one frames an issue in political decision making matters. Ignoring how issues are framed can make it difficult to understand how political issues are being decided and why.

Without considering framing, the Gramm-Rudman budget control system might seem a bizarre jury-rigged device created by Rube Goldberg. But the system forces Congress, as almost no other method does, to deal explicitly with the overall deficit consequences of their taxing and spending choices. It forces members to vote up or down on changing the deficit. If its discipline is enforced, increased spending on any specific program requires spending reductions elsewhere or a tax increase. Making such trade-offs explicit changes the way the issues are perceived by the voting public and the mass media and therefore is likely to change political choices. Economists may say that the trade-offs are ever-present and that the usual procedure for voting on spending increases simply means that some time later the budget costs of the program will be acknowledged. But not everyone is an economist, nor does every voter have the time—or incentive—to analyze everything their political agents in Congress do, given the tiny probability that the voter can affect political choices. Framing effects are important in determining political choice, and the Munnell-Ernsberger chapter would have benefited from the inclusion of a model of this or other political phenomena.

PART FOUR

Future Directions for Policy

7

Managing the Variability of the Social Security Balances with the Personal Income Tax

Lawrence B. Lindsey

Under the current set of economic and demographic assumptions used by policy makers, the U.S. social security program (Old-Age, Survivors, and Disability Insurance) is projected to run substantial surpluses during the 1990s and continuing through the first quarter of the twenty-first century.[1] Beginning in the 2030s, however, the program is projected to begin running substantial deficits. These deficits are projected to grow markedly, consuming by mid-century all the previously accumulated funds. This enormous fluctuation in the cash flow position of social security derives from a decision by policy makers to abandon effectively pay-as-you-go financing in the face of prospective demographic changes.

When introduced in 1935, social security was billed as an insurance program with a strong link between the taxes paid by individuals and the benefits they ultimately received. This original conceptualization of social security, which implied some substantial advance funding of future liabilities, rapidly evolved into one holding that rising real benefits for retirees could be financed by the rising real wages of workers.

Paul Samuelson and others provided the conceptual framework for this approach arguing that a growing economy could sustain benefits to each generation of retirees that greatly exceeded the taxes paid by that generation.[2] Under this pay-as-you-go model, benefit payments to retirees would be financed by the taxes paid by those currently working.

I am grateful to the National Bureau of Economic Research for the use of its TAXSIM model. I would also like to thank Andrew Mitrusi and John Navratil for their assistance in researching this material.

The sustainability of a public pension program financed on a pay-as-you-go basis is predicated on a stable or growing population. Unfortunately, recent demographic experience has not conformed to this population pattern. Instead, the United States experienced a rapid rise in the birthrate in the 1950s, after having experienced a rapid decline in the 1930s, before experiencing a rapid decline in the 1970s.

In the short run, these trends will increase the number of working-aged people relative to the number of retirees. In the late 1990s, for example, the number of people aged twenty-five to sixty-four will increase at an annual rate of 9.0 per thousand, whereas the number aged sixty-five and over will increase at the rate of only 7.7 per thousand.[3] In other words, the number of working-aged people will rise 17 percent faster than the number of people of retirement age. When the children of the 1950s retire, however, the wage base per retiree will begin to shrink, depressing real rates of return on tax payments and undermining the financing of social security.

Under the pay-as-you-go model, the rise in the number of workers per retiree in the 1990s would offer two possibilities. Either real benefits could be increased or the social security tax rate could be reduced. In the longer term, the rapid rise in the number of beneficiaries relative to workers in the twenty-first century would require either a sharp reduction in future real benefits or a dramatic rise in the payroll tax.

The 1983 Social Security Amendments moved toward partial reserve funding, ameliorating somewhat the necessary adjustments in social security. The legislation did nothing, however, to reduce the problem of managing fiscal policy in the context of rapid swings in the demands on social security.

Three major challenges remain. First, surpluses in the social security trust funds during the 1990s and early in the twenty-first century may tempt policy makers to run larger deficits in the rest of the budget than they otherwise would, thus depressing national saving. Second, even if the surpluses are not spent on other budget items, the purchase of assets by the social security trust funds may not increase national saving or investment. The accumulated funds are invested only in U.S. Treasury securities and thus can increase domestic investment only if the purchase of private assets is "crowded-in" because of a lower public sector borrowing rate. Alternatively, taxpayers may feel wealthier because of the lower public debt and therefore increase their consumption. Third, even if these problems can be worked out, social security will still face major deficits and ultimately an exhausted reserve fund. The Medicare or Hospital Insurance (HI) trust fund will be exhausted much sooner.

This chapter considers the efficacy of managing these problems by using the personal income tax system and a tax-based incentive program for saving. Such a program, termed Individual Saving Accounts (ISAs), could substantially alleviate the problems now facing fiscal policy planners as a result of the social security system. As this study reveals, the present income tax system is an enormously productive revenue source, particularly after long periods of sustained economic growth. In addition, under current trends, the aged population of the mid–twenty-first century will be quite wealthy by today's standards and will be making substantial income tax payments. These facts suggest that the existing income tax system may already possess some of the fiscal solutions to the long-term problem of income security for the aged.

The first section of this chapter evaluates the personal income tax as a revenue producer and income redistributor through the middle of the next century. The second section discusses the design of an ISA program and its likely effects on the level and timing of tax revenues to the government. The third section presents a set of simulations illustrating the impact of the ISA program on tax revenue, social security, and the incomes of the aged. The final section examines the combined effects of rising income tax revenue, the ISA program, and the long-term social security outlook on fiscal policy options in the first half of the twenty-first century.

The Income Tax over the Long Term

In the midst of current concerns about the federal budget deficit, we often forget that the federal income tax is a potent revenue producer, particularly during long periods of economic growth. Every 1 percent increase in real per capita income produces an additional 1.5 percent in real tax revenue.[4] In addition, the income tax system keeps pace, point for point, with both inflation and the growth in the working-age population. The power of the income tax can be seen by extrapolating revenue over the next five years, the federal government's budget horizon. Assuming 3 percent real economic growth (1.2 percent due to labor force growth and 1.8 percent due to a rise in real per capita incomes), real income tax revenue will grow at 3.9 percent per year. After five years we will have 21 percent more real income tax revenue than today, or roughly $80 billion in today's dollars. By that time, the excess growth of the income tax, above and beyond the growth in the economy, will amount to $6 billion annually. Over the sixty-year period considered here, this effect can be truly staggering.

To estimate the revenue effects of the income tax, we used the National Bureau of Economic Research TAXSIM program, which projected the path of income tax revenue into the next century. This computerized model, like those used by the Department of Treasury and the Joint Committee on Taxation, relies on a large disaggregated data base of actual tax returns. The model uses the short-term macroeconomic forecast employed by the Office of Management and Budget in preparing the federal budget to simulate the level and distribution of tax revenue for 1990 and the Social Security Administration's intermediate II-B economic and demographic assumptions to project events thereafter.[5]

It should be stressed that the resulting revenue figures are projections based on a long-term economic forecast and are quite sensitive to the assumptions used. A sustained drop of 0.5 percent in the annual rate of economic growth between 1990 and 2050, for example, implies an economy 26 percent smaller at the end of the period than would otherwise have been the case. Holding the tax system constant, it also implies that personal income tax collections will be 36 percent smaller in 2050.

Economic science has not developed sufficiently to make forecasts over many decades with any degree of confidence. Some scholars have expressed strong doubts about the government's economic and demographic assumptions. Aaron, Bosworth, and Burtless, for example, express deep reservations about the real interest rate and productivity growth assumptions used in the II-B intermediate projections.[6] They note, for instance, that while productivity growth in the period between 1975 and 1985 was only half that between 1946 and 1973, the II-B projections assume a sustained productivity increase at roughly the 1946–1973 pace.

We nevertheless rely on the II-B assumptions since our basic conclusion that social security should not be considered in isolation does not vary with the economic assumptions employed in the modeling process. In addition, the parameters for which sensitivity analysis would be useful are too numerous, and too interdependent, to make such an analysis within the scope of this chapter. By using the Social Security Administration's assumptions, we can compare our findings directly with the official projections.

The enormous revenue-producing power of the federal income tax is illustrated in figure 7–1. The figure presents the expected path of income tax returns, real adjusted gross income (AGI) per return, and real tax payments per return for the period 1990–2050. In each case, 1990 is given a value of 100 for comparison purposes. Over the sixty-year period illustrated, the number of tax returns is projected to increase by about 27 percent. More than three quarters of this growth occurs before 2020, with decade increases in returns of 9 million during

FIGURE 7–1

GROWTH IN INCOME, TAXES, AND TAX RETURNS, FOR ALL TAXPAYERS,
1990–2050
(1990 = 100)

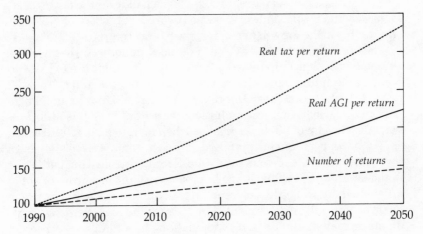

SOURCE: NBER TAXSIM Model.

the next two decades, slowing to 4.6 million during the 2010s, 2.9 million during the 2020s, and to virtually no growth thereafter. The reason for the projected slowing is that during the 2020s and 2030s the children of the "baby-bust" generation of the 1970s will start entering the labor force and thus start filing tax returns; at the same time, the individuals born during the baby boom of the 1950s will be dying. The combined effect is likely to be a marked slowing in the rate of growth of tax returns after 2030.

Aggregate real AGI, the definition of income used for income tax purposes, will nearly triple during these sixty years, reflecting a 1.76 percent annual rate of growth of personal income. Most of this growth reflects a growth in per capita income. Real AGI per tax return will grow 1.36 percent during this period. Stated differently, each taxpayer in 2050 will have a real income that is roughly two and a quarter times that enjoyed by taxpayers in 1990.

While income will nearly triple during this period, real tax payments will nearly quadruple. Assuming no changes in the tax law, taxes will rise automatically from 14.0 percent of AGI in 1990 to 21.3 percent in 2050—more than 50 percent. The reason for this is the revenue-producing power of the income tax. As real income rises, a greater percentage of income is taxed at higher tax rates. The result is a rise in the ratio of taxes to income. In the past, when inflation was the cause of the rise in the tax share of income, this effect was called "bracket creep." Under current tax law, which indexes the tax brackets to the consumer price index, all of the rise in the tax share of income is attributable to the growth of real income per tax return.

Historically, tax rates have been reduced periodically to offset the automatic rise in taxation. Two factors suggest that this is less likely to occur in the future. First, the maximum tax rate now in the law is 33 percent, with the vast majority of the public paying no more than 28 percent at the margin. Pressure for rate reductions from this historically modest level will not be as great as when marginal tax rates reached 50, 70, or 91 percent and promised to reach punitive levels for even moderate income taxpayers over time. Second, because the entire rise in the tax share of income is attributable to real income growth, not to inflation, there will be less pressure to take offsetting action. The rise in the tax share will be accompanied by a rise in the real after-tax income of the taxpaying, and voting, population. In addition, the pace of bracket creep induced by real growth is relatively modest, so that sharp, highly visible, and politically embarrassing increases in tax shares are not likely to occur.

Even if tax rate reductions are enacted, it is highly unlikely that they will be enough to eliminate the growth in real tax revenue. A more likely event is that the revenue windfall will be used to finance increased government spending, including social security spending. The magnitude of this windfall can be seen by comparing the amount of personal income taxes that will be collected in 2050 with the amount that would be collected if taxes as a share of AGI were to remain at its 1990 level of 14 percent. Rather than remaining constant, taxes as a share of AGI are expected to rise 7.3 percent to 21.3 percent in 2050, or $711 billion annually in real 1990 dollars. This revenue windfall is equal to two-thirds of total federal revenue collections from all sources in 1990 and is three and a half times the size of the real social security deficit projected for 2050.

If we assume that spending on programs other than social security keeps pace with economic growth, then income tax revenues will be so substantial that they will generate a surplus in the rest of the budget capable of completely offsetting the deficit in social security. This does not necessarily mean that income tax revenues should or need to be used to fund social security. In fact, social security reserves are projected to be sufficient to cover the deficit throughout the entire sixty-year period. This extra income tax revenue means that management of fiscal policy in the middle of the twenty-first century need not be made particularly difficult by the social security deficit and the resulting liquidation of reserves. There will be no need to sell the Treasury securities held by the trust funds to the public, which would strain fiscal management and create intense competition for the existing pool of saving. Instead, the Treasury securities can simply be retired.

It should be stressed that this is a theoretical possibility, not a prediction or endorsement of this course of action. This scenario entails a rapid expansion of the income tax relative to other revenue sources and a consequent redistribution of the federal tax burden. It is also based on the simplistic assumption that non-social-security programs will grow, on average, at the same rate as the economy. Arguments can be made either that such growth is insufficient to keep pace with a growing demand for public goods or that the implied tripling in the real size of government is excessive. The observation regarding the revenue-producing power of the income tax is made simply to point out that sufficient funds exist within the current tax framework to offset any deficit in the social security system over the time horizons now being considered.

Complicating this analysis is a fundamental change in the generational burden of the income tax in the next six decades. Figure 7–2 illustrates the rise in the number of returns, real AGI per return, and real tax payments per return for taxpayers who are sixty-five and over. The contrast with the first figure, which showed these trends for all taxpayers, is striking. The number of taxpayers sixty-five and over will more than double over the next six decades. As a result, most of the growth in the number of tax returns will be among taxpayers sixty-five and over, who will file 16 million of the 28 million additional returns.

Similar growth will occur in the share of income and the share of taxes paid by taxpayers over sixty-five. The share of AGI received by taxpayers over sixty-five will grow from 11 percent to 21 percent, and the share of taxes paid by this group will rise at roughly the same pace. Income per tax return and taxes per return will grow slightly faster for taxpayers over sixty-five than for the population as a whole. One important reason for this is the way in which social security benefits are taxed. Under the 1983 Social Security Amendments, half the benefits are taxable for individuals with AGIs over $25,000 ($32,000 for married couples). The thresholds are not indexed for inflation and thus will decline in value over time. Whereas in 1990, roughly $23 billion of social security benefits will be included in AGI, by 2050, the figure will be $253 billion in real 1990 dollars, or eleven times higher. The benefits of the great majority of social security recipients will be included in AGI even assuming that Congress does not increase the portion of

153

FIGURE 7–2

GROWTH IN INCOME, TAXES, AND TAX RETURNS FOR TAXPAYERS
SIXTY-FIVE AND OVER, 1990–2050
(1990 = 100)

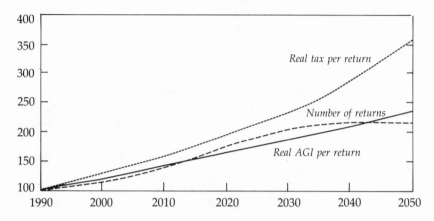

SOURCE: NBER TAXSIM Model.

benefits subject to taxation. Taxable benefits will rise from 5 percent of the AGI of the elderly in 1990 to 12 percent of their AGI in 2050.

The data also make clear that the real incomes of the elderly in 2050 will be quite high by today's standards. Figure 7–3 shows the distribution of real incomes for taxpayers sixty-five and over in 1990 and 2050. In 1990, 42 percent of elderly taxpayers have incomes under $15,000. By 2050, that share will shrink to 4 percent even after controlling for the effects of inflation. By contrast, the share of elderly taxpayers with real incomes over $50,000 will grow from 14 percent in 1990 to 48 percent in 2050. The number of elderly taxpayers with real incomes over $200,000 will grow thirteenfold over the same period. The reason for this is the rapid increase in the real incomes of all Americans assumed under the Social Security Administration's intermediate II-B projection. While the relative position of the elderly in the income distribution will change little, the entire population will be enjoying a considerably higher standard of living.

The rapid rise in the real incomes of elderly Americans raises three questions regarding the maintenance of social security as a transfer program at its current scale. First, is it fair to ask workers in the 1990s to contribute to the buildup of a social reserve for the payment of benefits

154

FIGURE 7–3

DISTRIBUTION OF REAL INCOMES FOR TAXPAYERS SIXTY-FIVE AND
OVER, 1990 AND 2050
(thousands of 1990 dollars)

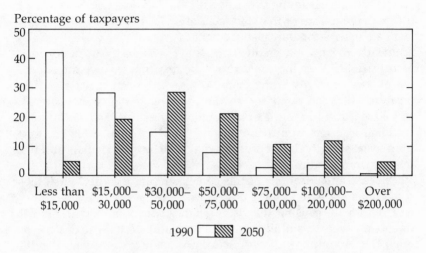

SOURCE: NBER TAXSIM Model.

in the middle of the next century? The typical retiree in 2050 will be enjoying a higher real income than the typical worker in 1990. Under these assumptions, an intertemporal transfer from the worker to the retiree makes little sense under most assumptions of social welfare maximization. Instead, a pay-as-you-go based reduction in social security taxes would seem the better course of action.

Second, will a massive program of transfers to the elderly be seen as necessary in 2050 as it was when the social security system was begun early in this century?

Third, will the rapid rise in income tax revenue generated by upper-income elderly Americans be sufficient to allow income safety net programs for the elderly to be financed without resort to massive intergenerational transfers? The recently repealed catastrophic care provisions of Medicare, for example, were to be financed largely by an income tax surcharge on elderly Americans who, as a group, were to benefit from the program. Total income tax collections from elderly Americans are expected to exceed $430 billion (in real 1990 dollars) in 2050, up from $55 billion in 1990. The funds clearly exist for using a within-generation transfer approach for other types of income security needs, although the experience with catastrophic care has shown us

155

that any such program must be structured with a sensitivity to political realities and perceptions.

This section has demonstrated that the current income tax is capable of producing sufficient revenue to offset projected shortfalls in social security, assuming expansion of non-social-security spending in line with the total growth of the economy. This prospect would greatly facilitate macroeconomic management by minimizing the federal government's reliance on credit markets. (The capacity to offset social security deficit with income tax revenue need not involve direct funding of social security with income taxes.) This section has also demonstrated that the rapid rise in the incomes of the elderly, and the consequent rise in their tax payments, reduces the need for intergenerational transfers to provide income security. As a result, the long-term social security deficit problem may well be more manageable than many current studies suggest.

Several qualifications of this conclusion are in order. First, these projections are based on the critical assumption that the government will refrain from using the rising share of income paid in taxes to finance an ever-expanding government relative to the size of the economy. This assumption allows for real growth in government spending but not for real growth beyond the rate of real economic growth. Given that roughly half of all non-social-security expenditures are for defense and that the defense share of gross national product (GNP) seems likely to decline in the foreseeable future, this does not seem like an overly restrictive assumption.

Second, these projections assume that SSA's intermediate II-B path of economic growth will be maintained. A substantial reduction in the rate of economic growth over the next sixty years from that assumed here will produce a very sharp drop in projected income tax revenues.[7] The management of the fiscal difficulties caused by social security, in turn, would be far less tractable.

Third, the analysis of this chapter is limited to the retirement and disability components of the social security system. Under current economic and demographic assumptions, the Medicare component will be in substantial deficit well before the social security component, possibly early in the next century. This will probably require an increased burden, financed either through taxes or through private insurance, which will likely be borne at least in part by the elderly population.

It should be noted that the use of income tax revenues to offset the long-term social security deficit does not solve two other problems with the system: fiscal management in the face of wide swings in social security balances and the need to increase domestic saving and investment rates. As a result, consideration of a supplementary ISA program is in order.

Individual Savings Accounts and Fiscal Policy

The concept of a tax-favored savings program is not new to tax policy. Pension programs, and retirement savings programs generally, have been in existence for many years. These programs became quite common after the passage of the Economic Recovery Tax Act of 1981, which extended Individual Retirement Account (IRA) eligibility to all working Americans. Under this program, taxpayers could make tax-free contributions to an account in which the funds could accumulate interest, dividends, and capital gains, tax free. Taxes were levied only when the funds were withdrawn from the account. The Tax Reform Act of 1986 sharply reduced access to IRAs. Only taxpayers who do not have other pension plans or who earn less than $25,000 ($40,000 if married) can make a fully deductible contribution to an IRA.

A broadening of the IRA concept to restore eligibility to all working Americans and to permit withdrawals under more circumstances offers one route to both increasing the national saving rate and managing the prospective swings in the social security balances in the next century. Such a liberalized program, an ISA program, would allow unlimited contributions to accounts that are tax favored in the same way as IRAs. To make saving more attractive, investors could withdraw their funds without any penalty beyond the normal tax due on withdrawal, provided the funds were deposited for at least four years.

The advantages to the individual of such a program are twofold. First, the taxpayer's tax rate while working and contributing to the account is likely to be greater than at the time of withdrawal. If this is the case, the ISA is clearly preferable to the ordinary savings account. Even if it is not, however, contributing to the ISA still might be preferable. The reason is that the ISA permits tax-free accumulation of interest.

The advantage of tax-free interest accumulation can be very powerful. One dollar invested at 8 percent interest grows to $4.66 in twenty years. If taxed at withdrawal at a rate of, say 28 percent, the taxpayer is left with $3.36. If, however, taxes are paid on the initial dollar contributed and each year on the interest earnings, the taxpayer is left with only $2.21, or 34 percent less after twenty years.

To date, analyses of individual savings account programs have focused on the present value of the tax savings to the taxpayer, described above. Often neglected are the implications for the timing of tax revenue from the perspective of the government. In the case just described, the use of an ISA lowers the government's revenue by twenty-eight cents the year the dollar is deposited into the account and by a few cents each year that the interest is compounded tax free; it then increases the government's revenue by $1.30 when the funds are withdrawn. The present value of the taxes received when the funds are withdrawn is twenty-eight cents, exactly equal to the taxes forgone when the funds are deposited in the account. Given the upcoming fiscal imbalances caused by the social security system, the intertemporal reallocation of government revenue becomes an important issue. The cost to the government of shifting tax receipts through time by this type of mechanism is the forgone taxes on the accruing interest.

It is important to stress that the transfer of revenue over time does not leave the present value of government revenue unchanged. Let us assume, for example, that the government must borrow at the same interest rate at which the individual must lend. Then, in the case just described, the present value of the revenue lost (in the form of the tax benefits offered by a twenty-year ISA program) amounts to twenty-five cents on each dollar invested in the program.

It is important to put this loss in perspective, however. Our prior analysis presumed that the government borrowed at the same interest rate at which the ISA money was invested. This is an overly restrictive assumption. If the individual is able to earn a higher return on the ISA than the one at which the government must borrow, then the present value of tax revenue may run in the government's favor. If, for example, the government must borrow at 8 percent to fund the forgone taxes on the ISA but the individual is earning 10 percent in the ISA account, then both the government and the individual are better off than if the investment were not made in the first place.

Why might we presume that individuals can lend, in an ISA, at a higher rate than the rate at which the government borrows? The principal reason is risk. The return on both corporate equities and corporate debt is now higher than the return on Treasury bonds of the same maturity. In addition, the very nature of ISAs entails a long-term investment perspective relative to other investments, also implying a higher return.

In sum, an individual savings account program would have several advantages for both the individual and the economy. The program would result in large initial revenue losses during the 1990s and early twenty-first century, which would, from the perspective of the federal government, offset the surpluses in social security. Later, when these funds were removed from the ISAs, the incomes of retired individuals would be raised, producing income tax revenue for the government.

This would occur at the same time that social security would be running large deficits. The ISA program would thus provide a means of redirecting income taxes intertemporally, transferring government tax receipts from a period of surplus to a period of deficits while ensuring that those funds are saved and invested in high-yielding assets.

Of course, an ISA program is not essential for fiscal management. One alternative is to keep the budget excluding social security roughly balanced, or at a relatively constant deficit relative to GNP, and allow the large swings in the social security balances to dominate the net fiscal position of the government. This alternative would imply large fiscal surpluses in the 1990s and the early twenty-first century followed by large deficits thereafter. The large fiscal surpluses would depress real interest rates and thus discourage domestic saving during the peak earning and saving years of the baby-boom generation. This is likely to produce a smaller long-run capital stock and consequently a lower long-run GNP than would a high saving policy during this same time. As the rest of the Western world experiences a similar demographic shift, America's public sector, and by extension the country as a whole, would become a net saving nation at the very time the world is awash in saving. The reversal of this net saving position later in the century would come at the very time saving is dearest. An ISA program would minimize these unprofitable swings in the fiscal position of the government and the adverse impacts on national saving behavior.

A second alternative is to return to pay-as-you-go financing of social security. This would ensure the long-run fiscal neutrality of the trust fund balances but allow the government's share of the economy to expand or contract according to the needs of social security. The major advantage in this approach is that it would allow a reduction in payroll taxes in the 1990s. But pay-as-you-go financing necessarily implies that short-term adjustments are left to the political process. Benefit increases, possibly in the health area, are at least as likely as tax reductions. The long-run sustainability of such benefit increases is open to serious question. They would necessitate either a significant increase in the intergenerational distortions now in the system or a dramatic increase in taxes as the twenty-first century progresses. A pay-as-you-go financed system that did not result in higher benefits would still require benefit reductions or tax increases, or both, in the twenty-first century.

A final alternative is to reduce social security tax rates and long-range benefit levels. This would move the system into balance by lowering both the near-term surplus and the long-term deficit. This alternative is attractive as a possible supplement to the ISA program. Current workers would be informed that they face lower benefits than

159

previously scheduled and would have more take-home-pay with which to provide for their retirement. In addition, the ISA program would encourage retirement saving. While clearly enhancing the advantages of the ISA program, such a proposal is politically less likely to be accepted than a simple ISA arrangement by itself.

Simulations of the Effect of ISAs

To simulate the effects of ISAs on the path of tax revenue, we developed a multigenerational model of population, income, and savings, which follows SSA's intermediate II-B economic assumptions. Each population cohort was assigned a level of income based on its age, the projected wages in the population for the year in question, and the historic pattern of relative wages for workers of that age to the national average.

The flow of savings from each group was based on average savings rates as reported by Aaron, Bosworth, and Burtless.[8] For these simulations, we assumed that half of all positive financial savings by cohorts aged thirty-five and over would be deposited in ISAs. It should be noted that this modeling of net contributions by cohorts produces substantially lower contributions than modeling net saving by individuals. This occurs because, on a cohort basis, the borrowing by individuals who do not save is assumed to offset the accumulation by those who do.

We also assumed no net increase in personal saving, simply a transfer of saving from ordinary investment vehicles to ISAs. Thus the high fraction of saving deposited in the ISA is attributable to a rearrangement of assets, not to a change in lifetime consumption or saving behavior. It should be noted, however, that any net saving that might occur would have zero present value revenue consequences since the present value of the tax on withdrawal just offsets the tax forgone when the funds are contributed to the ISA.

Withdrawals from the ISA program were assumed to begin at age sixty-five and to end at age eighty. Thus one-fifteenth of the accumulation of any cohort in the ISA was disbursed in each year the cohort was over age sixty-five. Remaining funds continued to accumulate interest and dividends. Thus, the total amount of funds withdrawn from the program during retirement are higher than the total amount of funds accumulated in the program by age sixty-five.

The tax consequences of such saving were estimated using NBER's TAXSIM model. In each year, the savings flowing into ISAs were apportioned among taxpayers under age sixty-five of different income classes based on the share of liquid wealth in that income class. The

FIGURE 7–4

TAX EFFECTS OF ISA PROVISIONS, 1990–2050

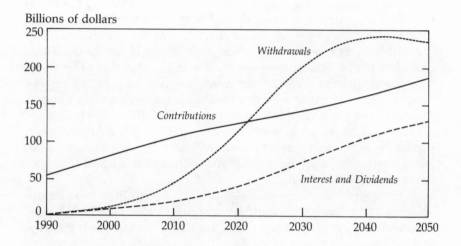

Billions of dollars

SOURCE: NBER TAXSIM Model.

distribution of the income tax effects of the ISA program were allowed to evolve over time as the underlying income distribution in the country changed. The withdrawals from the system were allocated according to the liquid wealth of taxpayers over age sixty-five in each income class.

Three key tax effects of ISAs were considered: the revenue forgone because of the tax deductibility of initial contributions, the revenue forgone because of the tax-free accumulation of earnings, and the revenue gain because of the taxation of funds at withdrawal. The effects of the ISA program were simulated to begin in 1990 and to continue indefinitely.

The impact of each of these tax effects over the next sixty years is presented in figure 7–4. In each case, the revenue impact is expressed in terms of real 1990 dollars. As the figure shows, the revenue consequences of contributions grow gradually over time. Underlying this trend is a very rapid percentage growth early in the program and a slower growth later. When the proportion of the population in the high-savings years, ages forty to sixty-five, is growing rapidly, contributions grow faster than overall income. This is especially true in the first decade of the program, when real contributions grow 44 percent.

The growth rate of savings slows precipitously in the 2010s and 2020s—to just 9 percent per decade in real terms—when the baby-bust generation of the 1970s is of prime saving age.

The tax consequences of withdrawals are small during the 1990s and the early part of the twenty-first century as the baby-boom generation accumulates its savings in the program. The extra taxes generated by withdrawals accelerate rapidly and ultimately equal the taxes forgone because of contributions shortly after 2020. After that point, there is a substantial net revenue gain from the program. In 2040, for example, the tax collected on withdrawals will exceed the taxes forgone because of new contributions by more than $90 billion in 1990 dollars. That is roughly equal to the real social security deficit for that year under the same set of economic assumptions. (The social security deficit is nominally $651 billion compared with the tax surplus from the ISA program of $644 billion.)

The government, however, also forgoes income from taxes on dividends and interest that would have been collected had the ISA program not been in place. The growth in these forgone taxes is roughly proportional to the stock of funds in the program. By 2040, these forgone taxes will exceed $100 billion (in real 1990 dollars). Some 40 percent of the interest and dividend income received by individuals in 2040 will accrue to funds invested in this program. On net, therefore, this program will make a positive contribution to deficit reduction for only a few years around 2030. After that time the combined effect of the tax deductibility of new contributions and the tax exclusion on investment income exceeds the taxes collected on withdrawals from the program.

While the program described here exacerbates the fiscal policy problems the country will face after 2035, it provides a useful way of channeling the social security surpluses of the 1990s and the early part of the twenty-first century. The forgone revenue from the ISA program amounts to roughly 85 percent of the social security surplus in 1990, 65 percent in 2000, and 40 to 50 percent during the first two decades of the twenty-first century. As such, the ISA program offers a use of fiscal policy surpluses that contributes to national saving and creates for government a statutory claim to future revenues. Equally important, the ISA program creates for individuals a statutory claim to the future income streams that their savings will generate. The potentially large fiscal surpluses in the next few decades would be less available to finance current government consumption but would produce revenue later in the century when needed.

To fine-tune the program to meet the prospective fiscal policy crisis of the mid–twenty-first century, we consider two options. The

FIGURE 7–5

TAX EFFECTS OF ISA PROVISIONS WITH TERMINATION IN 2030, 1990–2050
(in billions of real 1990 dollars)

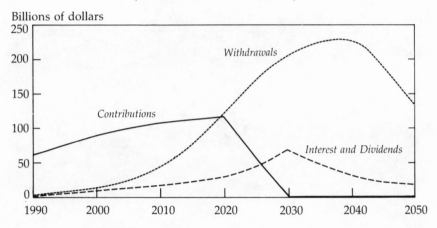

Billions of dollars

SOURCE: NBER TAXSIM Model.

first is to prohibit new contributions to the program beginning in 2030. The termination of contributions has three effects: (1) it eliminates the direct revenue lost on contributions; (2) it reduces the stock of funds ultimately in the program, thus lowering the forgone taxes on interest earnings; and (3) by lowering contributions, it ultimately reduces withdrawals and thereby depresses future tax revenue.

The results of terminating the program are shown graphically in figure 7–5. By eliminating $615 billion of real contributions in 2030, the program produces a surplus of roughly $130 billion in that year. By 2040, as withdrawals peak and the forgone revenue from the stock of funds in the program declines, the surplus reaches roughly $200 billion—over twice the social security deficit projected for that year. By 2050, when withdrawals are declining sharply, the program produces only $130 billion in real net revenue, $71 billion less than the social security deficit projected for that year.

The second option fine-tunes the program even more narrowly. In this case, new contributions are reduced by 50 percent in 2040 and are prohibited in 2050. This more gradual phase out eliminates the large surpluses associated with earlier termination. The ISA program results in a net surplus of nearly $70 billion in 2040 as the revenue cost of

163

FIGURE 7–6

TAX EFFECTS OF ISA PROVISIONS WITH 50 PERCENT LIMIT IN 2040 AND
CUT OFF IN 2050, 1990–2050
(in billions of real 1990 dollars)

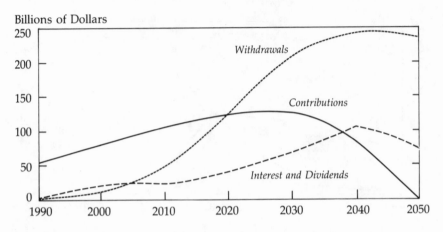

SOURCE: NBER TAXSIM Model.

contributions begins to decrease and a surplus of roughly $160 billion in 2050 as the revenue cost associated with contributions is eliminated. Figure 7–6 presents the tax consequences of this program in real 1990 dollars.

In practice, the fine-tuning of government programs half a century in the future is not particularly productive. Governments at that time will be able to gauge more closely the prospective deficits they face and will be able to adjust tax policy accordingly. This exercise demonstrates, however, that substantial amounts of revenue can be reallocated over time by allowing an up-front deduction for contributions to a savings plan and collecting taxes on the invested funds when they are withdrawn. As such, the income tax represents a potential mechanism for smoothing the fiscal policy fluctuations that are likely to occur with the interaction of demography and the social security system.

The Income Tax, the Social Security Deficit, and Fiscal Policy

This chapter has noted the enormous revenue-producing power of the federal income tax and the potential to use a savings program in conjunction with that tax to reallocate revenue over time. These factors are often overlooked in the discussion of the long-term implications of social security. When the income tax is considered in conjunction with social security, we can be optimistic that the government will be able to manage its long-term fiscal policy.

Traditionally, fiscal policy management has focused on the short-run management of aggregate demand, involving budget deficits in times of slack demand and budget surpluses in times of excess demand. Long-run fiscal policy should subsume these short-term macroeconomic fluctuations by considering the net position of the government's borrowing over the business cycle. In this regard, long-run fiscal policy should pursue two goals. The first is to raise the mean national saving rate. This can be done by minimizing the mean public sector borrowing requirement and fostering policies to encourage private saving. The second is to lower the long-term variability in public sector borrowing. This minimizes the variability of rates of capital formation and, in the case of open world trade, world capital flows.

Of these objectives, the first is least controversial but most difficult to attain. An increase in the mean rate of national saving requires a reduction in either public consumption or private consumption, or both. A tax-favored saving program, such as the ISA program described above, is one way of achieving such an increase in saving. Recent research shows that the IRA program in effect in the early 1980s did contribute to net national saving.[9] The 1990s appear to be a particularly fortuitous time to implement such a program as the baby-boom generation is just entering the traditional high-saving years.

It seems likely that the efficacy of such a program would be further enhanced if it were coupled with a short-term reduction in social security tax rates and a long-term reduction in social security benefits. The ISA program would provide the method, the lower tax rates would provide the means, and the reduction in long-term benefits would provide the objective for boosting personal saving.

The second objective of minimizing the variability of fiscal policy across business cycles is less directly beneficial but still provides several advantages to the nation. Swings between eras of budget surplus and deficit, other things equal, introduce a long-term cycle to real interest rates and thus to the attractiveness of capital formation. While such swings may be inevitable because of uncontrollable factors, such as the advent of new technologies, inducing further cyclicality through federal budget policy seems imprudent and unlikely to promote optimal rates of capital accumulation. In particular, demographically induced cycles should not be exaggerated by fiscal policies. Under current policy, social security surpluses coincide with periods of high private saving, and social security deficits coincide with periods of low private saving. If variable fiscal policy has any merit, it is to offset excesses in the private sector, not to enhance them.

Furthermore, political experience has shown that the variability of fiscal policy is unlikely to be symmetrical. Periods of large budget deficits are common, while continuing budget surpluses are infrequent. Establishing the principle of avoiding either deficit spending or surplus accumulation over the business cycle might well raise the long-term mean level of national saving as well as reduce its variability.

Again, the ISA program is designed to accomplish this goal. By depressing tax revenue in the near term and increasing tax revenue in the mid-twenty-first century, the ISA program can offset the scheduled variations in the financial position of social security. Augmenting such a program with short-term reductions in the social security tax rate and long-term reductions in benefits would also be helpful. With or without changes in social security, however, the most appropriate time to begin the ISA program is now, before the long-term variability of fiscal policy becomes established.

8
Controlling the Risks Posed by Advance Funding— Options for Reform

Carolyn L. Weaver

Social security and Medicare pose a staggering liability in the years ahead. The cost of benefits in the year 2025, when the retirement of the baby-boom is in full swing, is projected to be 21 percent of taxable payroll in the economy, up from 13 percent today.[1] In today's dollars, that amounts to some $900 billion annually. Between now and 2065, the social security actuaries' official long-range measuring period, the nation's giant retirement program is slated to spend $15 trillion (in present value terms). Counting Medicare, the projected liability is closer to $20–25 trillion. How this liability is met—indeed, whether it is met—will have a profound effect on individuals' retirement, saving, and insurance decisions; on families' living arrangements; on the nation's public finances; and, ultimately, on intergenerational wealth and equity.

Under the 1983 Social Security Amendments, the liability in the retirement program is scheduled to be met in the following way. The social security payroll tax, scheduled to peak in 1990 at 12.4 percent (Old-Age, Survivors, and Disability Insurance only, employee and employer combined), is projected to generate more revenues than necessary to meet benefits for the next twenty-five years. During this period, the trust funds will amass a large, interest-bearing reserve of U.S. government bonds. Interest earnings, together with tax income, are projected to keep the retirement program in surplus for another fifteen years. Beginning in 2030, when expenditures begin to outstrip tax and interest income, benefits are to be met by selling off the trust funds' bond holdings. Ultimately, when the children of the baby-boom generation are retiring, reserves are projected to be exhausted and the program insolvent. Medicare is financed in basically the same way,

167

only the projected surpluses are smaller, the deficits are larger, and the reserves are depleted more quickly.

Whether this financing arrangement makes sense is a matter of great concern. The question at hand is whether the advance funding of social security, as currently conceived, promotes national saving and economic growth and thereby enhances the affordability and security of future benefits. If not, what policies would promote these goals?[2]

I will argue that, without fundamental changes in the rules by which social security and federal budget decisions are made, the reserves now accumulating in the trust funds are unlikely to have lasting positive effects on the federal budget or on social security. Under current decision-making arrangements, any apparent saving through the social security system can be undermined by actions taken in the rest of the budget or even by subsequent actions involving social security. As a result, the financial condition of the trust funds is a poor indicator of the overall economic burden implied by social security in future decades. In effect, the trust funds are an accounting construct with little or no real economic import. To control the risks posed by advance funding, binding rules must be introduced to ensure that the social security surpluses are meaningfully saved for future years. Without such rules, the role of the government in accumulating and managing surplus funds should be reduced or eliminated.

The Economic Argument for Advance Funding

From an economic standpoint, it makes good sense to advance fund a pension program known to face a substantial and growing liability. Excess contributions invested in real capital help expand the productive capacity of the economy and increase real incomes in future decades. This lightens the burden of future pension benefits. In addition, interest helps defray the cost of future benefits, allowing for lower ultimate premiums.

Funding has another advantage, which is ensuring that pension participants recognize the cost implications of today's benefit promises. With a fully funded system, for example, where assets must cover accruing liabilities, increased benefit promises to present or future retirees must be met by increased premiums today. This ensures a degree of fiscal discipline that is largely absent in a pay-as-you-go system, where the cost of expansion can be deferred until the benefits come due.

A similar line of argument applies in the case of advance funding of a public pension system, where excess taxes are invested in government bonds rather than in private securities. As argued by Martin Feldstein, a strong proponent of advance funding, social security surpluses used to buy outstanding government debt from private investors add indirectly to the nation's real capital investment.[3] Private investors substitute new private securities for the government debt they relinquish, thus increasing the funds available for private investment. This, in turn, allows for increased capital formation and ultimately higher future real incomes with which to meet the cost of retirement benefits in the coming decades. Payroll taxes can be lower than otherwise because of the substantial interest accruing to the trust funds. Meanwhile, the income tax necessary to finance the interest payments need be no higher, since there is no change in the government's total indebtedness, only a change in the ownership of its debt from the public to the trust funds; money that would have been paid to private investors is paid to the trust funds instead. The total tax burden is thus lower as a result of advance funding.

Advance funding contrasts with pay-as-you-go financing, in which there is no reserve accumulation and no real capital backing up accumulating benefit promises. Benefits to future retirees must be met as they come due by increased taxes on future workers. In a very real sense, pay-as-you-go financing amounts to deficit financing, with wealth transferred from younger to older generations.

From this perspective, a shift toward advance funding, such as implied by the 1983 financing legislation, can potentially reverse some of the wealth transfers embodied in a pay-as-you-go system. With meaningful advance funding and real saving over time, a portion of workers' taxes—the extra taxes paid to accumulate the reserve—helps to finance their own future benefits. In Feldstein's words, advance funding in anticipation of the huge demographic bulge "eliminate[s] our dependence on a large tax increase self-imposed by future voters."[4]

Two critical assumptions underlie the expectation that economic benefits flow from advance funding. First, the social security surpluses result in a net reduction in outstanding federal debt held by the public: that is, there is net government saving. Second, net government saving translates into net national saving, with little or no offsetting reduction in private saving. Both statements must be true for advance funding to lead to aggregate welfare gains. While it is the responsiveness of private saving to changes in government saving on which economists generally focus, the assumption of net government saving also merits close attention.

The Contrast with Social Security

Unfortunately, upon closer scrutiny, the optimistic characterization of advance funding simply does not comport with the facts about social security.

For one thing, social security is not advance funded on a continuing basis, meaning that today's surpluses are not expected to result in a reserve fund that is maintained over time, nor is the program solvent over the long run. Large surpluses in the next twenty to thirty years, to the extent that they materialize, will be followed by even larger deficits in later decades. Trust fund reserves, projected to accumulate rapidly, will be drawn down as the baby-boom moves into retirement and exhausted as future cohorts retire. Social security is thus projected to be insolvent at the very time it faces an enormous continuing liability—one amounting to 16.7 percent of taxable payroll in 2050, as compared with 10.5 percent today, or nearly $1 trillion (in constant 1989 dollars) annually. Including Medicare, reserves will be depleted much more quickly and the liability will be substantially larger.

The primary implication is that the potential economic benefits of present financing arrangements are far more uncertain than might have been expected—both from the standpoint of the economy, or society as a whole, and from the standpoint of individuals contributing to the system. Just as the trust fund accumulations offer the potential for government saving (actually, for reduced government borrowing) that increases capital formation and future income and consumption, the depletion of trust fund assets in subsequent years brings with it the prospect of government borrowing that reduces capital formation and future income and consumption. In the end, there remains a very large unmet liability. Net welfare gains hinge on how long those surpluses last and how large they are relative to the deficits that follow, as well as on how solvency is ultimately restored: through tax increases, benefit cuts, or new federal borrowing. In the meantime, today's workers accept a lower standard of living on account of the extra payroll taxes necessary to build the reserve.

Second, social security complies with no funding rules, such as those imposed on private pension plans through the provisions of ERISA (the Employee Retirement Income Security Act). No legal requirement, for example, specifies that a certain level of reserves must be maintained against a portion of accruing liabilities or even that annual balance between spending and revenues must be maintained. The system can, and periodically does, operate with deficits and declining funding ratios. The reason is not just changes in the ratio of workers to beneficiaries or unexpected changes in the economy. Over the years, Congress has routinely increased benefits and met part of the cost by depleting reserves. The result has been wealth transfers from future generations to the present.

There is every reason to believe that Congress will take this route again as reserves begin to accumulate. The political pressures are strong to pay larger benefits to "particularly deserving" groups—whether aged widows, two-earner families, "notch babies," the incapacitated near-elderly, nonworking spouses, or any other group. And there is always Medicare, ever in need of a helping hand. The long-range Medicare deficit is so large that it alone could consume all available reserves and surplus funds in social security, rendering the entire system insolvent by 2030. Only the sheer unavailability of resources has arrested the expansion of the system since the early 1970s.

The primary implication is that, without a requirement in the law about necessary funding levels, there is every reason to believe that the social security reserves will be spent rather than saved. In this event, the extra payroll taxes levied today will underwrite an expansion of social security's long-range liability and the government's total indebtedness. A permanently higher structure of federal taxes is the likely result. As before, the economic benefits of advance funding are thus much more uncertain, with a reasonable prospect of very adverse outcomes. According to estimates by Michael Boskin, if the social security surpluses were fully dissipated through benefit increases, national saving would plummet over the next thirty years.[5]

Third, and more generally, no mechanism in the law ensures that the surpluses translate into meaningful saving—defined as a transfer of real resources from present to future generations. Under current law, all tax revenues not needed to meet current benefits are "invested" in new, special-issue government bonds. The trust funds are credited with a bond—an IOU from one part of the government to another—and the Treasury gets the cash. From the standpoint of the Treasury, this money is indistinguishable from any other money and is available to finance the general operations of the federal government. Only if Congress forgoes the opportunity to use the excess social security revenues to cut income or other federal taxes or to expand spending on other programs can the surpluses amount to net government saving. In other words, the surpluses must be devoted to retiring outstanding, publicly held debt.

The problem here is that the efficacy of the social security surpluses depends entirely on decisions made outside of social security, decisions regarding the rest of the budget. If the availability of surplus social security revenues relaxes fiscal restraint in the rest of the budget, the system's assets are effectively frittered away on current consumption. The $12 trillion reserve projected for the next century would amount to nothing more than social security's claim on the general fund of the Treasury—its accumulated spending authority—with no real capital backing up that claim.[6] And those huge interest payments, scheduled to amount to a quarter of trust fund income in the year 2020

($160 billion in constant 1989 dollars), would be an unprecedented drain on the federal budget. Rather than sums that would have been paid to private lenders, interest payments would amount to a new liability incurred on account of the trust fund buildup!

In this case, "advance funding" simply alters the mixture of taxes used to finance social security, from payroll taxes to general revenues, rather than lightening the overall burden. Wealth transfers toward present generations, taking place outside the social security system, negate the wealth transfers toward future generations that were sought through advance funding. The fiscal integrity of social security, as well as the rest of the budget, is undermined.

The concern here is not with the use of the social security surpluses to "fund the deficit," which we hear so much about these days. Presumably, funding the deficit means reducing the amount of new borrowing the federal government must do, which is as intended. The concern is that the surpluses allow for an *increase* in the deficit in the rest of the budget, in which case they have little or no beneficial impact on the federal deficit or the amount of outstanding public debt. Unfortunately, it is impossible to observe the size and composition of the budget to determine whether the social security surpluses are being spent in this way. Either we would have to know what the size and composition of the budget *would have been* in the absence of the trust fund buildup, or the budget excluding social security would have to be in balance.[7]

Uncharted Waters

It is worth bearing in mind that social security has never operated with a substantial share of income in the form of general fund transfers, whether for interest payments or any other purpose. Interest payments, for example, have averaged 3 or 4 percent of income to OASDI since 1960 and have exceeded 10 percent of income only four times (all before 1952). Yet, under the 1983 legislation, projections now show interest payments averaging 20 percent of trust fund income in the period 2005 to 2035, peaking at 24 percent (or $160 billion in real terms) in 2020. This compares with 6 percent, or about $19 billion, today.

Similarly, social security has never operated with a sustained period of substantial and growing operating deficits. Balances over the years (annual surpluses or deficits in an accounting sense, not taking into account changes in the system's real long-range indebtedness) have periodically been negative, but at no time has the deficit exceeded two- or three-tenths of a percent of GNP. This compares with the string of deficits projected to begin around 2030, on the order of 1 to 1½ percent of GNP (before exhausting the reserve). Including Medicare, the system is expected to run continuously rising deficits after 2015.

It is far from obvious, in our political and budget-making system, that these two developments would be greeted with equanimity. Whether the surpluses are frittered away, claims that "interest costs are no higher than they otherwise would have been" or that social security "carried its own weight" during the surplus years are likely to ring hollow in the next century when social security spending outstrips available tax income. At least as currently conceived, social security will have no private stash of claims to productive assets that will generate regular interest payments or that can be sold off for cash without affecting overall federal finances. Social security's fortunes will be completely entangled with those of the federal government.

The primary implication is that the accumulation of a social security reserve—a portfolio of government IOUs—reveals nothing, in and of itself, about the effect of social security on the federal debt or about the public's willingness and ability to meet the cost of benefits in the next century. The hoped-for economic benefits of advance funding are just that—hoped for.

Attention in 1983

The accumulation of large trust fund reserves, while appearing to enhance the well-being of social security and the federal budget, carries real risks of undermining both. These risks were not considered in 1983. In part, this was partly because the reform package was not seen as fundamentally altering the way social security was financed. The pattern of surpluses followed by large deficits was already established in the 1977 Social Security Amendments. In part, moreover, the prospect of sustained surpluses still seemed quite remote. Policy makers were coming out of a decade-long period in which the actuaries pronounced the program solvent only to find it insolvent again. In 1983, the debate over the investment and management of trust fund assets was limited to a relatively unimportant side issue: the interest rate to be paid on special-issue government bonds.

With the economy having performed far better than generally anticipated in 1983, surpluses are now a reality, and their effect on federal finances and on the well-being of present and future taxpayers must be critically evaluated. More than half of American taxpayers pay more in social security taxes than in federal income taxes. According to a recent study by Eugene Steuerle and Paul Wilson, the increase in payroll tax rates between 1978 and 1990 alone—almost 30 percent—exceeds any peacetime increase in the individual income tax burden to date.[8] Using this tax to relieve pressures on the income tax or to finance new government programs is bad economic policy and bad social policy.

Where Do We Go from Here?

There are two approaches for ameliorating the risks posed by social security funding, either of which would promote saving and economic growth while enhancing the predictability and affordability of future benefits. One approach is to restructure the rules by which social security and budget decisions are made so as to require government saving; the other is to reduce or eliminate the role of the government in accumulating and managing surplus funds so as to encourage private saving.

Binding Rules. As already noted, no mechanism now ensures that social security surpluses are saved on an ongoing basis. Reserves can be dissipated either directly by program liberalizations or indirectly by a loosening of control in the rest of the budget. If social security is to remain advance funded as currently conceived, meaning that investments continue to be restricted to government bonds, rules must be introduced to define the range of permissible fiscal outcomes and to constrain the political process. The need for binding rules is made clear by the nearly uninterrupted period of peacetime deficits since World War II.

One such set of rules would be the following. First, to ensure that each dollar of surplus social security revenues leads to a dollar increase in government saving (or reduction in outstanding public debt), the federal budget *excluding* social security must be balanced. Social security could be left in Gramm-Rudman or removed, provided the deficit-reduction targets were modified accordingly (long-range surplus targets in one case and zero-deficit targets in the other). What is essential is that the total federal budget be brought into balance in 1993 (as called for under Gramm-Rudman) and that the non-social-security portion of the budget be brought into balance thereafter.[9]

Second, to ensure that each dollar of surplus social security revenues leads to a dollar reduction in the system's unfunded liability, social security reserves must be maintained at a specified level relative to accruing liabilities. The "funding ratio" in the law may vary over time—a period of accumulation and partial depletion may well be deemed appropriate—but the chosen path must be retained.

The purpose of these rules, in combination, is to ensure that trust fund surpluses are used exclusively to lighten the burden of retirement benefits (and government spending generally) in the next century. Surplus funds could not be used to expand the general obligations of the government, nor could they be used to expand social security spending. Such an approach is based on the recognition that the relation between social security and the federal budget is a two-way proposition: a mishandling of one will undermine the well-being of future generations just as surely as a mishandling of the other.

Further gains could be achieved if these two rules were supplemented by another rule for social security, what might be termed an "automatic pilot." This rule would specify in advance how benefits or taxes would be adjusted in the event of unexpected changes in reserves. It would allow individuals to anticipate better the effect of periodic funding crises on their own future taxes and benefits and thereby to make more efficient private saving decisions.

This set of rules is not offered because of any supposed political feasibility. Congress has chafed under the constraints imposed by Gramm-Rudman, which merely calls for a phased elimination of the deficit—including the social security surpluses. Meeting the goal of budget *surplus* in the 1990s would dictate substantial additional spending reductions (or revenue increases) in the mid- to late-1990s. The resistance these proposals would likely meet, and the risk that budget surplus targets—even if enacted—would not be met on a long-term basis, highlights the flaw in present financing arrangements and the need to consider other more basic reforms.

Expanded Private Sector Role. Quite another approach, which recognizes the considerable reluctance of Congress to live with binding constraints, is to restructure social security so as to reduce or eliminate the role of the government in accumulating and managing surplus funds. An expanded role for the private sector would be at the heart of this approach.

Under one option, surplus revenues would be invested directly in the private sector, through individualized retirement accounts. To facilitate this, benefits would be restructured along the lines of a two-tiered system.[10] One tier would offer a flat or means-tested payment to retirees, financed on a pay-as-you-go basis. The other tier would offer an earnings-related payment, financed on a fully funded basis. Under the second tier, taxes would be channeled directly into individualized private savings accounts, possibly along the lines of individual retirement accounts (IRAs); benefits would be paid directly out of the proceeds of these accounts, based on contributions plus interest.[11] By design, there would be no surplus tax receipts to be managed by the federal government and thus no funds available to underwrite an expansion in the rest of the budget. The second-tier benefits would place no demands on the federal budget.

This option would allow for real saving to help lighten the burden of retirement payments in the next century—without involving the federal government in direct management and control of vast sums of private resources. Investment decisions would be fully decentralized and competitively determined. At the same time, individuals—directly involved in their retirement and savings decisions—would accumulate legally enforceable claims to future benefits.

It should be noted that this option is *not* equivalent to the government engaging in direct investment of trust fund assets in the private sector, as has been suggested by some. Were the power to control a portfolio of several hundred billion dollars, potentially several trillion dollars, delegated to a government entity, it is inconceivable that investment decisions would be made "as if" by individuals or portfolio managers in a competitive marketplace. By definition, investment decisions would be politically determined and resources would flow toward politically favored projects. One can easily imagine the list of disallowed investments, right alongside the list of preferred investments. It would be a fine line indeed between "investments" and public spending by another name.

Managers of a large public portfolio would have the capacity to make or break individual firms and to concentrate the ownership and control of American corporations to an unprecedented degree. Already there is concern, whether warranted or not, about the concentration of resources in corporate pension funds; the largest of these hold assets no larger than social security's *current* reserve.[12]

If the goal of reform is to short-circuit the direct and indirect spending of reserves and to achieve the full benefits of capital accumulation, a policy of government-directed investments is unlikely to be successful. Such a policy would put taxpayers' money at risk and likely distort the allocation of capital in the economy. The advantage of the two-tiered system described earlier is that it allows for direct investment through a highly decentralized, market-based mechanism.

Yet another option, which leaves more of the retirement decision to the individual, is simply to scale back long-range benefits and lower the payroll tax. Long-range benefits can be trimmed through any number of modest changes, including increasing the retirement age (raising the age to sixty-eight or seventy or speeding the transition to sixty-seven), indexing the retirement age to longevity, raising the age at which early retirement benefits are payable, or revising the way benefits are computed for new retirees.[13] Moving to a price-indexed system (where the benefit formula is indexed to price growth, rather than wage growth, as is now done for postretirement benefits), for example, would generate savings equal to two-thirds of the social security deficit (including Medicare), while still allowing for real benefit growth in future decades.[14] Such a change could be implemented as part of a more comprehensive package of tax and regulatory changes designed to promote private saving.

If properly designed, this option would reduce the great imbalance between social security income and outgo in the coming decades, thereby ameliorating the social security funding problem as well as some of the implied pressures on the federal budget. At the same time, it would return the system closer to pay-as-you-go financing but without leaving the full liability implied by today's benefit structure to be met as it comes due.

From the standpoint of the individual, this option would encourage rather than mandate private savings. With less income taxed away for the purpose of retirement saving and less offered by the government in the way of future benefits, individuals and families would have increased flexibility—and incentive—to structure their savings to meet their needs. They would have more freedom to decide when to save as well as how to save. (At present, a young family with substantial debt must "save" through social security at the same rate as a couple nearing retirement with peak wealth. In addition, they must allocate a substantial portion of their saving to one particular investment—social security, with its own unique risk and return characteristics—irrespective of the diversity of their portfolios.) To the extent that younger workers perceived that the scaled-back benefit promises posed a more realistic cost burden and were thus more likely to be met, they would be better able to plan their retirement savings around social security.

Conclusion

To sit back and hope that we have entered, or are about to enter, a new era of fiscal responsibility is foolhardy at best. Pressures to increase government spending and to obscure and defer costs are as great as ever. Social security's looming surpluses pose an irresistible target. Amassed through hefty increases in the payroll tax, these surpluses must be managed so that they are channeled into productive investments that promote capital formation and economic growth. Otherwise, there is no sound basis, economically or socially, for taxing American workers at a rate higher than necessary to finance current benefits. Controlling the risks posed by advance funding, and protecting the interests of future as well as present generations, will necessitate either basic changes in the rules by which social security and budget decisions are made or a reduction in the role of the government in accumulating and managing surplus funds.

Protecting the Social Security Surplus through Institutional or Fundamental Reform?

A Commentary by William D. Nordhaus

After a number of careful studies of the social security system, including the Brookings and ICF reports[1] and two symposiums sponsored by the Social Security Public Trustees in 1988, a general consensus is emerging on the financial future of social security. The consensus holds that social security is running and will continue to run a large surplus until well into the next century. Moreover, this surplus is economically desirable as a way of anticipating a demographic shift that will produce a significant deficit sometime in the middle half of the next century. The current surplus will therefore help reduce fluctuations in the payroll tax and will require current workers to pay for a larger fraction of their own pensions.

Most of us would presumably see this as a wonderful development after years of fretting about social security deficits. But whenever a group of economists get together, these dismal scientists can discern a gray cloud on even the sunniest day. In this instance, the social security surplus is not being translated into social savings. In particular, even though there are pious intentions to keep social security "off-budget," Gramm-Rudman-Hollings includes the social security surplus in the deficit targets. For the foreseeable future, the actual impact of the surplus will be to compensate for lower taxes or higher spending elsewhere.

The present course of overall fiscal policy is undesirable, because the nation should be taking steps to increase its lagging savings rate. As is well known, the national savings rate has fallen to a postwar low. Although economists differ on the most efficient and equitable way to raise savings, most strategies involve moving the fiscal-monetary mixture away from a large fiscal deficit toward a fiscal surplus.

179

The concern about the social security system, however, is more than a statement that the nation needs to raise its saving rate; in fact we need to raise the saving rate by an extra amount to prepare for the demographic shifts over the next century. Net saving and investment (domestic and foreign), for example, came to about 8 percent of net national product (NNP) for the three decades before 1980; in the past two years, the net national savings rate fell to slightly above 2 percent. It is reasonable to suppose that we should take steps to achieve the earlier rate of national savings. But in addition, if we include the need for a social security surplus, likely to be 1 to 2 percent of NNP over the next few years, our national savings target should be 9 to 10 percent— that is, equal to the earlier rate of 8 percent of NNP plus the additional 1 to 2 percent for prefunding social security.

In the context of overall economic policy, then, "validating the social security surplus," which is the current jargon for ensuring that the surpluses actually do raise government saving, should be treated as a need to raise national savings above the normal target. But if we take 9 to 10 percent of NNP as a savings target for the turn of the century, protecting the social security surplus is only a small part of our total saving problem.

Many economists familiar with social security finances would probably not disagree violently with my summary to this point. The problem is that—while everyone agrees in principle—the people, the Congress, and the president do not agree in practice. The Bush administration's budgets have made no substantial inroads in the total federal deficit, and a realistic projection shows a widening of the non-social-security deficit.

The reasons for the failure of political will are fascinating and have been thoroughly addressed by the chapters in this volume. The chapters by Lawrence Lindsey and Carolyn Weaver as well as by Herman Leonard address a somewhat different aspect of the issue. Having agreed that we want to save more, how should we force ourselves to behave the way we want?

I am struck by the parallel between our wrestling with the social security surplus and discussions about various addictions. We are not talking about whether it is fair to tax the current generation to pay for uncertain future benefits or whether it is appropriate to run a fiscal surplus at this time. Rather, like smokers who are trying to kick the habit, we are trying to figure out how to deceive ourselves into actually saving the social security surplus rather than frittering it away on non-social-security purposes. We are trying to wean ourselves from "surplus illusion," which involves aggregating social security and other government programs in our budgetary calculations.

The problem with setting up devices to overcome fiscal illusions resembles the problem of quitting smoking. Are devices like setting up separate accounts or investing in different kinds of securities not like hiding the cigarettes on top of the refrigerator or playing poker against yourself? Isn't it hard to devise a game where you force yourself voluntarily to give up something you don't want to give up?

One special difficulty with breaking the deficit habit is the problem of knowing when you have won. You know when you have quit smoking or are a fully reformed alcoholic. But, given the analytical difficulties in defining the deficit, we cannot be sure that we are in fact saving the surplus. As Robert Eisner and Laurence Kotlikoff have reminded us many times, in relying upon cash flow methods, the federal budget follows the most primitive accounting techniques known to humanity. So even if we were to put social security off budget, we have no guarantee that the desired level of government saving or spending would lead to the optimal amount of national saving.

Many economists are concerned with setting up incentives, accounting conventions, management processes, or investment procedures so that government decisions will not aggregate the social security accounts with the rest of the budget. At this point a well-trained neoclassical economist will argue that setting up such artificial boundaries is doomed to failure. According to what might be called the Hypothesis of the Irrelevancy of Institutions, or the Irrelevance Hypothesis for short, people see through the veil of accounting conventions or institutional boundaries. The Irrelevance Hypothesis is well known in theories such as the Robert Barro hypothesis that the timing of taxes cannot trick people into changing their consumption patterns or in the proposition that households pierce the veil of corporate accounts or that markets see through management accounting gimmicks.

A little reflection will reveal, however, a great deal of evidence that the Irrelevance Hypothesis fails the test of experience. People apparently are spending their supply-side tax cuts. Moreover, state and local governments do *not* aggregate local pensions into their budget decisions, and the national accounts show a corresponding state and local budget surplus. According to Alicia Munnell and C. Nicole Ernsberger, the extent to which foreign public pension funds have been insulated from general budget pressures has varied according to the institutional structure. And, Eisner's arguments notwithstanding, Congress does pay a great deal of attention to the conventionally defined budget deficit and generally tends to ignore economist's suggestions about alternative budget concepts. Hence, a carefully designed set of rules and procedures might have a significant impact on the extent to which the social security surpluses are translated into social saving.

The changes that could help insulate social security finances from the rest of the budget naturally divide into two types: (1) institutional changes that retain the essential nature of social security but modify the administration in more or less profound ways; and (2) fundamental changes that radically redesign the social security system itself.

In the category of institutional changes, the most important would clearly be to exclude social security from a target of a balanced budget, say in extended Gramm-Rudman-Hollings targets. This step would impose additional deficit reductions rising to an estimated $107 billion in 1993.[2] The choice about whether to do this is a pure referendum on whether to increase the amount of government saving. Another option would be to create a separate or independent agency and to restructure the board of trustees—although it is hard to see how this change could have a perceptible impact upon fiscal policy. I would rate the chances of the success of such measures in validating the surplus as moderate.

The Lindsey and Weaver chapters have laid out the options for fundamental changes. As I understand Lindsey's proposal for individual savings accounts, it is purely supplementary to the social security system. As such, it might be part of a national strategy to increase the national savings rate, but it appears to have little to do with managing social security finances.

As a device for promoting saving, the verdict of the 1980s seems to be skepticism toward policies that rely on raising the real return on saving as a stimulant to personal saving. Conventional wisdom before the 1980s held that the saving rate is insensitive to the return on saving. The 1980s constituted a grand experiment in the use of "price-affecting" policies to bolster saving. These included higher real interest rates, lower tax rates on income, and special incentives for saving. One measure of the impact of these policies was that the real posttax return (measured by the real return on tax-free bonds) rose from *minus* 2½ percent in 1979 to *plus* 3 percent in 1988. Yet personal saving declined. This experiment, along with the volumes of corroborating sophisticated econometric work, should give pause to those who propose price-affecting policies to raise our saving rate.

Another fundamental reform is Weaver's two-tier option, which in essence unscrambles the social security omelette into a "yolk" part, which is an actuarially fair pure annuity, and a "white" part, which is a means-tested redistribution program. This unscrambling would represent more than a cosmetic change and would indeed have real effects on government behavior. But it does so by changing the character of the current social security system in two fundamental ways. First, it puts the means-tested part of the system on a pay-as-you-go basis, which reverses the philosophy of the 1983 amendments. The burden of taxation to pay for the means-tested part would presumably rise sharply in the next century, so this would seem to undermine the decision to prefund future expenditure increases incorporated in the 1983 amendments. Second, the Weaver plan converts the annuity part into a defined contribution plan from a defined benefit plan. I believe that the defined benefit plans are more suitable for pensions than defined contribution plans, as they allow a broader sharing of the risks about the return on pension savings. Finally, we have to confront the possibility that, once the omelette is unscrambled, the consensus that has led to its remarkable political success will come unstuck as the whites and the yolks battle for a larger share of the meal.

A final set of changes, which might fall somewhere between the institutional and the fundamental, would be to change the social security investment policy. I am skeptical about Leonard's proposal to overcome surplus illusion by investing in private bonds. Given the close-to-infinite substitutability of different kinds of bonds, the impact upon markets is likely to be nil.

On the other hand, I think that Weaver is too harsh on proposals to direct the government to invest surplus funds in assets other than federal securities. The Munnell and Ernsberger chapter indicates that this has been successful in some countries. Clearly, careful rules would need to be put in place, and a separation of investment from politics would have to be thorough.

There is some confusion about whether changing investment policies would have any effect on real economic magnitudes. The answer to this depends upon the preferences of investors, but the weight of the evidence is that changing investments to marketable bonds would not affect real investment or saving. Because different securities (outside of bonds) are not perfect substitutes, though, changes in relative supplies of fixed-interest and equity investments in the hands of the public would change real yields and therefore affect investment patterns.

The stakes of such a policy are substantial because the difference between the yield of a social security portfolio and a modern pension portfolio is substantial—on the order of 5 to 6 percent per year in recent decades. I am puzzled over why we should penalize those who have public pensions, which happens when we impose below-par returns upon their pension investments, which must be invested in government bonds.

It is well to remember, however, that in the end this discussion is primarily about federal policy to increase the level of national saving. To protect the social security surplus, we need to face up to the need for some combination of higher taxes or lower expenditures on items other than social security. We are making little progress on this central task. It would be fair to characterize the current fiscal policy as an "eat-as-you-go" approach, one in which we are eating our nest egg before it is hatched.

Controlling Social Security Expansion and Increasing Private Saving

A Commentary by Stephen J. Entin

Carolyn Weaver has produced a clear and rigorous statement of the realities of the social security financing mechanisms after 1983. She points out that the surpluses in the Old-Age, Survivors, and Disability Insurance (OASDI) trust funds are not true budget surpluses and that the investments are accounting artifacts, and suggests that the money is being spent, not saved. She then addresses the question of whether we should try to convert these surpluses into real advance funding or if there is a better way to address the retirement needs of the aging population.

Although Weaver states the case for advance funding very fairly, she also lists its assumptions very fairly, and that is where the option begins to look decidedly seedy. She then offers a private sector alternative that has much to recommend it.

Weaver notes the large economic literature on whether government saving becomes national saving and does not address it further. She focuses instead on the difficult political problem of establishing a budget process that would bind Congress to follow the rules of an advance-funded system and turn the social security surplus into a real government surplus. In my view, this is an impossible task. The reason Congress is attracted to advance funding in the first place is the opportunity to spend the money or mandate its investment for industrial, regional, or political policy. Sensible rules would eliminate any reason for Congress to choose this route.

I should like to pick up on the issue of whether government saving becomes national saving. This is critical because only greater saving and investment will raise gross national product (GNP) and make it easier to provide goods and services for the baby-boom generation when it retires without lowering the living standard of future workers. We hear calls for balancing the non-social-security portion of the budget in the near future and turning the OASDI surpluses into total budget surpluses to prefund the baby-boom's retirement. It is an act of faith that total budget surpluses would somehow raise national saving, reduce interest rates, and promote investment. I call it an act of faith, because there is surely no research to support the notion.

The case for advance funding is based on the critical assumption that, first, the OASDI surpluses result in a net reduction in outstanding federal debt held by the public and, second, net government saving translates into net national saving, with little or no offsetting reduction in private saving. I would add a third condition: the higher saving needs to result in higher domestic investment in human or physical capital.

The assumption behind the prosurplus view is that, if the government borrows less from a supposedly fixed private sector saving pool, more saving is left over to finance investment and growth. In fact, the saving pool is not fixed; budget surpluses brought about by tax increases on business or on individuals would cut private saving by a similar amount, and national saving would not rise.

In particular, consider the sort of tax increase in which the entire amount comes directly out of the earnings of capital, as in the Tax Reform Act of 1986. By what magic mechanism can a $100 billion tax increase on capital, coming straight out of business saving dollar for dollar, result in greater national saving and investment? To perform this sleight of hand, the $100 billion tax hike would have to produce a cut of more than $100 billion in the deficit and, in spite of being anticapital, encourage the net saving to flow into new investment. This is impossible. Clearly, there are some types of tax increases that would not permit the taxes-are-national-saving notion to hold, even without resorting to Keynesian multipliers that suggest the economy would weaken and reduce saving. Leaving cash flow notions and tautological GNP accounting identities aside, any reasonable view of real world behavior would suggest that higher taxes on capital (or the labor it works with or the products they produce) discourage capital investment by reducing its rate of return, that is, by driving up the cost of capital. For proof, ask any corporate planning officer whether a higher corporate tax rate or less favorable tax treatment of depreciation would improve or worsen the expected profitability of a proposed project. This method of reducing the government deficit would reduce national saving rather than increase it and would discourage investment.

Budget surpluses may also arise from spending restraint. Indeed, less government spending on goods and services frees real resources for private investment and consumption. It is the spending restraint, however, not the surplus per se, that potentially improves the investment climate. Furthermore, spending restraint alone could increase either consumption or investment, depending on which resources the government surrendered. It is saving and investment that are needed to prepare for the aging of America; how can we ensure that investment gains the lion's share of the liberated resources?

Let us assume for a moment that spending cuts were about to produce a budget surplus and free real resources for nongovernment use. Other things being equal, there is a given desired domestic capital stock for a given tax regime. To ensure that the freed resources go chiefly to investment, Congress should offset the surpluses with tax reductions structured to increase the amount of capital the country wants to hold. The business community and the advocates of budget surpluses might consider which would raise investment more, a budget surplus or accelerated depreciation. Clearly, tax incentives are better than budget surpluses for promoting investment and growth.

I disagree with those who claim that personal saving is not responsive to tax incentives, such as individual retirement accounts (IRAs). Work by Steven S. Vinti and David Wise, Daniel Feenberg and Jonathan Skinner, and others and the evidence from Canada indicate that IRAs generated considerable new saving by removing the double tax on saving.[1] This literature is well worth looking at before casually dismissing the idea that individuals are rational in their saving behavior. One does not have to subscribe to the ultrarationalist Barro model to assume that people take advantage of a bargain when they see one.

As for the hope that lower deficits will reduce interest rates, this is quashed by a study entitled "The Effect of Deficits on Prices of Financial Assets: Theory and Evidence," by Manuel Johnson and Jacob Dreyer from the Office of Economic Policy at Treasury.[2] The study surveyed the economic literature on the question. Clearly, the literature shows that random deficit reduction will do little to reduce interest rates. It is government spending, not the deficit per se, that seems to be linked to interest rates. Even this link seems to be through the effect on real resources, not through the effect on credit markets.

Finally, note that the Federal Reserve cannot increase the marginal physical product of capital, which is the amount of additional real output produced by an additional unit of plant, equipment, or structures, and which represents the demand for real capital. All the Federal Reserve can do to aid saving and investment is to encourage saving by reducing inflation and risk. The Federal Reserve can do this only by pursuing stable policies; it may drive down nominal interest rates in the short run by injecting funds, but ultimately it can lower interest rates only by controlling inflation. It will only drive real interest rates higher if it pursues risky and destabilizing policies. Interest rates cannot be forced down through monetary manipulation to increase the desired real capital stock or to expand investment. In short, there are problems with every link in the chain connecting government surpluses to investment and growth.

I agree with the section of the Weaver chapter outlining the advantages of expanding the role of the private sector in providing for retirement income. I share her concern that, in the unlikely event that surpluses were to become real, government has no business managing investments that could make or break private sector firms. Consequently, I support the idea of using expanded IRAs to encourage, but not mandate, higher private saving. As for social security, I urge postponement of the 1990 payroll tax increase and a return to a more nearly pay-as-you-go system.

Weaver lists options for scaling back the growth of social security in the future, so that it may live within its scheduled tax rate indefinitely. These options are certainly workable. Substantial budget savings could be realized by shifting to less generous indexation of the formula that determines initial benefits for new retirees. Currently, the dollar amounts (so-called bend points) in the formula are increased annually by the percentage growth in average wages nationwide. Each worker's earnings history is also wage indexed before his "averaged indexed monthly earnings" are computed for use in the formula. Shifting from wage to price indexing of the earning histories and bend points for adjustments beginning in 1990 would produce savings, in 1988 constant dollars, of $1 billion annually by 1995. The annual savings would exceed $6 billion by the year 2000, $34 billion by 2010, $127 billion by 2025, $300 billion by 2050, and $442 billion by 2065 (see table 4C–1).

The change would result in slower but still substantial growth of real retirement benefits per retiree. The initial benefit of a college-educated retiree, age sixty-five, and spouse, averaged $14,477 in 1988. Under current law, it would be $39,366 in constant 1988 dollars for a similar couple retiring in 2065, a 172 percent real increase; price indexing would hold the 2065 benefit to $23,422, a 62 percent increase. For a high school graduate and spouse, the 1988 benefit was $13,101; it would be $32,697 in 2065, a 150 percent increase. Price indexing would limit the 2065 benefit to $18,022, a 38 percent real rise (see table 4C–2).

Lawrence Lindsey joins Weaver in acknowledging that the current social security surpluses are not real saving and worries about the temptation to spend them. He has an ingenious solution: a greatly expanded savings incentive program to shift revenues from the present to the future, from years of social security surpluses to years of deficits.

TABLE 4C–1

OASDI OUTLAYS UNDER PRESENT LAW AND UNDER PRICE INDEXING
OF BEND POINTS AND EARNINGS HISTORIES, 1990–2065
(billions of 1988 dollars)

Year	Present Law	Price Indexing the Bend Points and Earnings Histories	Savings
1990	231.26	231.25	.01
1991	236.44	236.41	.03
1992	241.30	241.19	.12
1993	245.82	245.53	.29
1994	250.13	249.54	.59
1995	254.47	253.41	1.06
2000	276.22	269.62	6.59
2005	302.39	284.91	17.48
2010	344.90	310.07	34.83
2015	413.21	352.88	60.33
2020	500.93	408.39	92.55
2025	591.22	463.88	127.35
2030	671.79	509.94	161.85
2035	736.83	542.49	194.34
2040	788.28	563.19	225.09
2045	843.19	583.70	259.49
2050	910.36	610.04	300.32
2055	986.49	640.53	345.96
2060	1064.23	670.82	393.41
2065	1142.95	700.35	442.60

NOTE: Proposal effective in 1990. Numbers may not add because of rounding.
SOURCE: Based on estimates by Aldonna Robbins, Fiscal Associates, updated by
IRET for alternative II-B assumptions in the *1988 OASDI Trustees' Report*. See
Board of Trustees of the Federal Old-Age and Survivors Insurance Trust Fund
and Federal Disability Insurance Trust Fund, *1988 Annual Report of the Board of
Trustees of the Federal Old-Age and Survivors Insurance Trust Fund and Federal
Disability Insurance Trust Fund* (Washington, D.C.: GPO, 1988).

I agree completely that saving incentives are the right approach to the
problems of an aging population. I question some of his analysis, however. I also believe there are stronger arguments to support the recommendation than he offers, and many of the arguments appearing in the
chapter are a bit off the mark.

The general perspective of the proposal is intriguing. Its apparent
purpose is not so much to improve the security and living standards of
a billion Americans over the next four generations as it is to make life

TABLE 4C–2

BENEFITS FOR RETIRED WORKER (AND SPOUSE) BY EDUCATION
UNDER PRESENT LAW AND UNDER PRICE INDEXING OF BEND POINTS AND
EARNINGS HISTORIES, 1990–2065

(1988 dollars)

	College Education		High School Graduate	
Year	Present law	Price indexing	Present law	Price indexing
1990	15,327	15,327	13,834	13,834
1995	16,138	15,895	14,477	14,289
2000	17,973	16,660	15,729	14,523
2005	19,403	17,015	16,460	14,324
2010	20,244	16,886	16,835	13,883
2015	21,671	17,295	18,000	14,143
2020	23,025	17,676	19,124	14,401
2025	23,190	17,206	19,261	13,964
2030	24,653	17,727	20,476	14,338
2035	26,358	18,387	21,892	14,771
2040	28,180	19,092	23,406	15,227
2045	30,129	19,847	25,024	15,713
2050	32,212	20,653	26,755	16,234
2055	34,439	21,515	28,604	16,790
2060	36,821	22,437	30,582	17,386
2065	39,366	23,422	32,697	18,022
Percentage increase	172	62	150	38

NOTE: Proposal effective in 1990. Benefits computed for retirees age sixty-five, before tax.
SOURCE: Based on estimates by Aldonna Robbins, Fiscal Associates, updated by IRET for alternative II-B assumptions in the *1988 OASDI Trustees' Report*. See Board of Trustees of the Federal Old-Age and Survivors Insurance Trust Fund and Federal Disability Insurance Trust Fund, *1988 Annual Report of the Board of Trustees of the Federal Old-Age and Survivors Insurance Trust Fund and Federal Disability Insurance Trust Fund* (Washington, D.C.: GPO, 1988).

easier for future administrations and congressional budget planners. Its chief rationale seems to be to rearrange the timing of federal receipts and borrowing to make it easier to manage fiscal policy over the next seventy-five years. I would hate to have to sell a major overhaul of social security and tax policy to the country on the grounds that it will let future White House budget officials get home earlier and reduce aspirin consumption among Capitol Hill budget staffers.

Lindsey states that a rapid increase in the ratio of beneficiaries to workers in the next century would require either a sharp cut in real benefits or a sharp rise in the payroll tax. In fact, it would not require a cut in benefits, merely a reduction in the projected increase from a near-tripling of real benefits per recipient under current law to a bit less than doubling. The current benefit formula is promising some rather spectacular benefit increases. We must be careful to abandon the "current services" approach to federal spending programs and measure outlays against what was actually spent in the past, rather than against what we optimistically hoped they would be in the future.

Lindsey's chapter lays out with great care the expected pattern of rising receipts from the income tax under the alternative II-B economic assumptions in the trustees' report. This is most interesting, as it is not available elsewhere. He makes the point that the budget has room to accommodate the projected outlays of the social security program. This comes dangerously close to endorsing the program's current scope. The income tax is indexed to inflation but not to real income growth. As incomes rise in real terms, people will rise through the tax brackets. By 2050, real incomes will triple, while real tax revenues from the income tax will nearly quadruple; and the excess revenue available for demographic-related initiatives, assuming all other programs grow only in line with the real economy, will reach an *annual* rate of $711 billion in real 1990 dollars. This shows the importance of continued economic growth to our ability to keep our promises to the elderly.

Lindsey points out that the elderly will pay a disproportionate amount of the increased income tax burden and that the elderly of 2050 will be richer than the workers of 1990. This raises two questions. First, why raise taxes on the elderly just to pay them higher benefits, when we could cut taxes and benefits and avoid the disincentives and economic distortions that high tax rates cause? Second, why strain to preserve the current benefit formula if the elderly are projected to become that rich?

I view the projected $711 billion revenue figure for the year 2050 with some skepticism. This revenue projection assumes we do not have periodic tax cuts and that we allow tax revenue to rise from about 14 percent of adjusted gross income to over 21 percent. Lindsey says that this should be politically possible because it will occur gradually, so there will be no "politically embarrassing rise in tax shares" and because aftertax income will continue to increase in spite of the rising tax burden. This misses the point.

The damage done by bracket creep is more than a little political embarrassment, as we clearly demonstrated in the 1970s. Tax rates had to be reduced in 1981 after the inflation of the 1970s because of the real economic costs of the higher rate structure. Higher marginal tax rates drove up labor and capital costs at the margin, reduced employment and the capital stock, and shrank real output. If we leave real bracket creep unchecked, the same will happen again, and the revenue will not materialize. Factoring in the payroll tax and state income tax rates, taxpayers would find that a shift from the 15 percent federal income tax bracket to the 33 percent bracket would reduce aftertax income at the margin by 20 to 30 percent. It is useless to expect workers, savers, and investors to ignore such an assault on incentives.

Even if the $711 billion figure were to materialize, it would not be enough to preserve our social security unscathed. Lindsey cautions that his analysis applies to OASDI and omits computations of the Hospital Insurance (HI) program (Medicare Part A). HI will begin to run deficits in the mid-1990s, deficits which will reach 1.8 percent of GNP between 2050 and 2060.[3] Even this caution does not go far enough. In federal programs, where there is a Part A, there is surely a Part B, which in this case is the Supplemental Medical Insurance (SMI) program covering physicians' fees and outpatient care. SMI is 75 percent paid for out of general revenues and will be running a deficit of nearly 1.6 percent of GNP between 2050 and 2060.[4] Furthermore, Lindsey assumes that non-social-security programs grow only as fast as the economy, which is distinctly not the case for either part of Medicare.

Assume, optimistically, that medical costs stop rising faster than the general rate of inflation in twenty-five years and grow in real terms thereafter only with the demographic factors. By 2050, the combined social security, HI, and SMI deficit will exceed $690 billion in 1990 dollars. This is a shade under $711 billion, but then the situation becomes very adverse. By 2060, the combined deficit will be just over $1,100 billion in real 1990 dollars, while the $711 billion bracket creep windfall will come only to $888 billion by 2060.

I do share Lindsey's enthusiasm for instituting a sort of super-IRA with unlimited contributions, which he calls an individual savings account, or ISA. I wish, though, that he had based the recommendation on a less restrictive set of assumptions. He points out that the initial year tax deduction of IRA-type contributions costs the government nothing in present value terms, as the tax on withdrawals from the compounded buildup of principal is equal in present value to the first year tax break. He dwells on the revenue loss in present value from the deferral of taxation of the accruing interest, however. This cost occurs only because he assumes that all the saving in the ISA is shifted in from other accounts. He points out later that, in the case of net new saving, there is no such cost, as the interest would not otherwise have been present to tax. He cites work by Feenberg, Rosen, and Wise, which would have justified an assumption of considerable net new saving.

STEPHEN J. ENTIN

More recent work by Vinti and Wise and by Feenberg and Skinner makes the case even more convincingly.[5]

Because Lindsey assumes no net new saving, he must rely on a differential in rates of return to the government and the private investor to get any improvement in saving and investment from his initiative. This is very weak ground. As he acknowledges, there is a risk differential in the rate of return between government and private sector debt instruments. In a perfectly functioning capital market, this reflects real factors, such as defaults, failed real estate projects, and unprofitable widgets. It is not fair to state that the private sector gets a higher return, in the aggregate, than the government.

Lindsey views the ISA not as a way to promote saving and investment but as a way to eliminate the temptation to spend the near-term surpluses by shifting government revenue from the present to the future. If this were the only reason for ISAs, one could achieve the same thing with less trouble by cutting the payroll tax now and raising it later, as Robert Myers has recommended. The real reason, then, to support the ISA initiative is not because of an interest rate differential on an existing pool of saving but because of the enlarged national pool of saving created by the ISA. An ISA would eliminate the double tax on saving implicit in the income tax. It would create a tax system that was far closer to neutrality in the treatment of current versus future consumption than at present, resulting in less current consumption and more saving for future consumption. It would raise the rate of return to saving and lower the cost of capital, encouraging an expansion of the capital stock. This is what is needed to improve the productive capacity of the economy to meet the needs of an aging population.

The current tax system is not neutral because the income tax falls more heavily on income that is saved than on income that is consumed. Income is taxed when earned, and is not taxed again if spent. However, if the aftertax income is transformed from a lump sum into an income stream, say by buying a bond, the stream is taxed again, even though in present value the stream is just equal to the principal. This imposes a double tax burden on income saved. An ISA eliminates the double tax by permitting a tax deduction for income saved, thereby moving the tax code from its current approximation of a pure income tax system toward a consumed income tax system.

The Lindsey proposal to fine-tune the budget over time by first instituting ISAs and then repealing them is most unattractive. Why, after removing a major distortion in the tax code, should it be reintroduced at a later date? If there were any need for more revenue at that time, a more neutral means of raising it could be found. Better yet would be restraint of spending over the period; not all forms of government spending need to grow in proportion to the real economy, and we have fifty years to find them.

Lindsey's concern over avoiding fiscal swings is overdone, and his willingness to see enormous increases in the income tax to finance the projected expansion of an unreformed social security program is alarming. His best recommendation is his last, that the swings in the budget due to social security be reduced by trimming the growth of social security so that it may survive within its current law tax rate. It is likely that we shall need a mixture of policies to deal with the issue. Weaver's list of options to scale back the system and Lindsey's ISA proposal would make an excellent package.

Notes

CHAPTER 1: INTRODUCTION, *Carolyn L. Weaver*

1. Data on reserves (here and elsewhere in this chapter) as of start of year, adjusted for advance transfers. Projections based on data underlying the Board of Trustees of the Federal Old-Age and Survivors Insurance Trust Fund and the Federal Disability Insurance Trust Fund, *1989 Annual Report* of the *Board of Trustees of the Federal Old-Age and Survivors Insurance Trust Fund and the Federal Disability Insurance Trust Fund* (Washington, D.C.: GPO, 1989), hereafter referred to as *1989 OASDI Trustees' Report*, supplied by the Office of the Actuary, Social Security Administration. See also the Board of Trustees of the Federal Hospital Insurance Trust Fund, *The 1989 Annual Report* (Washington, D.C.: GPO, 1989).

2. Ibid. Projections based on 1989 intermediate II-B assumptions.

3. This is the amount the actuaries project the system will pay out in present value terms over the next seventy-five years, given the benefit structure now in the law and expected work and demographic patterns in the future. Estimates supplied by the Office of the Actuary, Social Security Administration.

4. While there actually are three separate trust funds, it is common to merge the trust funds in this way for purposes of discussion. Legislation would be needed to authorize the use of resources in any of the three trust funds to finance benefits out of another trust fund.

5. See the *1989 OASDI Trustees' Report*. While questions have been raised about the reasonableness of the intermediate assumptions, the same patterns of surpluses and reserve accumulation followed by deficits and reserve depletion are observed with the more pessimistic cost assumptions, referred to as alternative III. In addition to the alternative II-B and III assumptions, the trustees' reports also contain alternatives I and II-A (the latter based on the president's budget assumptions), which are more optimistic from the standpoint of costs.

While it is traditional for policy makers to rely on the intermediate II-B assumptions, 1983 was an exception. The National Commission on Social Security Reform, which developed the package of proposals adopted in the 1983 Social Security Amendments, used the alternative III (pessimistic) assumptions for the short range. The economy has performed substantially better than projected using these assumptions, and consequently the annual surpluses have been, and continue to be, considerably larger.

6. The reserve ratio (reserves as a percentage of outgo) generally regarded to be adequate and appropriate for pay-as-you-go financing is 100–150 percent

of annual outgo. A ratio of 9 percent is the minimum necessary to meet monthly benefits, but reserves must be considerably higher than this if the trust funds are to weather periodic economic downturns.

7. On a fiscal year basis. See President of the United States, *The 1989 Economic Report of the President* (Washington, D.C.: GPO, 1989).

8. For future cohorts of retirees. For example, an age-sixty-five retiree (and spouse) in 1990 with average lifetime earnings will draw annual benefits of $12,430 in 1990; a comparable couple in 2035 would draw $18,400 (in real 1989 dollars), roughly 50 percent higher in real terms. See the *1989 OASDI Trustees' Report*, table F6. For more on this, see commentary by Stephen Entin in this book.

9. These alternatives vary in all important respects; among the assumptions with the greatest long-range impact is the fertility rate assumption, which varies from 2.2, to 1.9, and to 1.6 children per woman under alternatives I, II-B, and III, respectively. (The U.S. fertility rate hit a low of 1.74 children per woman in 1976, and has remained below 2.0 children per woman since that time.)

10. These interest payments do not represent a drain on the federal treasury until the trust funds are in deficit, and additional income is needed to help meet benefit costs.

11. See *1989 Economic Report of the President*, pp. 98–101. See also Statement of Stephen J. Entin before the Subcommittee on Social Security and Family Policy, Committee on Finance, U.S. Senate, June 30, 1980, *Treasury News*.

12. Alicia H. Munnell, "Social Security and the Budget," *New England Economic Review* (July–August 1985), pp. 5–18.

13. The HI trust fund is scheduled to become an off-budget item in 1993.

14. The Moynihan proposal does not address the large projected deficits in the HI trust fund. Information supplied by the Office of the Actuary, Social Security Administration. See also statement by Sen. Daniel Patrick Moynihan, *Congressional Record*, January 23, 1990, S149–154.

15. The Congressional Budget Office now estimates that over two-thirds of families that pay taxes pay more in social security taxes (including the employee and employer share) than in federal income taxes; the proportion was closer to 50 percent in 1977. See "Background Materials on Federal Budget and Tax Policy for Fiscal Year 1991 and Beyond," Committee on Ways and Means, U.S. House of Representatives, 101st Cong., 2d sess., WMCP:101–21 (Feb. 6, 1990), p. 24.

16. It is worth noting that the question of how the reserves are invested and whether there is any meaningful saving remains important even under pay-as-you-go financing. Under the Moynihan proposal, for example, OASDI reserves still grow by $20–40 billion annually during the 1990s, reaching a level of $450 billion ($360 billion in real 1989 dollars) in the year 2000.

CHAPTER 2: NEW CLOTHES FOR THE EMPEROR? *Laurence J. Kotlikoff*

1. See Laurence J. Kotlikoff, "Deficit Delusion," *The Public Interest* (Summer 1986); Laurence J. Kotlikoff, "Taxation and Savings: A Neoclassical Perspective," *Journal of Economic Literature* (December 1984); and Laurence J. Kotlikoff,

"The Deficit is Not a Meaningful Measure of Fiscal Policy," *Science*, September 1988.

2. Martin Feldstein, "Social Security, Induced Retirement, and Aggregate Capital Accumulation," *Journal of Political Economy* (September–October 1974), pp. 905–26.

3. Hans Christian Andersen, "The Emperor's New Clothes," in *Forty-Two Stories*, trans. M. R. James (New York: A. S. Barnes and Company, 1959), pp. 104–7.

4. Ignoring changes in excess burden, changes in factor prices serve only to redistribute resources; they do not alter the economy's intertemporal consumption possibility frontier (its resources). See Alan J. Auerback and Laurence J. Kotlikoff, *Dynamic Fiscal Policy* (Cambridge, England: Cambridge University Press, 1988), for fiscal policy simulations illustrating the redistribution across generations arising from general equilibrium changes in factor prices.

5. If labor supply is variable, the economy's intertemporal budget constraint states that the present value of resources (human capital measured at full-time hours plus nonhuman capital) equals the present value of government consumption plus the present value of private expenditures on consumption and leisure.

6. See Franco Modigliani and Richard Brumberg, "Utility Analysis and the Consumption Function: An Interpretation of Cross-Section Data," in *Post-Keynesian Economics*, ed. Kenneth K. Kurihara (New Brunswick, N.J.: Rutgers University Press, 1954), pp. 388–436; and Albert Ando and Franco Modigliani, "The Life Cycle Hypothesis of Saving: Aggregate Implications and Tests," *American Economic Review* (March 1963), pp. 55–84.

7. Reported in telephone conversations with the Office of the Actuary, Social Security Administration. This figure represents an estimate of the reduction in the closed-group social security liability due to the 1983 Social Security Amendments, based on intermediate II-B assumptions.

8. The Reagan "deficits" and the 1983 Social Security Amendments are the major policies that have affected generational accounts in the 1980s. There appears to have been some reduction in government consumption, properly measured. See Michael J. Boskin, Alan Huber, and Mark Robinson, "Government Saving and Capital Formation in the United States, 1948–1985," in R. E. Lipsey and H. Tice, eds., *The Measurement of Saving and Investment* (Chicago: University of Chicago Press, 1989). In addition, the enactment of the Accelerated Cost Recovery System in 1981 may have tightened fiscal policy considerably in the early 1980s by redistributing roughly $300 billion from older to younger generations via changes in the value of the stock market. See "How Tight Was the Reagan Administration's First Term Fiscal Policy," in *Assessing the Reagan Years*, David Boaz, ed., Washington, D.C.: The Cato Institute, 1988 and Alan J. Auerbach and Laurence J. Kotlikoff, "Investment versus Savings Incentives: The Size of the Bang for the Buck and the Potential for Self-Financing Business Tax Cuts," in *The Economic Consequences of Government Deficits*, ed. L. H. Meyer (Boston: Kluwer-Nijhoff, 1983).

9. Andersen, "The Emperor's New Clothes," p. 107.

BOOSTING NATIONAL SAVING: *A Commentary by James M. Poterba*

1. A more detailed discussion of the empirical evidence suggesting that the current flow of tax revenue affects consumption decisions may be found in James M. Poterba and Lawrence H. Summers, "Finite Lifetimes and the Effects of Budget Deficits on National Saving," *Journal of Monetary Economics*, vol. 20 (September 1987), pp. 369–93.

INEFFECTIVENESS OF SURPLUSES: *A Commentary by John H. Makin*

1. See John H. Makin and Kenneth A. Couch, "Saving, Pension Contributions and the Real Interest Rate," *The Review of Economics and Statistics* (August 1989).
2. See Michael J. Boskin and Lawrence A. Lau, "An Analysis of U.S. Postwar Consumption and Saving," National Bureau of Economic Research, Working Paper nos. 2605 and 2606, 1988.

CHAPTER 3: BUDGETARY POLITICS, *James M. Buchanan*

1. For presentations of the results of simulation models that examine those effects under several sets of assumptions, see Joseph M. Anderson, Richard A. Kuzmak, Donald W. Moran, George R. Schink, Dale W. Jorgenson, and William R.M. Perradin, "Study of the Potential Economic and Fiscal Effects of Investment of the Assets of the Social Security Old-Age and Survivors and Disability Insurance Trust Funds: Final Report to the Social Security Administration," (Mimeo, May 1988); and Henry J. Aaron, Barry P. Bosworth, and Gary T. Burtless, "Final Report to the Social Security Administration on Contract No. 600-87-0072" (Mimeo, 1988).
2. See intermediate II-B projections contained in the Board of Trustees of the Federal Old-Age and Survivors Insurance Trust Fund and the Federal Disability Insurance Trust Fund, *1989 Annual Report of the Board of Trustees of the Federal Old-Age and Survivors Insurance Trust Fund and the Federal Disability Insurance Trust Fund* (Washington, D.C.: GPO, 1989).
3. It may be suggested that there is no increase in the size of the debt, properly measured. If retirement benefits are promised in future periods, the present value of these benefits is a liability of the federal government that should be included in properly measured debt totals. The "funding" process serves merely to make these real liabilities explicit.
In the strict independence scenario, by contrast, there will be an explicit reduction in the size of the debt, properly measured, as trust fund surpluses emerge.
4. See Carolyn L. Weaver, "Controlling the Risks Posed by Advance Funding—Options for Reform," in this volume for more on this.

CHAPTER 4: THE POLITICAL ECONOMY OF THE RESERVES, *Herman B. Leonard*

1. For a discussion of the debate on this question early in the history of social security, see Carolyn Weaver, *The Crisis in Social Security: Economic and*

Political Origins (Durham, N.C.: Duke Press Policy Studies, 1982). For a view of the modern debate, see Alicia Munnell, "Should We Fund Social Security?" Federal Reserve Bank of Boston, Mimeographed.

2. This does not imply that having reserves has no impact on national savings; the buildup of the reserves would certainly contribute to national saving if it were financed out of taxes that reduce consumption spending and were funneled effectively into public or private investments in ways that do not reduce other investment. The assumption here is that the existence of the reserves does not, by itself, change the impact of social security on people's private saving.

3. To see whether it has, we have to compare the amount of non-social-security deficit spending that occurs in response to the 1983 amendments with the deficit spending that would otherwise have taken place (which, of course, we cannot know precisely).

4. The strong political logic of righteous entitlement, which indicates that benefits will be paid, also indicates who should be thought of as owning the reserves. They are a down payment against future benefits. What is most certain is the benefit level; whether the reserves will cover it is less clear. Any higher than anticipated return reduces future taxpayer burdens rather than expanding benefits. If we are to be guided by the risk preferences of the owners in establishing the investment policy, then the relevant preferences are those of future taxpayers, not future beneficiaries.

5. To be precise, an amount equal to the estimated tax on social security benefits collected by the Treasury is transferred each year from the general fund of the Treasury to the social security system. The transfer from the general fund is not perceived by the recipients, taxpayers, or by social security's political supporters as general revenue financing.

6. Even under the current arrangement, Congress has one strong reason to increase the taxation of social security benefits: each dollar of taxes reduces the overall federal budget deficit as measured under Gramm-Rudman. If social security is separated from the remainder of the budget, however, the taxability of benefits will merely increase what to some may seem to be an already too large reserve.

7. See Carolyn L. Weaver, "Social Security's Looming Surpluses: Panacea or Mirage?" Statement before the Social Security Public Trustees' Symposium on the Social Security Trust Fund Buildup, Washington, D. C., September 16, 1988.

8. Senator Moynihan, who argues that the existence of the social security reserves (under the policy of lending them directly to the Treasury) is making it harder to achieve fiscal balance in the non-social-security budget, has recently proposed a payroll tax reduction to force greater responsibility in the rest of the budget. There is real irony in the proposal: based on a concern about a lack of balance in one part of the budget, it would plunge the overall budget into a deeper deficit.

9. Interestingly, this may be a result, but may not have been the intent, of the recommendations of the National Commission on Social Security Reform. According to its executive director, Robert Myers, the intent was to finance the

long-term deficit with level payroll tax rates. Given the population dynamics of the baby-boom generation, this implied partial funding of the system between roughly 1990 and 2025.

10. Obviously, if the social security reserves are all invested in a fixed-supply asset (like land in a particular location), then the returns to that asset would decrease markedly. But if they are invested either in a large and growing asset (like federal government debt issues) or in a reasonably diversified portfolio of other assets, they are unlikely to shift returns markedly.

11. The second round of funding would come from general revenues, called forth to pay off the social security debt as it was presented to the Treasury for repayment. Some of this debt might be "rolled over," building up debt held by the public. But if what holds the budget in check is the public's willingness to absorb Treasury debt (or Congress's willingness to accept the consequences of issuing additional debt), the need to roll over former social security "inside" debt to "outsiders" will create the same strain Congress had sought to avoid (or, at least, defer).

12. Current law permits some investments of this kind (for example, in FNMA securities), but in practice all funds are invested in Treasury obligations.

POLITICAL EFFECTS OF SOCIAL SECURITY SURPLUSES: *A Commentary by Alan S. Blinder*

1. This underscores my warning about political forecasting. Less than a year after the conference at which these remarks were delivered Congress was debating Senator Moynihan's proposal to cut the payroll tax!

CHAPTER 5: FOREIGN EXPERIENCE WITH SURPLUSES, *Munnell and Ernsberger*

1. See the intermediate II-B projections contained in the Board of Trustees of the Federal Old-Age and Survivors Insurance Trust Fund and the Federal Disability Insurance Trust Fund, *1989 Annual Report of the Board of Trustees of the Federal Old-Age and Survivors Insurance Trust Fund and the Federal Disability Insurance Trust Fund* (Washington, D.C.: GPO, 1989).

2. Henry J. Aaron, Barry P. Bosworth, and Gary Burtless, *Can America Afford to Grow Old? Paying for Social Security* (Washington, D.C.: Brookings Institution, 1989), table 5–4.

3. Until fiscal 1969, the financial activity of social security and other trust funds was reported separately from the administrative budget; after fiscal 1969, trust fund activity was integrated with other functions and the total reported as the unified budget. The Gramm-Rudman-Hollings legislation enacted in 1985 moved social security off-budget but retained it for the purpose of calculating whether Congress meets the deficit targets. When Gramm-Rudman-Hollings expires in 1993, social security will be off-budget for all purposes.

4. U.S. Congress, Senate, Committee on Finance, Subcommittee on Social Security and Income Maintenance Programs, *Review of Social Security Trust Fund Policy*, 98th Congress, 1st session, 1986, S. Hearing 99-528, November 7,

1985. General Accounting Office, *Disinvestment of the Social Security Trust Funds* (Washington, D.C.: General Accounting Office, February 1986).

5. David Koitz, "Social Security: Its Funding Outlook and Significance for Government Finance" (Washington, D.C.: Congressional Research Service, June 1, 1986).

6. The OECD uses the System of National Accounts (SNA), developed by the United Nations, to calculate government surpluses or deficits and government saving. According to the SNA, a government's surplus or deficit equals the amount that it has to lend or needs to borrow after financing its total expenditures. In other words the surplus or deficit equals total revenue minus total outlays.

Total revenue falls into two classifications: current and capital. Current revenue includes tax receipts (other than those from estate or inheritance taxes), property income, proceeds from nonindustrial and incidental sales, cash operating surpluses of departmental enterprises, fees and charges, fines, forfeits, private donations, and financial grants from other governments. Capital revenue equals proceeds from sales of capital items plus capital transfers from other sectors and governments. Capital transfers also includes death duties, such as inheritance taxes, as well as donations of durable goods made by the private sector or by other governments.

Like revenues, expenditures are categorized as current or capital. The SNA defines current outlays as purchases of services and nondurable goods, financial transfers to individuals, financial grants to other governments, and all military expenditures. Capital outlays include expenditures for acquisitions of land, intangible assets, government stocks, or nonmilitary durable goods with a life expectancy of more than one year. Transfers of capital assets to other governments and sectors are also considered capital outlays.

Government saving, according to the SNA, equals the surplus or deficit plus net capital investment (capital outlays minus capital income minus depreciation). Depreciation is defined as a government's consumption of fixed capital, or the reduction in value of its reproducible fixed assets resulting from normal wear and tear and foreseen obsolescence. The SNA calculation includes wear and tear of government buildings but does not depreciate other forms of government construction, such as roads. Reductions in value that result from unforeseen catastrophes and depletion of natural resources are also not included in depreciation.

Because the U.S. Bureau of the Census does not distinguish between current and capital receipts and outlays of governments, U.S. economists typically consider a government's saving equal to its surplus or deficit. Since this chapter is more concerned with productivity than the level of government expenditure, we use the SNA definition of saving. See International Monetary Fund, *A Manual on Government Finance Statistics* (Washington, D.C.: IMF 1986) and United Nations, *Demographic Yearbook, 1962* (New York: UN, 1962).

7. The Swedish Institute, *Sweden in Brief*, 3rd ed. (Uddevalla, Sweden: Bohuslaningens Boktryckeri AB, 1986).

8. Sweden's basic pension program provides old-age, survivors, and disability benefits. Resident citizens are eligible for the basic retirement pension at

age sixty-five (sixty-seven before July 1976), regardless of employment or income status. Citizens not domiciled in Sweden may qualify for reduced benefits, while foreign nationals must fulfill a minimum residency requirement. Benefit amounts are calculated with reference to a base sum and automatically adjusted for changes in the price level. The annuity for an individual equals 96 percent of the base amount, and the annuity for a married couple equals 157 percent of the base. Actuarially adjusted pensions may be collected as early as age sixty or postponed until age seventy.

ATP pays earnings-related old-age, survivors, and disability benefits to persons who have been credited with at least three years of pensionable income. Pensionable income includes all earnings under an annually adjusted cap. Workers with thirty years of contributions are eligible for the full ATP old-age pension, which amounts to 60 percent of their average pensionable income. (Average pensionable income is calculated from a participant's fifteen best-paid years.) ATP offers the same rights as the basis pension to advance or postpone collection of benefits.

9. Aleksander Markowski and Edward E. Palmer, "Social Insurance and Saving in Sweden," in *Social Security versus Private Saving*, George M. von Furstenberg, ed. (Cambridge, Mass.: Ballinger, 1979), p. 188.

10. Comparative Studies Staff, Social Security Administration, "Social Security in Sweden" (Baltimore, Md.: U.S. Department of Health and Human Services, August 1980, Mimeographed).

11. Markowski and Palmer, "Social Insurance and Saving in Sweden," p. 188.

12. While the ATP eligibility requirement would have postponed payment of full benefits until 1991, special introductory provisions forgave some contribution requirements for older workers. This allowed participants ages forty-seven to sixty-four in 1960 to receive more generous partial benefit payments than they would have otherwise, and for participants ages thirty-seven to forty-six in 1960 eventually to collect full benefits. These introductory provisions would have caused the first full benefits to be paid in 1981. Legislation passed in 1979, however, lowered the retirement age from sixty-seven to sixty-five, making 1979 the first year in which full benefits were paid.

13. Edward M. Gramlich, "Rethinking the Role of the Public Sector," in *The Swedish Economy*, Barry P. Bosworth and Alice M. Rivlin, eds. (Washington, D.C.: Brookings Institution, 1987), pp. 250–70.

14. Actually, costs are rising faster than the number of pensioners because new beneficiaries, having been covered by the ATP system for a longer time, have above-average entitlements.

15. Swedish National Pension Fund, *Summary of Activities* (Stockholm: Swedish National Pension Fund, 1987), p. 6.

16. Ministry of Finance, *Summary of The Swedish Budget 1988/1989* (Stockholm, Sweden: Norstedts Tryckeri AB, 1988), p. 11.

17. Swedish National Pension Fund, *Summary of Activities* (Stockholm: Swedish National Pension Fund, 1985), p. 14.

18. From the outset, however, the three funds elected to administer the

program jointly and have come, for all intents and purposes, to function as a single unit. As a result references to the funds are traditionally in the singular.

19. Since 1959, seven additional funds, entitled to invest in private securities, have been created. The Fourth Fund was developed amid great controversy in 1974. Start-up capital was provided by the boards of the First, Second, and Third Funds, and subsequent infusions of capital from ATP premiums have been frequently granted by Parliament. The five Wage-Earner Funds were established in 1983 and derive their funding from two sources: a 0.2 percentage point increase in the ATP contribution rate earmarked for the Wage-Earner Funds and a special profit-sharing tax levied on businesses. Finally, a tenth fund, similar to the Fourth Fund in revenue source and investment regulation, was recently approved by the Parliament. To ensure that the seven funds are productively invested, they are required to earn a minimum real return of 3 percent on their assets.

While the Socialist implications of these funds and the controversy surrounding them are quite interesting, they are of little relevance for the United States since it is unlikely that such an approach would ever be taken here. Additionally the impact of these funds on the ATP system has necessarily been quite small since their combined assets are only 7 percent of the assets held by the First, Second, and Third Funds. See Swedish National Pension Fund, *Summary of Activities* (Stockholm: Swedish National Pension Fund, First, Second, and Third Boards, 1987).

20. The following discussion draws heavily on Jonas Pontusson, *Public Pension Funds and the Politics of Capital Formation in Sweden* (Goteborg, Sweden: Tryckt va Graphic Systems AB, 1984).

21. Until late 1986, the Swedish central bank used three basic approaches for controlling the supply of assets available in the credit markets. First, the bank supervised the release of all bonds (both public and private) to the general public. This enabled the central bank to regulate the interest rate on bonds in a detailed fashion and to determine the volume and sectoral distribution of bond issues at any time. The release of corporate bonds was commonly postponed to make room for government or housing bonds. Second, the central bank influenced the distribution and volume of bank lending through liquidity requirements. The bank not only dictated what assets were liquid—government and housing bonds were always defined as liquid assets—but also regulated the required ratio of liquid assets to liabilities for banks. By changing this ratio or redefining liquid assets, the central bank could induce commercial banks to purchase specific securities. Third, the central bank directly regulated the lending practices of nonbank suppliers of credit through a system of annual agreements. Most notable were the bank's agreements with the insurance companies. When the first agreement was struck in 1952, the insurance companies merely agreed to restrict their lending to the previous year's level, but subsequent agreements usually entailed more extensive and detailed commitments.

22. By keeping interest rates low, the central bank hoped to stimulate the economy and facilitate the financing of low-income housing. The government had announced in 1964 a goal of constructing 1 million new housing units

between 1965 and 1974. See Pontusson, *Public Pension Funds and the Politics of Capital Formation in Sweden*, p. 33.

23. Ibid., p. 50.

24. Ministry of Finance, *Summary of the Swedish Budget 1988/1989*, p. 41.

25. Actually Sweden's elderly dependency ratio is expected to decline for a brief period early in the next century, after which Sweden will experience further population aging. Presumably the AP fund will accumulate additional reserves during the period of de-aging and then rely once again on interest earnings to help meet benefit costs.

26. Kishimoto Koichi, *Politics in Modern Japan: Development and Organization* (Tokyo: Japan Echo, 1982).

27. Four mutual aid associations provide coverage to workers not participating in EPI. These mutual aid associations represent central government employees, local government workers, private school teachers, and workers in agricultural cooperatives.

28. More precisely, EPI participants make all contributions to the EPI program, and a designated proportion of their contribution is then transferred on their behalf to the NP account. One-third of this transfer is paid out of general revenues. General revenues also subsidize one-third of benefit costs for persons contributing exclusively to the NP. See Foreign Press Center/Japan, "Social Security in Japan," in *About Japan*, no. 17 (Tokyo: Foreign Press Center, 1988), pp. 13–22.

29. John Creighton Campbell, "Social Welfare," in *Kodansha Encyclopedia of Japan* (New York: Kodansha International, 1983), p. 211.

30. Japanese Social Insurance Agency, *Outline of Social Insurance in Japan* (Tokyo: Japanese Social Insurance Agency, 1982), p. 77.

31. Before the 1985 reforms (implemented in April 1986), the EPI and NP covered about 90 percent of the working population. The EPI program insured all wage and salary workers in firms with five or more workers. EPI participants constituted 44 percent of all insured persons. The NP program was established in 1969 as a catchall for any economically active Japanese not otherwise insured and included workers in small businesses, farmers, and the self-employed. The NP covered 46 percent of all insured persons. In addition Japan had four mutual aid associations (see note 27) and a special program for seamen.

EPI provided an earnings-related pension financed by equal employee and employer payroll tax contributions and a general revenue supplement equal to 20 percent of benefit costs. The benefit consisted of a flat-rate amount plus 1 percent of a retiree's average indexed earnings, both multiplied by the number of years of participation. The NP provided a flat-rate pension, only varying with years of earnings, that was financed by a flat-rate contribution from the insured and a general revenue subsidy amounting to one-third of benefit costs. Income-tested allowances were also provided by the NP program to the needy aged and disabled. Benefits under both the EPI and NP were automatically adjusted for annual changes of 5 percent or more in consumer prices and adjustments for smaller price increases were frequently approved by the Diet.

See Japanese Social Insurance Agency, *Outline of Social Insurance in Japan* (Tokyo: Japanese Social Insurance Agency, 1982), and U.S. Department of Health and Human Services, Comparative Studies Staff, Social Security Administration, "Social Security in Japan" (Baltimore, Md.: U.S. Department of Health and Human Services, April 1983, Mimeographed).

As a result of the reform, the NP was expanded to include all residents ages 20 to 59 and the seamen's insurance system was merged with the EPI program. The principal cost-cutting measure of the reform was a large reduction in benefits, phased in over twenty years. The new NP offers a full pension only to retirees with fifty years of participation; benefits are actuarially reduced for workers with twenty-five to forty-nine years of contributions, and no benefits are paid to workers with fewer than twenty-five years of participation. The EPI also requires twenty-five years of participation. Additionally the EPI no longer provides the flat pension component and its earnings-related component has been reduced by 25 percent.

32. For an excellent discussion of intragenerational and intergenerational inequities of the previous system, see Martha N. Ozawa, "Social Security Reform in Japan," *Social Service Review* (September 1985), pp. 476–95.

33. See Japan Foundation for Research and Development of Pension Schemes, *National System of Old-Age, Disability and Survivors' Benefits in Japan*, 2d ed. (Tokyo: Japan Foundation for Research and Development of Pension Schemes, 1986), for a description of the transitional provisions.

34. Lillian Liu, "Social Security Reforms in Japan," *Social Security Bulletin* (September 1987), pp. 29–37.

35. Yukio Noguchi, *The Failure of the Government to Perform its Proper Task: A Case Study of Japan*, vol. 34 of *Ordo; Jahrbuch fur die Ordnung von Wirtschaft und Gesellschaft* (New York: Gustav Fisher Verlag, 1983), pp. 559–70.

36. Douglas Ostrom, "Japan's Fiscal Policy," *Japan Economic Institute Report*, no. 18A (May 6, 1988), p. 5.

37. Ministry of Finance, Budget Bureau, *The Budget in Brief* (Tokyo: Ministry of Finance, 1987).

38. Ostrom, "Japan's Fiscal Policy," p. 8; Organisation for Economic Cooperation and Development, *OECD Economic Surveys: Japan 1987/1988* (Paris: OECD, 1988).

39. Gardner Ackley and Hiromitsu Ishi, "Fiscal, Monetary, and Related Policies," in *Asia's New Giant: How the Japanese Economy Works*, Hugh Patrick and Henry Rosovsky, eds. (Washington, D.C.: Brookings Institution, 1976), p. 212.

40. Yukio Noguchi, "Public Finance," in *The Political Economy of Japan: The Domestic Transformation*, vol. 1, Kozo Yamamura and Yasukichi Yasuba, eds. (Stanford, Calif.: Stanford University Press, 1987).

41. The agreement provided that "appropriate measures" would be taken to repay the suspension but did not state explicitly what these measures should be. The Diet understood from the agreement that at a minimum the principal would be repaid once fiscal policy was loosened. The first principal repayment was made in the fiscal year 1988 budget.

42. Noriyuki Takayama, "Japan," in *The World Crisis in Social Security*,

Jean-Jacques Rosa, ed. (San Francisco: Institute for Contemporary Studies, 1982), pp. 93–120.

43. Legislation in 1987 loosened restrictions on FILP's interest rates. The rate is now determined by government ordinances that consider market rates. In 1980 FILP's rate was 0.8 percentage points lower than the long-term prime rate, but in 1987 both rates were 5.2 percent. The same legislation created the Pension Welfare Corporation, which typically provides returns that are higher than the prime rate. Roughly one-third of EPI and NP assets are invested via the Pension Welfare Corporation.

44. The full Old Age Security pension is paid to persons age sixty-five and over who have resided in Canada for forty years after reaching age eighteen. Persons who are older than age thirty-seven in 1988 and have lived in Canada for ten consecutive years immediately preceding application are also eligible for full benefits. Any person may collect a partial pension after meeting a ten-year residency requirement.

The fully reciprocal Canada and Quebec Pension Plans provide earnings-related old-age, survivors, and disability benefits for Canadian workers. Persons with at least ten years of contributions collect an annuity equal to 25 percent of their average indexed earnings regardless of labor force status. Participants with more than ten years of contributions may drop periods of low earnings (up to 15 percent of the total career period) when calculating average earnings. Actuarially reduced pensions are payable to retired participants who are between ages sixty and sixty-four. Workers may also postpone benefit payments until age seventy and use the additional periods to calculate average earnings.

45. While in favor of reform, the New Democrats were opposed initially to the trust fund buildup, which they considered regressive. Since then, however, the prefunding policy has gained widespread support throughout all three parties. See Ken Bryden, M. P. P. Morton, and Des Morton, *New Democrats Look at the Canada Pension Plan* (Toronto: Ontario New Democratic Party, 1965).

46. Kenneth Bryden, *Old-Age Pensions and Policy Making in Canada* (Montreal: McGill-Queen's University Press, 1974).

47. Department of Insurance Canada, *Canada Pension Plan Statutory Actuarial Report No. 10 as of December 31, 1985* (Canada: Department of Insurance Canada, 1985), p. 3.

48. This tradition was initiated by the Conservatives in 1985. See Ministry of Finance, *The Canadian Budgetary Process: Proposals for Improvement* (Ottawa: Ministry of Finance, 1985).

49. A 1976 study by the province of Ontario provides one example of how the provinces might eliminate their debt to the CPP. The study argues that if a fully funded system is not possible, then the next best alternative is pay-as-you-go in which current contributions are used to cover benefit payments and administrative expenses. Under the proposed scheme the existing fund would not be used but would rather continue to accrue interest; the interest paid by the provinces on the existing debt would be used to purchase new provincial debt. Although the CPP fund would continue to grow, this plan could amount to the equivalent of the forgiveness of debt. (See Ontario Ministry of Treasury,

Economics, and Governmental Affairs, *Review of Issues in Financing the Canada Pension Plan*, 1976.)

50. J. E. Pesando and S. A. Rea, *Public and Private Pensions in Canada: An Economic Analysis* (Toronto: University of Toronto Press for the Ontario Economic Council, 1977), p. 91.

51. Ontario Ministry of Treasury, *Budget Statements* (Toronto: Ontario Ministry of Treasury, 1974), pp. 26–27.

52. Richard M. Bird, *Charging for Public Services: A New Look at an Old Idea* (Toronto: Canadian Tax Foundation, December 1976).

53. Keith Patterson, "The Effect of the Provincial Borrowings from Universal Pension Plans on Provincial and Municipal Government Finance," Discussion Paper 192 (Ottawa: Economic Council of Canada, 1981).

54. Ministry of Finance, *Quarterly Economic Review: Annual Reference Tables* (Ottawa: Ministry of Supply and Services, June 1987), table 52.

55. Advisory Commission on Intergovernmental Relations, *Significant Features of Fiscal Federalism, 1988 Edition*, vol. 1 (Washington, D.C.: Advisory Commission, December 1987), tables 42 and 43.

56. Robert M. Ball, *Social Security Today and Tomorrow* (New York: Columbia University Press, 1978), pp. 458–60; U.S. Congress, House of Representatives, Committee on Ways and Means, Subcommittee on Social Security, *Report on the Study of Social Security as an Independent Agency: Hearing before Committee on Ways and Means, House of Representatives*, 98th Congress, 2d session, July 30, 1984, serial 98-92.

CHAPTER 6: SOCIAL SECURITY AND THE BUDGET, *Crain and Marlow*

1. See Michael L. Marlow, "Tax and Spend Hypothesis" (1988, Unpublished).

2. See William Anderson, Myles S. Wallace, and John T. Warner, "Government Spending and Taxation: What Causes What?" *Southern Economic Journal*, January 1986, pp. 630–39; Paul R. Blackley, "Causality between Revenues and Expenditures and the Size of the Federal Budget," *Public Finance Quarterly*, April 1986, pp. 139–56; Neela Manage and Michael L. Marlow, "The Causal Relation between Federal Expenditures and Receipts," *Southern Economic Journal*, January 1986, pp. 717–29; and George von Furstenburg, Jeffrey R. Green, and Jin-Ho Jeogn, "Tax and Spend or Spend and Tax," *Review of Economics and Statistics*, May 1986, pp. 179–88.

3. At least two different issues were being raised in this debate. One issue was the appropriate size of government. Once one agreed to a certain desired level of government, it was easy to determine whether the budget deficit reflected over- or undertaxation. Second, the different policy recommendations reflected different behavioral assumptions concerning the probable effects of a tax or spending change on budget activities. The major opposing view centers on whether one accepts the budget constraint hypothesis. See Marlow, "Tax and Spend Hypothesis," for the argument that formal discussion of the ap-

propriate size of government is a prerequisite for solving the federal budget deficit problem.

4. See Milton Friedman, *Tax Limitation, Inflation and the Role of Government* (Dallas: Fisher Institute, 1978).

5. Ibid., p. 5.

6. See John Cogan, "The Evolution of Congressional Budget Decisionmaking and the Emergence of Federal Deficits," Working Paper, Hoover Institution, Palo Alto, Calif., August 1988.

7. See C. W. Granger, "Investigating Causal Relations by Economic Models and Cross Spectral Methods," *Econometrica*, July 1969, pp. 424–38.

8. See Manage and Marlow, "Causal Relation between Federal Expenditures and Receipts."

9. See Rati Ram, "Additional Evidence on Causality between Government Revenue and Government Expenditure," *Southern Economic Journal*, January 1988, pp. 763–69.

10. See David Joulfaian, "The Causal Effects of Government Expenditures on Government Revenues" (Washington, D.C.: U.S. Treasury, 1988, Mimeographed).

11. Blackley uses both Granger and Sims causality tests. The main difference between these tests is that Sim's definition includes information on future values of variables (leads rather than lags) as well as past values (lags) of the variables. See Blackley, "Causality between Revenues and Expenditures and the Size of the Federal Budget."

12. See Michael L. Marlow and Neela Manage, "Testing for Causality in State and Local Government Finances," *Public Choice*, vol. 53, no. 2 (1987). Twenty-five states, for example, limit the amount of debt they may sell, twenty states forbid appropriations to exceed estimated revenues, eighteen states require governors to submit balanced budgets, and so forth. Similar to the case of the federal government, which operates subject to a quasi-binding debt ceiling, the states are not actually constrained by these devices or appear to have developed sophisticated means of circumventing many of them. In addition to the growth of off-budget enterprises, states have increased their use of non-guaranteed debt and other creative financing. See James T. Bennett and Thomas J. DiLorenzo, "Off-Budget Activities of the Local Governments: The Bane of the Tax Revolt," *Public Choice*, vol. 39, no. 3 (1982), pp. 333–42.

13. See Abdur R. Chowdhry, "Expenditures and Receipts in the State and Local Levels of Government," *Public Choice*, vol. 59, no. 3 (1988), pp. 277–85.

14. See Douglas Holtz-Eakin, Whitney Newey, and Harvey Rosen, "The Revenues-Expenditures Nexus: Evidence from the Local Government Data," Working Paper 2180, National Bureau of Economic Research, March 1987.

15. See Anderson, Wallace, and Warner, "Government Spending and Taxation: What Causes What?" The authors only consider inflation-adjusted measures of expenditures and tax receipts. When one uses real spending and taxes, however, a new problem emerges because of the high correlation between inflation and inflation lagged one or more periods.

16. Von Furstenburg, Green, and Jeogn, "Tax and Spend or Spend and Tax."

17. Moreover, without showing any significant relation—casual or other-

wise—between taxes and spending, the study implies that past increases in taxes are unrelated to current spending and past increases in spending are unrelated to current tax levels. In other words past fiscal policy bears little relation to current policy, or fiscal policy is random.

18. Even if one does not accept the budget constraint hypothesis, the empirical evidence suggests that one cannot reasonably reject the hypothesis that any time taxes are raised expenditures will also rise. Plans to increase taxes as a way to reduce deficits thus carry the potential of raising government spending and possibly future deficits.

19. See U.S. Office of Management and Budget, *Historical Tables, Budget of the United States, Fiscal Year 1989* (Washington, D.C.: U.S. Government Printing Office, 1988), tables 1.1 and 13.1. Social security revenues includes all sources of cash income to the four trust funds, including interest and other transfers from the general fund.

Since 1986, the OASI and the DI trust funds have been excluded from the unified budget; they continue to be used in the calculations of spending reductions necessary to meet Gramm-Rudman-Hollings.

20. After first-differencing the data once, we transformed it into log * first-difference form, which is the annual growth rate. We then regressed this transformed data on a simple (linear) time trend. When the time trend coefficient was not statistically different from zero, we assumed that the variable exhibits stationarity. When the time coefficient was statistically different from zero, we transformed the variable once more by taking an additional first-difference (but without another log transformation). In the event the second transformation continued to be related statistically to the time trend, we transformed it, and so on.

21. See D. K. Guilkey, "Small Sample Properties of Three Tests for Granger-Causal Ordering a Bivariate Stochastic Series," *Review of Economics and Statistics*, November 1982, pp. 668–80, and Marlow and Manage, "Testing for Causality in State and Local Government Finances: Reply," *Public Choice*, vol. 59, no. 3 (1988), pp. 287–90, for discussion of these important issues.

22. This is the standard approach taken in previous studies using Granger-causality tests where the null hypothesis is that $\beta_1 = \beta_2 = \ldots \beta_n = 0$.

23. This follows Joulfaian, "Causal Effects of Government Expenditures on Government Revenues."

24. Consider the following: Let $SB = sr - ss$, where sr and ss refer, respectively, to social security revenues and spending. Then, when we regress ss on $SB (= sr - ss)$, there must exist an inverse relation between ss and SB.

25. See Office of Management and Budget, *Historical Tables, Budget of the United States, Fiscal Year 1989*, table 3.1.

26. Ibid., table 1.1.

27. These findings bear on the question of how social security's net contribution to the federal deficit should be measured. Before 1986, for example, when social security was included in the unified budget, its net contribution was determined as the difference between direct outlays and direct receipts, ignoring intragovernmental transfers, such as interest payments. Alicia Munnell argues that this is not appropriate:

> The crux of the issue is whether this [interest] payment is simply a transfer among different sectors of the federal government that would not occur in the absence of social security or an outlay that would have to be paid to the public if it were not paid to the trust funds (Munnell, "Social Security and the Budget," *New England Economic Journal*, July/August 1985, p. 9).

Munnell argues that interest payments by the Treasury to social security trust funds are paid-off borrowings by the U.S. government and therefore reflect past deficits in the non-social-security portion of the federal budget. She therefore suggests that we calculate the effect of social security on the overall federal budget by including interest received on the trust funds investments (and all other components of intragovernmental transfers) as well as direct receipts.

From a broader perspective, Munnell is basically arguing that trust fund surpluses are effectively saved. If this were correct—and our empirical findings suggest it is not—there would be no reason for concern about the misuse of trust fund surpluses, a concern which she shares. See Munnell, pp. 5–18.

BENEFITS OF ADVANCE FUNDING: *A Commentary by John B. Shoven*

1. See Henry J. Aaron, Barry P. Bosworth, and Gary T. Burtless, "Final Report to the Social Security Administration on Contract No. 600-87-0072" (Washington, D.C.: Social Security Administration, 1988, Mimeographed).

2. Henry J. Aaron, Barry P. Bosworth, and Gary T. Burtless, *Can America Afford to Grow Old? Paying for Social Security* (Washington, D.C.: Brookings Institution, 1989).

CHAPTER 7: MANAGING THE BALANCES WITH THE INCOME TAX, *Lawrence B. Lindsey*

1. Board of Trustees of the Federal Old-Age and Survivors Insurance Trust Fund and the Federal Disability Insurance Trust Fund, *1989 Annual Report of the Board of Trustees of the Federal Old-Age and Survivors Insurance Trust Fund and the Federal Disabilty Insurance Trust Fund* (Washington, D.C.: GPO, 1989), hereafter referred to as *1989 OASDI Trustees' Report*.

2. See Paul Samuelson, "An Exact Consumption Loan Model on Interest with or without the Social Contrivance of Money," *Journal of Political Economy* (December 1958), pp. 467–82.

3. See *1989 OASDI Trustees' Report*.

4. See, for example, U.S. Congressional Budget Office, *Indexing the Individual Income Tax* (Washington, D.C.: GPO, 1980). Calculations for this chapter were done using the NBER TAXSIM model, which produces an elasticity of 1.5 under the current tax code.

5. See *1988 OASDI Trustees' Report*, tables 10 and 11.

6. See Henry J. Aaron, Barry P. Bosworth, and Gary T. Burtless, "Final Report to the Social Security Administration on Contract No. 600-87-0072" (Washington, D.C.: Social Security Administration, 1988, Mimeographed).

7. For example, a rate of per capita AGI growth of only 0.86 percent per year instead of 1.36 percent will mean that the income tax share of AGI will grow to 18.4 percent instead of 21.3 percent. In addition, the economy will be 26 percent smaller under the slower-growth assumption. The combined effect of lower income and a smaller income tax share will mean a sharply lower revenue windfall of only $110 billion (real 1990 dollars) in 2050.

8. See Aaron, Bosworth, and Burtless, "Final Report."

9. See Steven Vinti and David Wise, "Tax Deferred Accounts, Constrained Choice and Estimation of Individual Savings," *Review of Economic Studies*, vol. 53 (1986), pp. 579–601; and Daniel Feenberg and Jonathan Skinner, "Sources of IRA Saving," in L. Summers, ed., *Tax Policy and the Economy*, vol. 3 (Cambridge, Mass.: MIT Press, 1989), pp. 25–46.

CHAPTER 8: RISKS OF ADVANCE FUNDING, *Carolyn L. Weaver*

1. Data and projections on costs and financial condition of the trust funds presented here and elsewhere in this chapter are based on the intermediate II-B assumptions contained in the Board of Trustees of the Federal Old-Age and Survivors Insurance Trust Fund and the Federal Disability Trust Fund, *1989 Annual Report of the Board of Trustees of the Federal Old-Age and Survivors Insurance Trust Fund and the Federal Disability Insurance Trust Fund* (Washington, D.C.: GPO, 1989), hereafter referred to as *1989 OASDI Trustees' Report*. (Under less optimistic assumptions, costs would be higher and the financial condition of the trust funds would be more adverse.) Data on liabilities provided by the Office of the Actuary, Social Security Administration.

2. These questions remain important and of immediate concern even if the trustees' long-range projections prove to be too optimistic. Already, the system (OASDHI) has amassed a reserve fund on the order of $208 billion and is adding to that reserve at a rate exceeding $1 billion *weekly*. (Roughly one quarter of the surplus receipts today are due to interest payments from the general fund of the Treasury.)

3. Martin Feldstein, "The Social Security Fund and National Capital Accumulation," *Funding Pensions: Issues and Implications for Financial Markets*, Conference Series No. 16 (Boston: Federal Reserve Bank of Boston, 1976).

4. Ibid., p. 45.

5. Michael Boskin, "Future Social Security Financing Alternatives and National Saving," National Bureau of Economic Research, Working Paper No. 2256, 1987.

6. Twelve trillion dollars is the estimated reserve of social security in 2030, in current dollars; in constant 1989 dollars, this amounts to $2.5 trillion. Including HI, the reserve peaks at $5.8 trillion in 2020, which is $1.8 trillion in constant 1989 dollars. All projections are based on intermediate II-B assumptions in *1989 OASDI Trustees' Report*.

7. Alternatively, the surplus or deficit in the rest of the budget could bear some fixed relation to GNP. The key is that the rest of the budget be unaffected by changes in social security reserves.

8. Eugene Steuerle and Paul Wilson, "The Taxation of Poor and Lower-Income Workers," *Tax Notes*, vol. 34, no. 7 (February 16, 1987), pp. 695–712.

9. It is immaterial whether social security is actually on or off budget in an accounting sense.

Since such a plan would result in aggregate fiscal policy being driven by social security, a careful reconsideration of the social security financing arrangement—both the wisdom of the implied rate of government saving and spending and the quality of the underlying economic and demographic assumptions—would be imperative. A desired or "optimal" level of surpluses or rate of saving was not debated in 1983; the projected path is simply the byproduct of a particular tax schedule combined with projected economic and demographic developments. See Carolyn L. Weaver, "Social Security Shouldn't Drive U.S. Fiscal Policy," *Wall Street Journal*, April 18, 1989.

10. Congressman John Porter has proposed privatizing the investment and ownership of the surpluses. (See John Porter, *Fact Sheet: Individual Social Security Retirement Accounts*, 1990.) He has not, however, specified how benefits would be restructured. If individuals are to be granted ownership of the proceeds of these accounts, some restructuring of benefits relative to taxes is unavoidable. The reason is that, under present arrangements, only a small portion of each individual's taxes is potentially available to finance his or her own future benefits; most will be used to finance someone else's benefits—someone older or someone poorer, for example.

The system described here (actually the second tier) would embrace the concept of "individual equity," closely linking the individual's tax payments and expected benefits.

11. Michael Boskin has proposed a two-tiered system that is similar in the structure of benefits but different in its financing. Under his proposal, the earnings-related payments would be made by the federal treasury, as is now the case, and financed on a pay-as-you-go basis. There would be no private sector accounts. See Michael Boskin, *Too Many Promises: The Uncertain Future of Social Security* (Homewood, Ill.: Dow-Jones Irwin, 1986), pp. 139–71.

12. For more on this, see Carolyn L. Weaver, "Social Security Investment Policy," Statement before the Social Security Advisory Council, Washington, D.C., March 8, 1990.

13. Under the 1983 amendments, the retirement age (actually, the age at which full benefits are payable) does not begin to rise until 2000. It takes sixteen years to reach sixty-six and another six years to reach sixty-seven, with the full transition to sixty-seven completed in 2022. Early retirement benefits continue to be payable at 62.

14. Based on informal estimates provided by the Office of the Actuary, Social Security Administration.

PROTECTING THE SURPLUSES: *A Commentary by William D. Nordhaus*

1. See Henry J. Aaron, Barry P. Bosworth, and Gary T. Burtless, "Final Report to the Social Security Administration on Contract No. 600-87-0072"

(Mimeographed, 1988); and Joseph M. Anderson et al., "Study of the Potential Economic and Fiscal Effects of Investment of the Assets of the Social Security Old-Age and Survivors and Disability Insurance Trust Funds: Final Report (Mimeographed, May 1988).

2. Budget estimate as of 1989.

CONTROLLING SOCIAL SECURITY EXPANSION: *A Commentary by Stephen J. Entin*

1. Steven S. Vinti and David Wise, "Have IRA's Increased U.S. Saving? Evidence from Consumer Expenditure Surveys," National Bureau of Economic Research, Working Paper no. 2217, 1987; Steven S. Vinti and David Wise, "IRA's and Saving," in *Taxes and Capital Formation*, M. Feldstein, ed. (Chicago: University of Chicago Press, 1986); and Steven S. Vinti and David Wise, "Tax Deferred Accounts: Constrained Choice and Estimation of Individual Saving," *Review of Economic Studies* (August 1986).

2. Manuel H. Johnson and Jacob Dreyer, "The Effect of Deficits on the Prices of Financial Assets: Theory and Evidence," Office of the Assistant Secretary of Economic Policy, U.S. Treasury, Washington, D.C., 1984.

3. Board of Trustees of the Federal Old-Age and Survivors Insurance Trust Fund and the Federal Disability Insurance Trust Fund, *1989 Annual Report of the Board of Trustees of the Federal Old-Age and Survivors Insurance Trust Fund and the Federal Disability Insurance Trust Fund* (Washington, D.C.: GPO, 1989).

4. Institute for Research on the Economics of Taxation, Washington, D.C.

5. See Daniel Feenburg and Jonathan Skinner, "Sources of IRA Saving," in Lawrence H. Summers, ed., *Tax Policy and the Economy* (Cambridge, Mass.: MIT Press, 1989); Steven S. Vinti and David Wise, "Evidence on IRA's," *Tax Notes*, January 25, 1988.

Bibliography

Aaron, Henry J., Barry P. Bosworth, and Gary Burtless. *Can America Afford to Grow Old? Paying for Social Security.* Washington, D.C.: Brookings Institution, 1989.

———. "Final Report to the Social Security Administration on Contract No. 600-87-0072" (1988). Mimeographed.

Ackley, Gardner, and Hiromitsu Ishi. "Fiscal, Monetary, and Related Policies." In *Asia's New Giant: How the Japanese Economy Works.* Edited by Hugh Patrick and Henry Rosovsky. Washington, D.C.: Brookings Institution, 1976, pp. 153–249.

Andersen, Hans Christian. "The Emperor's New Clothes." In *Forty-Two Stories.* Translated by M. R. James, pp. 104–7. New York: A. S. Barnes and Company, 1959.

Anderson, Joseph M., Richard A. Kuzmak, Donald W. Moran, George R. Schink, Dale W. Jorgenson, and William R. M. Perradin. "Study of the Potential Economic and Fiscal Effects of Investment of the Assets of the Social Security Old-Age and Survivors and Disability Insurance Trust Funds: Final Report to the Social Security Administration" (May 1988). Mimeographed.

Anderson, William, Myles S. Wallace, and John T. Warner. "Government Spending and Taxation: What Causes What?" *Southern Economic Journal* (January 1986), pp. 630–39.

Ando, Albert, and Franco Modigliani. "The Life Cycle Hypothesis of Saving: Aggregate Implications and Tests." *American Economic Review* (March 1963), pp. 55–84.

Auerbach, Alan J., and Laurence J. Kotlikoff. *Dynamic Fiscal Policy.* Cambridge, England: Cambridge University Press, 1987.

———. "Investment versus Savings Incentives: The Size of the Bang for the Buck and the Potential for Self-Financing Business Tax Cuts." In *The Economic Consequences of Government Deficits.* Edited by L. H. Meyer. Boston: Kluwer-Nijhoff, 1983.

Ball, Robert M. *Social Security Today and Tomorrow.* New York: Columbia University Press, 1978.

Bennett, James T., and Thomas J. DiLorenzo. "Off-Budget Activities of the Local Governments: The Bane of the Tax Revolt." *Public Choice*, vol. 39, no. 3 (1982).

Bird, Richard M. *Charging for Public Services: A New Look at an Old Idea.* Toronto: Canadian Tax Foundation, December 1976.

Blackley, Paul R. "Causality between Revenues and Expenditures and the Size of the Federal Budget." *Public Finance Quarterly* (April 1986), pp. 139–56.

Board of Trustees, Federal Old-Age and Survivors Insurance and Disability Insurance Trust Funds. *1988 Annual Report of the Board of Trustees of the Federal Old-Age and Survivors Insurance and Disability Insurance Trust Funds.* Washington, D.C.: GPO, 1988.

——. *1989 Annual Report of the Board of Trustees of the Federal Old-Age and Survivors Insurance and Disability Insurance Trust Funds.* Washington, D.C.: GPO, 1989.

Boskin, Michael J. "Future Social Security Financing Alternatives and National Saving." National Bureau of Economic Research Working Paper no. 2256 (1987).

——. *Too Many Promises: The Uncertain Future of Social Security.* Homewood, Ill.: Dow-Jones Irwin, 1986.

Boskin, Michael J., Alan Huber, and Mark Robinson. "Government Saving and Capital Formation in the United States, 1948–1985." In *The Measurement of Saving and Investment.* Edited by R. E. Lipsey and H. Tice. Chicago: University of Chicago Press, 1989.

Boskin, Michael J., and Lawrence J. Lau. "An Analysis of U.S. Postwar Consumption and Saving." National Bureau of Economic Research, Working Paper no. 2605-06 (1988).

Bosworth, Barry P., and Alice M. Rivlin, eds. *The Swedish Economy.* Washington, D.C.: Brookings Institution, 1987.

Bryden, Kenneth. *Old-Age Pensions and Policy Making in Canada.* Montreal: McGill-Queen's University Press, 1974.

Bryden, Kenneth, M. P. P. Morton, and Des Morton. *New Democrats Look at the Canada Pension Plan.* Toronto: Ontario New Democratic Party, 1965.

Buchanan, James M., and Richard E. Wagner. *Democracy in Deficit: The Political Legacy of Lord Keynes.* New York: Academic Press, 1978.

——. *The Limits of Liberty: Between Anarchy and Leviathan.* Chicago: University of Chicago Press, 1975.

Campbell, John Creighton. "Social Welfare." In *Kodansha Encyclopedia of Japan.* New York: Kodansha International, 1983, pp. 210–13.

Canada. Ministry of Finance. *The Canadian Budgetary Process: Proposals for Improvement.* Ottawa: Ministry of Finance, 1985.

——. *Quarterly Economic Review: Annual Reference Tables.* Ottawa: Ministry of Supply and Services, June 1987.

——. *Budget Papers: Securing Economic Renewal*. Ottawa: Ministry of Finance, February 10, 1988.

Canada. Ministry of Health and Welfare. "Expenditure Plan." Part 3 of *1988-89 Main Estimates*. Ottawa: Ministry of Health and Welfare, 1988.

——. *Inventory of Income Security Programs in Canada: Recent Initiatives and Statistical Update as of January 1987*. Ottawa: Ministry of Health and Welfare, February 1988.

——. *Canada Pension Plan Account Monthly Report*. Ottawa: Ministry of Health and Welfare, April 1988.

——. *Monthly Statistics: Income Security Programs*. Ottawa: Ministry of Health and Welfare, August 1988.

Chowdhry, Abdur R. "Expenditures and Receipts in the State and Local Levels of Government." *Public Choice*, vol. 59, no. 3 (1988).

Cogan, John. "The Evolution of Congressional Budget Decisionmaking and the Emergence of Federal Deficits." Hoover Institution Working Paper (August 1988).

Comiez, Maynard S., and Fred L. Lynn. "Notes on Budget Concepts in Selected Developed Countries and Other Materials." In *Staff Papers and Other Materials Reviewed by the President's Commission*, pp. 117–58 (Report prepared for the President's Commission on Budget Concepts). Washington, D.C.: GPO, October 1967.

Denny, Michael, and Samuel Area, Jr. "Pensions and Saving in Canada." In *Social Security versus Private Saving*. Edited by George M. von Furstenberg, pp. 135–65. Cambridge, Mass.: Ballinger, 1979.

Department of Insurance Canada. *Canada Pension Plan Statutory Actuarial Report No. 10 as of December 31, 1985*. Canada: Department of Insurance Canada, 1985.

Dole, Robert J., and Barber B. Conable, Jr. "Additional Views of Senator Robert J. Dole and Congressman Barber B. Conable, Jr." Report of the National Commission on Social Security Reform. Washington, D.C.: GPO, January 1983.

Economic Council of Canada. *One in Three: Pensions for Canadians to 2030*. Hull: Ministry of Supply and Services, 1979.

Entin, Stephen J. "Statement before the Subcommittee on Social Security and Family Policy, Committee on Finance, U.S. Senate." *Treasury News* (June 30, 1988).

Feenberg, Daniel, and Jonathan Skinner. "Sources of IRA Saving." In Lawrence H. Summers, ed. *Tax Policy and the Economy*. Cambridge, Mass.: MIT Press, 1989.

Feldstein, Martin. "The Social Security Fund and National Capital Accumulation." *Funding Pensions: Issues and Implications for Financial Markets*. Conference Series no. 16. Boston: Federal Reserve Bank of Boston, 1976.

———. "Social Security, Induced Retirement, and Aggregate Capital Accumulation." *Journal of Political Economy* (September–October 1974), pp. 905–26.

Ferrara, Peter J. *Social Security: Prospects for Real Reform*. Washington, D.C.: Cato Institute, 1988.

Flanagan, Robert J., David W. Soskice, and Lloyd Ulman. Chap. 6 in *Unionism, Economic Stabilization, and Income Policies: European Experience*. Washington, D.C.: Brookings Institution, 1983.

Foreign Press Center/Japan. "Social Security in Japan." In *About Japan*, no. 17. Tokyo: Foreign Press Center/Japan, March 1988.

Friedman, Milton. *Tax Limitation, Inflation, and the Role of Government*. Dallas: Fisher Institute, 1978.

Furstenburg, George M. von, Jeffrey R. Green, and Jin-Ho Jeogn. "Tax and Spend or Spend and Tax." *Review of Economics and Statistics* (May 1986), pp. 179–88.

Goss, Stephen C., Milton P. Glanz, and Esperanza Lopez. *Economic Projections for OASDHI Cost and Income Estimates: 1987*. Washington, D.C.: U.S. Department of Health and Human Services, Office of the Actuary, May 1988.

Gramlich, Edward M. "Rethinking the Role of the Public Sector." In *The Swedish Economy*. Edited by Barry P. Bosworth and Alice M. Rivlin. Washington, D.C.: Brookings Institution, 1987, pp. 210–13.

Granger, C. W. "Investigating Causal Relations by Economic Models and Cross Spectral Methods." *Econometrica*, July 1969, pp. 424–38.

———. *Forecasting in Business and Economics*. New York: Academic Press, 1980.

Gravelle, Jane G. "Deficit Targets, National Savings, and Social Security." Congressional Research Staff Report for Congress. Washington, D.C., July 1988.

Guest, Dennis. *The Emergence of Social Security in Canada*. 2d ed. Vancouver: University of British Columbia Press, 1985.

Guilkey, D. K. "Small Sample Properties of Three Tests for Granger-Causal Ordering a Bivariate Stochastic Series." *Review of Economics and Statistics* (November 1982), pp. 668–80.

Hayck, Friedrich A. von. "Social Security." *The Constitution of Liberty*. Chicago: Henry Regnery Co., 1960, pp. 285–305.

Heller, Peter S., Richard Hemming, and Peter W. Kohnert. "Aging and Social Expenditure in the Major Industrial Countries, 1980–2025." Occasional Paper 47. Washington, D.C.: International Monetary Fund, September 1986.

Holtz-Eakin, Douglas, Whitney Newey, and Harvey Rosen. "The Revenues-Expenditures Nexus: Evidence from the Local Government Data." National Bureau of Economic Research Working Paper no. 2180 (March 1987).

International Monetary Fund. *A Manual on Government Finance Statistics*. Washington, D.C.: IMF, 1986.

International Society for Educational Information. *Government*. Facts about Japan Series. Japan: International Society for Educational Information, 1988.

Japan. Ministry of Finance, Budget Bureau. *The Budget in Brief*. Tokyo: Ministry of Finance, 1987.

Japan Foundation for Research and Development of Pension Schemes. *National System of Old-Age, Disability and Survivors' Benefits in Japan*. 2d ed. Tokyo: Japan Foundation for Research and Development of Pension Schemes, 1986.

Japanese Social Insurance Agency. *Outline of Social Insurance in Japan*. Tokyo: Japanese Social Insurance Agency, 1982.

———. *Outline of Social Insurance in Japan*. Tokyo: Japanese Social Insurance Agency, 1985.

Johnson, Manuel H., and Jacob Dreyer. "The Effect of Deficits on the Prices of Financial Assets: Theory and Evidence." Office of the Assistant Secretary of Economic Policy, U.S. Treasury, Washington, D.C., 1984.

Joulfaian, David. "The Causal Effects of Government Expenditures on Government Revenues." Washington, D.C.: U.S. Treasury 1988. Mimeographed.

Kerns, Wilmer L. "Federal Employees' Retirement System Act of 1986." *Social Security Bulletin* (November 1986), pp. 5–10.

Koichi, Kishimoto. *Politics in Modern Japan: Development and Organization*. Tokyo: Japan Echo, 1982.

Koitz, David. "Social Security: Its Funding Outlook and Significance for Government Finance." Washington, D.C.: Congressional Research Service, June 1, 1986.

Kotlikoff, Laurence J. "Deficit Delusion." *Public Interest* (Summer 1986).

———. "The Deficit Is Not a Meaningful Measure of Fiscal Policy." *Science* (September 1988).

———. "Taxation and Savings: A Neoclassical Perspective." *Journal of Economic Literature* (December 1984).

Leonard, Herman B. "Shadows in Time: The Perils of Intergenerational Transfers." *Generational Journal* (April 15, 1988), pp. 1–2.

———. Chap. 2 in *Checks Unbalanced: The Quiet Side of Public Spending*. New York: Basic Books, 1986.

Lindbeck, Assar. *Swedish Economic Policy*. Berkeley: University of California Press, 1974.

Liu, Lillian. "Social Security Reforms in Japan." *Social Security Bulletin* (September 1987), pp. 29–37.

Makin, John H., and Kenneth A. Couch. "Saving, Pension Contributions and the Real Interest Rate." *Review of Economics and Statistics* (1989).

Manage, Neela, and Michael L. Marlow. "The Causal Relation between Federal Expenditures and Receipts." *Southern Economic Journal* (January 1986), pp. 717–29.

Markowski, Aleksander, and Edward E. Palmer. "Social Insurance and Saving in Sweden." In *Social Security versus Private Saving*. Edited by George M. von Furstenberg. Cambridge, Mass.: Ballinger, 1979, pp. 167–228.

Marlow, Michael L. "Tax and Spend Hypothesis." 1988. Unpublished manuscript.

Marlow, Michael L., and Neela Manage. "Testing for Causality in State and Local Government Finances." *Public Choice*, vol. 53, no. 2 (1987).

———. "Testing for Causality in State and Local Government Finances: Reply." *Public Choice*, vol. 59, no. 3 (1988).

Modigliani, Franco, and Richard Brumberg. "Utility Analysis and the Consumption Function: An Interpretation of Cross-Section Data." In *Post-Keynesian Economics*. Edited by Kenneth K. Kurihara. New Brunswick, N.J.: Rutgers University Press, 1954.

Moynihan, Daniel P., *Congressional Record* (January 23, 1990), S149–154.

Munnell, Alicia H. "Projected Trust Fund Build-Up: Social Security Issues." Paper prepared for the Technical Symposium on the Economic Implication of the Trust Fund Buildup, Washington, D.C., September 16, 1988.

———. "Social Security and the Budget." *Federal Reserve Bank of Boston Economic Review* (July/August 1985), pp. 5–18.

———. "Should We Fund Social Security?" Boston: Federal Reserve Bank of Boston. Mimeographed.

Munnell, Alicia H., and Lynn E. Blais. "Do We Want Large Social Security Surpluses?" *Generational Journal*, April 15, 1988, pp. 21–36.

Myers, Robert J. "Investment Policies and Procedures of the Social Security Trust Funds." *Social Security Bulletin* (January 1982), pp. 3–7.

Noguchi, Yukio. "Budget, National." In *Kodansha Encyclopedia of Japan*. New York: Kodansha International, 1983, pp. 210–13.

———. *The Failure of the Government to Perform Its Proper Task: A Case Study of Japan*, vol. 34 of *Ordo; Jahrbuch fur die Ordnung von Wirtschaft und Gesellschaft*. New York: Gustav Fisher Verlag, 1983.

———. "Public Finance." In *The Political Economy of Japan: The Domestic Transformation*, vol. 1. Edited by Kozo Yamamura and Yasukichi. Stanford, Calif.: Stanford University Press, 1987, pp. 186–222.

Olson, Sven. "Sweden." *Growth to Limits*, vol. 1. Edited by Peter Flora. New York: Walter de Gruyter, 1986, pp. 4–114.

——. "The People's Old-Age Pension in Sweden: Past, Present and Future." *International Social Security Review* (April 1987), pp. 361–72.

Ontario Ministry of Treasury. *Budget Statements*. Ontario: Ontario Ministry of Treasury, 1974.

Ontario Ministry of Treasury, Economics, and Governmental Affairs. *Review of Issues in Financing the Canada Pension Plan*. Ontario: Ontario Ministry of Treasury, 1976.

Organization for Economic Cooperation and Development. "Aging Populations: Implications for Public Finance and the Macroeconomy." Paris: OECD, 1988. Photocopy.

——. Department of Economics and Statistics. *National Accounts: 1974–86*. Detailed tables, vol. 2. Paris: OECD, 1988.

——. *OECD Economic Surveys: Japan 1987/1988*. Paris: OECD, 1988.

Ostrom, Douglas. "Japan's Fiscal Policy." *Japan Economic Institute Report*, no. 18A, May 6, 1988.

Ozawa, Martha N. "Social Security Reform in Japan." *Social Service Review* (September 1985), pp. 476–95.

Patrick, Hugh, and Henry Rosovsky, eds. *Asia's New Giant: How the Japanese Economy Works*. Washington, D.C.: Brookings Institution, 1976.

Patterson, Keith. "The Effect of the Provincial Borrowings from Universal Pension Plans on Provincial and Municipal Government Finance." Discussion paper 192. Ottawa: Economic Council of Canada, 1981.

Pechman, Joseph A. *The Rich, the Poor, and the Taxes They Pay*. Boulder, Colo.: Westview Press, 1986.

Pesando, J. E., and S. A. Rea. *Public and Private Pensions in Canada: An Economic Analysis*. Toronto: University of Toronto Press for the Ontario Economic Council, 1977.

Pontusson, Jonas. *Public Pension Funds and the Politics of Capital Formation in Sweden*. Goteborg, Sweden: Tryckt va Graphic Systems AB, 1984.

Porter, John. *Fact Sheet: Individual Social Security Retirement Accounts (ISSRAs)*, 1990. Mimeographed.

President of the United States. *Economic Report of the President*. Washington, D.C.: GPO, January 1989.

Ram, Rati. "Additional Evidence on Causality between Government Revenue and Government Expenditure." *Southern Economic Journal* (January 1988), pp. 763–69.

Robertson, A. Haeworth. *The Coming Revolution in Social Security*. McLean, Va.: Security Press, 1981.

Samuelson, Paul. "An Exact Consumption Loan Model on Interest with or without the Social Contrivance of Money." *Journal of Political Economy* (December 1958), pp. 467–82.

Schieber, Sylvester J. *Social Security: Perspectives on Preserving the System*. Washington, D.C.: Employee Benefit Research Institute, 1982.

Smith, Lee. "Trim That Social Security Surplus." *Fortune* (August 29, 1988), pp. 84–89.

Stahl, Ingemar. "Sweden." In *The World Crisis in Social Security*. Edited by Jean-Jacques Rosa. San Francisco: Institute for Contemporary Studies, 1982, pp. 93–120.

Steuerle, Eugene, and Paul Wilson. "The Taxation of the Poor and Lower-Income Workers." *Tax Notes*, vol. 34, no. 7 (February 16, 1987), pp. 695–712.

Sweden. Ministry of Finance. Summary of *The Swedish Budget 1988/1989*. Stockholm: Norstedts Tryckeri AB, 1988.

Swedish Institute. *Sweden in Brief*. 3d ed. Uddevalla, Sweden: Bohuslaningens Boktryckeri AB, 1986.

Swedish National Pension Fund. *Annual Report*. Stockholm: Swedish National Pension Fund, First, Second, and Third Boards, 1985.

——. *Summary of Activities*. Stockholm: Swedish National Pension Fund, First, Second, and Third Boards, 1987.

Takayama, Noriyuki. "Japan." In *The World Crisis in Social Security*. Edited by Jean-Jacques Rosa. San Francisco: Institute for Contemporary Studies, 1982, pp. 93–120.

United Nations. *Demographic Yearbook, 1962*. New York: UN, 1962.

——. Department of Economic and Social Affairs. *A System of National Accounts*. 2d ser., no. 2, rev. 2. New York: UN, 1968.

U.S. Advisory Commission on Intergovernmental Relations. *Significant Features of Fiscal Federalism, 1988 Edition*, vol. 1. Washington, D.C.: Advisory Commission on Intergovernmental Relations, December 1987.

U.S. Congress. House. Committee on Ways and Means. "Background Materials on Federal Budget and Tax Policy for Fiscal Year 1991 and Beyond." 101st Cong., 2d sess., WMCP 101-21 (February 6, 1990).

U.S. Congress. House. Committee on Ways and Means. Subcommittee on Social Security. *Disinvestment of the Social Security Trust Funds to Finance the Public Debt*. 99th Cong., 1st sess., 1985. Committee Print WMCT 99-12.

U.S. Congress. House. Committee on Ways and Means. Subcommittee on Social Security. *Report on Study of Social Security as an Independent Agency: Hearing before Committee on Ways and Means, House of Representatives*. 98th Cong., 2d sess., July 30, 1984. Serial 98-92.

U.S. Congress. Senate. Committee on Finance. Subcommittee on Social Security and Income Maintenance Programs. *Review of Social Security*

Trust Fund Policy. 99th Cong., 1st sess., 1986. Committee Print WMCT 99-12.

U.S. Congressional Budget Office. *The Economic and Budget Outlook: An Update.* Washington, D.C.: GPO, August, 1988.

———. *Indexing the Individual Income Tax.* Washington, D.C.: GPO, 1980.

U.S. Department of Health and Human Services, Comparative Studies Staff, Social Security Administration. "Social Security in Japan." Baltimore, Md.: U.S. Department of Health and Human Services, April 1983. Mimeographed.

U.S. Department of Health and Human Services, Social Security Administration. "Social Security Programs Throughout the World: 1985." Research Report 60. Washington, D.C.: GPO, 1986.

U.S. General Accounting Office. *Disinvestment of the Social Security Trust Funds.* Washington, D.C: GAO, February 28, 1986.

———. *Social Security: Past Projections and Future Financing Concerns.* Washington, D.C.: GPO, March 1986.

U.S. Office of Management and Budget. *Historical Tables. Budget of the United States, Fiscal Year 1989.* Washington, D.C.: GPO, 1988.

Vinti, Steven S., and David Wise. "Evidence on IRA's." *Tax Notes,* January 25, 1988.

———. "Have IRA's Increased U.S. Saving? Evidence from Consumer Expenditure Surveys." National Bureau of Economic Research Working Paper 2217 (1987).

———. "IRA's and Saving." In *Taxes and Capital Formation.* Edited by Martin Feldstein. Chicago: University of Chicago Press, 1968.

———. "Tax Deferred Accounts, Constrained Choice and Estimation of Individual Saving." *Review of Economic Studies,* vol. 53 (August 1986), pp. 579–601.

Wade, Alice. *Social Security Area Population Projections 1988.* Washington, D.C.: U.S. Department of Health and Human Services, Office of the Actuary, June 1988.

Weaver, Carolyn L. "Social Security Shouldn't Drive U.S. Fiscal Policy." *Wall Street Journal.* April 18, 1989.

———. *The Crisis in Social Security: Economic and Political Origins.* Durham, N.C.: Duke Press Policy Studies, 1982.

———. "Social Security Investment Policy." Statement before the Social Security Advisory Council, Washington, D.C., March 8, 1990.

———. "Social Security's Looming Surpluses: Panacea or Mirage?" Statement before the Social Security Public Trustees' Symposium on the Social Security Trust Fund Buildup, Washington, D.C., September 16, 1988.

Wilson, Dorothy J. "Sweden." In *Pensions, Inflation and Growth: A Com-*

parative Study of the Elderly in the Welfare State. Edited by Thomas Wilson. London: Heinemann Educational Books, 1974, pp. 155–200.

Winterthur Swiss Insurance Co. *Social Security Survey 1987/88.* New York: Winterthur Swiss Insurance, 1988.

Index

proposals for United States, 70–73,
77, 175–76
in public versus private sector
obligations, 69–73, 82, 88
for Swedish AP and APT funds,
96–99
Irrelevance Hypothesis, 181

Jeogn, Jin-Ho, 124
Johnson, Manuel, 187
Joulfaian, David, 124

Kotlikoff, Laurence, 181

Life-cycle model, 24

Manage, Neela, 124
Marlow, Michael L., 124
Medicare
effect with off-budget status for,
81–82
estimated deficit in, 156, 167, 170,
171
Moynihan, Daniel P., proposal, 11–12, 76
Munnell, Alicia, 9

National Commission on Social Security
Reform: 1983 (the Greenspan Commission), 11, 55, 82
National Economic Commission, 75, 76,
82
National Pension Fund (Allman Tillaggspension: ATP), Sweden
funding of, 90–91
lending policy of, 96–97
National Pension Insurance Fund
(Allmanna Pensionfoden: AP), Sweden
function of reserve funds in, 91–92
lending practices of, 96–98
separate subfunds of, 96
National Pension (NP), Japan
coverage, financing, and reform for,
99–101
treatment in budget process for,
102–3

Old-Age, Survivors, Disability, and
Hospital Insurance (OASDHI), 2
Old-Age, Survivors, and Disability Insurance (OASDI). See Social security
trust fund surplus and reserves, 1, 2

Payroll tax
effect of, 136, 173

proposals for reduction of, 11–12,
64–65, 171
rates for, 7, 12, 61, 173–74
revenues from, 58, 167
Pension programs
pay-as-you-go financing for, 168–69
prefunding (advance funding) for,
168–69
prefunding in Canada for, 107–14
prefunding in Japan for, 99–106
prefunding in Sweden for, 90–99
Pension Welfare Agency, Japan, 102–3
Policy recommendations
to change reserve investment policy,
73
to create independent agency, 115
Gramm-Rudman-Hollings changes,
137, 174, 182
for individual savings account, 149,
158–64
rules of conduct for decision
making, 134
scaling back benefits, 176–77
two-tier system, 175–76, 182–83, 185
Politics
as driving force for social security,
59–65
framing effects in, 142–43
Politics of righteous entitlement, 59–60,
67, 72
Postal Life Insurance Fund, Japan, 102
Prefunding (advance funding). See Pension programs; Reserves, social
security

Quebec Pension Plan (QPP), 107–8, 113

Ram, Rati, 124
Reserves, social security
current level and investment of, 1,
3, 4
effect of buildup of, 57–58
effect of no requirement to maintain
levels of, 170–71
effect on and of federal spending of,
65–69
hypothetical use of, 61–65
partial funding for, 148
prefunding (accumulation or nonac-
cumulation) of, 85–86, 170
projected level of, 1, 4–5
proposals to protect, 69–72
surpluses in Canada for, 118
surpluses in Japan for, 101, 118
surpluses in Sweden for, 118

A NOTE ON THE BOOK

This book was edited by Dana Lane and Ann Petty
of the publications staff of the American Enterprise Institute.
The text was set in Palatino, a typeface designed by the twentieth-century
Swiss designer Hermann Zapf. Harper Graphics, of Waldorf, Maryland, set
the type, and Edwards Brothers Incorporated, of Ann Arbor, Michigan,
printed and bound the book, using permanent acid-free paper.

The AEI PRESS is the publisher for the American Enterprise Institute for
Public Policy Research, 1150 17th Street, N.W., Washington, D.C. 20036:
Christopher C. DeMuth, publisher; *Edward Styles,* director; *Dana Lane,* editor;
Ann Petty, editor; *Cheryl Weissman,* editor; *Susan Moran,* editorial assistant
(rights and permissions). Books published by the AEI PRESS are distributed
by arrangement with the University Press of America, 4720 Boston Way,
Lanham, Md. 20706.

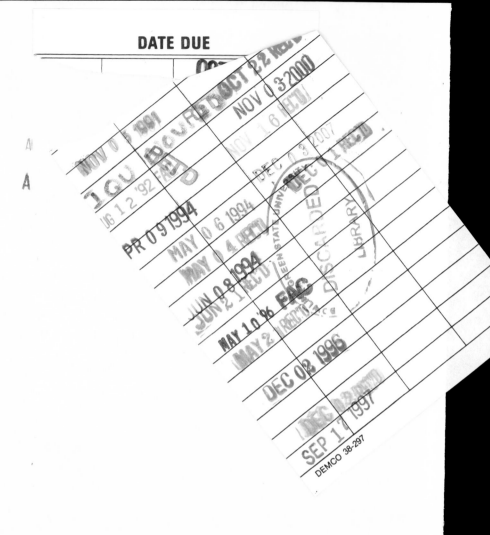